Confessions of
A STEAM-AGE
FERROEQUINOLOGIST

KEITH WIDDOWSON

Confessions of
A STEAM-AGE
FERROEQUINOLOGIST

JOURNEYS ON BR'S LONDON MIDLAND REGION

Every effort has been made to source and contact
copyright holders of illustrated material. In case
of any omission, please contact the author via
the publishers.

Cover illustrations: *Front:* A crowded scene at Liverpool Lime Street on
Saturday, 4 June 1966 as Stockport-allocated Brit 70004 *William Shakespeare*
prepares to take the LCGB Fellsman rail tour forward the 135 miles to Scotland.
Back: Haulage bashers congregate at Warrington Bank Quay; a ticket offered to
the guard after leaving Wigan.

First published 2019

The History Press
97 St George's Place, Cheltenham,
Gloucestershire, GL50 3QB
www.thehistorypress.co.uk

© Keith Widdowson, 2019

The right of Keith Widdowson to be identified as the Author
of this work has been asserted in accordance with the
Copyright, Designs and Patents Act 1988.

British Library Cataloguing in Publication Data.
A catalogue record for this book is available from the British Library.

ISBN 978 0 07509 9197 1

Typesetting and origination by The History Press
Printed and bound in Great Britain by TJ International Ltd.

CONTENTS

ABOUT THE AUTHOR

Keith Widdowson was born to his pharmacist father and secretarial mother during the calamitous winter of 1947 at St Mary Cray, Kent – attending the nearby schools of Poverest and Charterhouse. He joined British Railways in June 1962 as an enquiry clerk at the Waterloo telephone bureau – 'because his mother had noted his obsession with collecting timetables'.

Thus began a forty-five-year career within various train planning departments throughout BR, the bulk of which was at Waterloo but also included locations at Cannon Street, Wimbledon, Crewe, Euston, Blackfriars, Paddington and finally Croydon – specialising in dealing with train-crew arrangements. After spending several years during the 1970s and '80s in Cheshire, London and Sittingbourne, he returned to his roots in 1985 and there he finally met the steadying influence in his life, Joan, with whom he had a daughter, Victoria, now a primary school teacher. In addition to membership of the local residents' association (St Pauls Cray), the Sittingbourne & Kemsley Light Railway and the U3A organisation, he keeps busy writing articles for railway magazines and gardening.

INTRODUCTION

Welcome to the fifth tome on my steam-chasing years between 1964 and 1968. Having exhausted my memories of steam in Europe, Southern England, Yorkshire and Scotland I have turned my attention to where steam in Britain died – the London Midland Region. By default it has become the largest publication of them all, influenced probably as being, after October 1967, the only place to be.

Perhaps using the irrational logic that 'there will always be steam on LMR metals', I had initially, excepting a brief Leicester-based foray in the August of 1964, concentrated on other regions during the formative years of my railway travels – the only LMR-orientated steam-train travels during 1965 were afternoon trips out of Marylebone and overnights to Scotland.

The majority of this book therefore depicts my visits to the LMR from the March of 1966 until the end. My self-imposed mission was to travel behind as many different steam locomotives as feasible and as the months went by and the steam passenger services became fewer, the waits for them – the remaining ones being confined to the night hours – became lengthier.

Here then is a travelogue of those expeditions undertaken during my teenage years. Along with like-minded friends, we led a carefree existence untroubled by world events. Yet to be burdened with mortgages, relationships and career prospects, we, using the generic overview, trainspotters, were able to roam the railway network in a frenzied pursuit of the centrepiece of our hobby – the steam locomotive.

Please join me on my quest: the successes, the disappointments, the scenarios I encountered and above all the realisation that history was being enacted, i.e. one of the last vestiges of the Industrial Revolution, the Iron Horse, was being extinguished.

1

IN THE BEGINNING

My parents met at a Somerset holiday camp just prior to the outbreak of the Second World War. Having qualified as a pharmacist, Dad was in the Medical Corps (behind the lines) at Dunkirk when, in 1940, the historic retreat was ordered by the government. After his inevitable capture by the Germans he endured a five-day train journey across Europe, becoming a POW in a camp in Austria before, in 1945, being liberated. Returning home, my parents married and settled in Kent – just a stone's throw from the railway line at St Mary Cray. Born at home in the calamitous winter of 1947 (the midwife couldn't get through because of the snow – Grandma having to deliver me!) I was to gain a brother four and a half years later.

The road in which we lived was initially just a cul-de-sac, at the end of which was an extensive orchard. During the early 1950s, in line with a great many other areas in the Home Counties, the orchard was cleared and an estate was built to house Londoners whose homes had been damaged by the war or were in sub-standard accommodation. As an integral part of the development, a church, shops, dentist, doctor, public house and a school were all built.

Directly opposite my house, however, because the ground was unable to sustain house construction, a wooded area was left untouched – and still is to this day. This parallels the London-bound railway line west of St Mary Cray station and, although it was our playground, it was only after the acquisition of a dog, whose predilection was to race against the passing trains, that I took any notice of the railway itself. Unlike many railway authors who commence a book detailing their earliest memories of what they spotted, even though the ideal environment presented itself I retrospectively regret failing to document anything passing along the former London & Chatham Main Line.

Attending the aforementioned primary school, a lack of common sense/inattention led me to fail the eleven-plus and although it seemed I was destined to attend the nearest secondary modern just a mile away, my parents, because of its reputation re poor discipline, etc., registered me to one more than 3 miles away – south of Orpington.

Although, after gaining my Cycling Proficiency badge – a prerequisite insisted upon by the school – during the summer I used my bicycle, the bulk of my journeys were made using London Transport buses. They weren't as frequent back then as nowadays and it was necessary to purchase a local timetable. I became proficient, fascinated even, by it. So much so that, having purchased adjacent area issues, my brother and I embarked on days out exploiting the myriad of bus routes available using the Red (or Green) Rover tickets.[1] Available on weekends only at 2s 6d (12½p), what a bargain they were – inevitably leading to Ian Allan books being purchased and serious spotting being undertaken. All the above was funded from my job(s) delivering papers. I had a morning round from the local newsagent and a Saturday evening round patrolling the streets of Petts Wood hollering out 'classified' – the 6d (2½p) pink edition, with all that day's football results, having been delivered by train at about 6 p.m..

I had attended the obligatory Sunday school and cubs and now, as a teenager, progressed onto Scouts and youth hostels. Collecting stamps, tea cards and vinyl records of Cliff Richard and Adam Faith (played on my Dansette), it was only the partial destruction of 'my' woods opposite my home (in connection with the Kent Coast Electrification scheme that, at St Mary Cray, made it a four-track railway), that the earliest indication of an interest in trains manifested itself. Normally served by a mundane selection of EMUs at about 6 a.m., just as I was getting up for my paper round a coast-bound steam train deigned to call there. Then, about midday, witnessed only during the school holidays, a steam-hauled freight train, worked by a class later recognised as an N or U, called there collecting empty coal wagons and letting all around know when it was struggling away up the 1 in 100 with its increased load.

---

[1] London Transport Red Rovers covered all Red Routes 1–299 that operated within Central and Outer London, while Green Rovers were for Country Routes 300 onwards that operated within the surrounding Home Counties.

Then there were the twice-yearly trips to Dad's home city of Leicester. My brother went with him during the summer whilst I, being older and more able to carry the presents, went with him each December. The only day Dad wasn't running his pharmacy was a Sunday and, after waving to Mum from the departing train at St Mary Cray, we made our way to Marylebone for a journey down the ex GC to Leicester Central. Met by relatives, we called at his brother's for dinner at Evington Close, his sister's for tea at The Highway (where I noted the maroon and cream-liveried Leicester Corporation buses passing the window whilst everyone else was talking) and his dad's at Dulverton Road. It was always the same circuit – being returned to the station about 7 p.m. courtesy of someone's car. What locomotives were we hauled by? Nothing was noted. Gresley A3s or V2s – who knows!

There was, however, change afoot. During 1960 the Sunday services out of Marylebone were withdrawn and we had to travel out of St Pancras to Leicester's London Road station. Stanier Scots and Jubilees must surely have been at the front – all regrettably not being recorded! The cross-London journey was now from Elephant and Castle via the Northern (City branch). I can still visualise the single 12ft-wide island-platformed Angel station, which was deemed sufficiently unsafe to be rebuilt in the early 1990s. Upon departure, from there I looked forward in anticipation to the deep drop, akin to a roller coaster, before arriving into King's Cross/St Pancras.

As to the return journey, I remember there was one occasion when, having been delayed by thick fog and snow en route, Dad and I eventually arrived at Elephant and Castle in the early hours of Monday morning. Not to worry, with trains departing at 01.25, 01.56 and 02.23 for Orpington we were still able to reach home. The SR ran these trains to entice Fleet Street print workers to live in the suburbs. Annoyingly, I was still dispatched to school that morning!

Meanwhile, following a series of must-do-better reports from school together with slipping down a stream, Dad decided (I was 15½) that it was pointless me staying on in order for me to fail the Royal Society of Arts examination (a qualification he said would get me nowhere) and I might as well follow his advice to 'get yourself a job'. Parents are in life to guide their offspring and I can never thank them enough for setting me up in a career within the railway industry. They had noted my interest in timetables and wrote to the SR HQ at Waterloo on the off chance of a position in the Telephone Enquiry Bureau – whose prime objective was to assist prospective customers with their journey arrangements by reading timetables. Having passed the necessary entrance exam and medical, I commenced working for BR in June 1962 – the catalyst of a fulfilling forty-five-year career at a dozen or so train planning offices.

So now I was *in situ*, so to speak, to commence my lifelong love affair with the steam locomotive. But, as so often when such opportunities happen in life, one tends to miss the beckoning signs. I had joined BR purely as a job. Initially, I had little or no interest in steam. It was others I worked with who highlighted that it would be naive of me not to take advantage of the travel perks associated with my employment, thus enabling me to see the world at a far cheaper cost than Joe Public.

And so I began, cautiously at first and concentrating on my home patch of the Southern Region, to venture out to destinations to which I had often directed callers. Into 1963 and I began visiting lines threatened under that year's 'The Reshaping of British Railways' as compiled by Doctor Richard Beeching. I discovered that the majority of those lines retained steam traction and, coupled with lunchtime visits to the 'spotters' end of Waterloo's platform 11 to witness the 13.30 Pacific-powered Weymouth departure, slowly and surely the attraction became irresistible, intoxicating even.

As the steam locomotive's reign was coming to an end the numbers of followers increased dramatically. For sure the majority were platform-enders, filling their ABCs with whatever came along, but a minority were hard-core haulage bashers. Without initially appreciating it, I was to morph into one of them – gallivanting around the country purely to travel behind as many different locomotives as possible before their inevitable demise. Our remit was to have actually travelled on the train that was worked by a particular locomotive and then, and only then, could you score though or underline it in your ever-present Ian Allan *Locoshed/ABC/Combined Volume*. Indeed, Ian Allan (1922–2015) has long been considered the spiritual father of trainspotters. His publications, which in turn provided the necessary detail so central to a 'gricer', are alleged to have kept thousands of teenagers off of the streets and out of trouble. What would today's adolescent generation think if we stated that it was a completely acceptable, normal even, activity to undertake during the early hours of a Sunday morning, rather than any of the more typical goings-on they might have been up to back in the 1960s, to be aboard steam trains arriving at and leaving Manchester! Other innocuous pastimes similar-aged lads undertook were collecting records, stamps, Dinky toys, matchbox labels, birds' eggs, butterflies; we collected steam locomotive numbers – so what?

It had to be done. We felt obliged to record the end of steam. As time went by, with fewer and fewer trains being steam operated it was inevitable that our paths began crossing on a far more frequent scale. The camaraderie that was created back then is still prevalent amongst today's survivors. You don't need confirmatory documents as to where you were and what trains you were on. It is all stored within each individual's memory bank. These days, as soon as like-minded haulage bashers from the 1960s see each other, the greatest likelihood being at the wonderfully organised galas most of the larger preserved railways run, the conversation quickly returns to those halcyon days. If one of the visiting locomotives, having been specially brought in by road for the event, had been caught back in its BR operational days by one of us but not the other, a somewhat (with a waving motion in front of the mouth as if muting a trumpet) exaggerated yawn, indicating boredom at the fact that was so common back then, pervades the carriage. The followers were classless. Rich or poor, privileged or working class – all backgrounds with a common aim. I often wondered how those who did not obtain cheap travel as an employment perk could afford it all – but then again ticket checks on trains were infrequent and there were no automatic barriers back then!

It was alleged in an article in *The New Society* magazine (August 1986, author Lincoln Allison) that there were, at the most, a mere 300 genuine haulage bashers. Nearly all were English, a surprisingly high (he wrote) proportion of whom were BR employees – usually from the clerical or lower management grades, and that, their activity being incompatible with stable relationships with the opposite sex, they didn't bother to wash, when in full cry of their hobby, for several days. He went on to say that, unlike a great many other hobbies, no trophies were presented, no collections mounted – their sole achievement being books, which, on relevant pages, have lists of numbers underscored. As to my response to all the above; I plead guilty!

Anyway, back to the centre of attention – the steam locomotive itself. The condition many of the steam locomotives were to be found in can be seen in the photographs accompanying this tome. Filthy, run down, externally neglected (but by necessity safe to run), numbers and names missing – it only added to the aura. To many older enthusiasts, reared in the days of smart, gleaming locomotives proudly displaying their companies' colours, the sight of them in the depth of their degradation must have been abhorrent. For more recent generations such as myself, however, it was all we ever knew and photographs of that era are still fondly cherished as the years slip by.

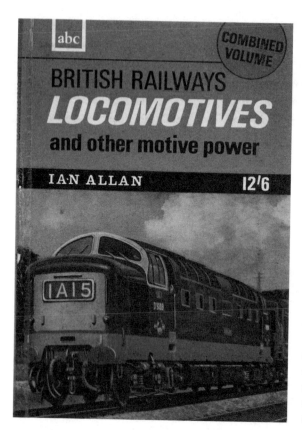

The April 1965 edition of the *Ian Allan Combined Volume*. This contained all steam, diesel and electric numbers for the entire country and was an essential guide for any serious spotter.

For sure, the drivers and firemen worked their socks off in attempting to get their steeds to perform the Herculean tasks demanded of them. The writing was, however, on the wall. The sword of Damocles was hanging over the steam locomotive; it didn't fit in the newly emerging modern era of BR – and indeed Britain itself. Sheds, falling into dereliction, had become surrounded in an abominable amount of dirt and neglect. They were knee deep in ash and coal, making them hazardous to negotiate, hence the foreman's frequent retort upon being requested for permission to have a look around: 'I haven't seen you.' The locomotives themselves seemed to leak steam and smoke from all manner of orifices not designed for such an activity. They usually, however, unlike their replacement modes of power, which would fail at the wrong turn of a switch, got you where you wanted to go. I was part of a fortunate generation criss-crossing the country on steam trains. From the magnificent Pacifics to the humble tanks, the smoke and sulphurous smell of burning coal, the whistles and a myriad of noises associated with a living machine – it all made it worthwhile.

For many of us we were discovering the world at large. Allowed away from our comfortable existence at home, we had to deal with all those situations never encountered before – strange locations, different dialects, inebriated waiting-room occupants having missed their last train home. We made mistakes. We were tired and hungry. We misread timetables, overslept – it was all part and parcel of life's experiences – and I wouldn't have missed it for the world. The sights seen, places visited – they would never have warranted attention if steam hadn't taken us there. Like acne, homework and the first pair of trousers, it wasn't just a hobby, it was part of growing up, our life – and our best friend was to be taken from us in August 1968.

Ian Allan appreciated that trainspotters' pocket money might not have stretched to purchase the *Combined Volume* and so he published two steam extracts at the more affordable price of 2s 6d. Here is the May 1964 issue of part 2, where all locomotives numbered from 40000 upwards were listed – part 1 being those up to 39999.

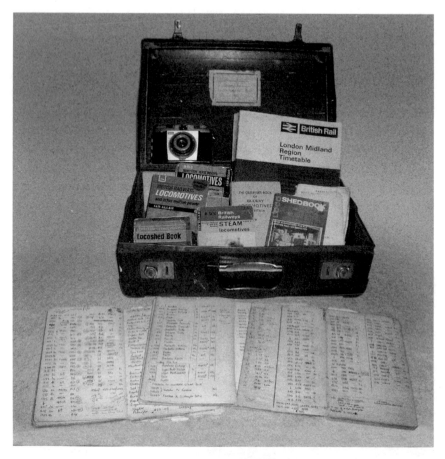

My case and equipment – always with me as if attached by an umbilical cord.

Through all the travels contained within this tome my small attaché case (16in × 10in × 4in) went with me. All necessary requirements were contained within it: timetables, camera, Ian Allan books, notebooks, Lyons fruit pies, Club biscuits, pens, flannel, handkerchief, stopwatch, cartons of orange drinks, sandwiches and, of course, a BR1 carriage key – for use in emergencies! Sturdy enough to sit on in crowded corridors of packed trains and doubling up as a pillow (albeit hard!) on overnight services, it was in regular use through the final years of BR steam and even travelled with me throughout Europe. Having survived many domestic upheavals over the years, it now enjoys a comfortable retirement at the bottom of my railway cupboard at home – containing all the documented travel information, without which I could never have contemplated writing a book such as this.

As for apparel, the anorak was not in existence then – to the best of my knowledge it was either a raincoat or a duffle coat with its attendant toggle fasteners. A selection of clothing we all wore back then can be seen within the group photographs at various locations throughout the book. Usually having commencing weekend travels directly after a day's work at the office, the obligatory tie (modern and straight edged) was always worn – albeit at peculiar angles after many nights out.

As mentioned in the introduction, this, my fifth tome, concentrates on the former London Midland Region. Even with the Carlisle area having being adequately catered for within *Scottish Steam's Final Fling* (published 2017) and my travels over the former GWR Paddington to Birkenhead main line and Wales being held over for a future book, if I was to detail every train travelled on throughout the LMR I suspect the publisher/reader would suffer apoplexy. I have therefore compacted my travels into a series of chapters, which, I hope, will enable the reader to read at leisure, perhaps allowing a drip feed of their own memories to infiltrate them.

My Kodak Colorsnap 35 camera.

BRITISH RAILWAYS LOCOMOTIVE SHEDS AND SHED CODES

The following list of sheds has been officially checked against British Railways records. Engines may, however, be seen at other sheds which, although officially " closed ", are used as stabling or servicing points. Sub-sheds, which are not given a special code number by British Railways, are included in this list, but locomotives allocated to them carry the shed code of the parent depot, whose number appears immediately above them in the list of shed codes. Sheds listed in bold type are chief sheds of a motive power district.

LONDON MIDLAND REGION

LMW	**Western A.C. Lines**	6A	**Chester**	9C	Reddish
		6B	Mold Junction	9D	Newton Heath
		6C	Croes Newydd	9E	Trafford Park
ML	**Midland Lines**	6D	Shrewsbury		Glazebrook
			Builth Road	9F	Heaton Mersey
1A	**Willesden**	6F	Machynlleth		Gowhole
1B	Camden		Aberystwyth	9H	Patricroft
1C	Watford		(V. of R.)	9J	Agecroft
1D	Marylebone		Portmadoc	9K	Bolton
1E	Bletchley		Pwllheli	9L	Buxton
1F	Rugby	6G	Llandudno		Middleton
1H	Northampton		Junction		
		6J	Holyhead	10A	**Carnforth**
				10C	Fleetwood
2A	**Tyseley**	8A	**Edge Hill**	10D	Lostock Hall
	Stratford-on-Avon		(Liverpool)	10E	Accrington
2B	Oxley	8B	Warrington	10F	Rose Grove
	(Wolverhampton)		(Dallam)	10G	Skipton
2C	Stourbridge	8C	Speke Junction	10H	Lower Darwen
2D	Banbury	8E	Northwich	10J	Lancaster
2E	Saltley	8F	Springs Branch		(Green Ayre)
2F	Bescot		(Wigan)		
2G	Ryecroft (Walsall)	8G	Sutton Oak	12A	**Carlisle**
2H	Monument Lane	8H	Birkenhead		(Kingmoor)
2J	Aston	8J	Allerton	12B	Carlisle (Upperby)
		8K	Bank Hall	12C	Barrow
		8L	Aintree	12D	Workington
5A	**Crewe North**	8M	Southport	12E	Tebay
5B	Crewe South				
5C	Stafford	9A	**Longsight**	D14	**London (Midland) Division**
5D	Stoke & Cockshute		(Manchester)	14A	**Cricklewood East**
5E	Nuneaton	9B	Stockport	14B	Cricklewood West
			(Edgeley)	14C	Bedford
D15	**Leicester Division**	D16	**Nottingham Division**	16C	Derby
15A	**Leicester (Midland)**				Cromford
	Market Harborough				Sheep Pasture
				16D	Nottingham
		16A	**Toton (Stapleford & Sandiacre)**	16E	Kirkby-in-Ashfield
15B	Wellingborough			16F	Burton
15E	Coalville	16B	Annesley		Overseal
				16G	Westhouses

List of London Midland Region sheds extant at the beginning of my travels.

Furthermore, I would respectfully point out that this book is by no means a definitive account of the last days of steam. There have been a myriad of publications, usually circulated whenever a commemorative date occurs, over the years dealing with that aspect. This is one man's personal observations and travelogue of what he witnessed and photographed during the final forty-eight months of steam on BR's London Midland Region. Having confessed to all the reasons behind my belated appearance on the steam scene, here we go ...

2

VOYAGE OF DISCOVERY: 1964

Initially concentrating on the many line closures throughout Southern England, it was in August 1964 that, having been invited to use their Leicester home as a base, my father's brother's family offered me the opportunity to explore the world away from my home territory. Many hours of studious scrutiny of the maroon LMR timetable, together with magazines such as *The Railway World* detailing the latest lists of proposed line closures, led me to compile the itinerary as followed in this chapter.

Manfred Mann's 'Do Wah Diddy Diddy', having displaced The Beatles' 'A Hard Day's Night', was holding the top spot and, earlier that month, the last British hangings at Strangeways and Walton jails had taken place. Other UK newsworthy events were John Surtees winning the German Grand Prix; the first broadcast of TV's *Match of the Day* with Kenneth Wolstenholme and Great Train Robber Charlie Wilson escaping from Birmingham's Winson Green prison. World events such as the escalation of the Vietnam War, The Beatles touring the USA and Canada to packed stadiums and the deaths of James Bond creator Ian Fleming and singer Jim Reeves were far from my thoughts – I was totally preoccupied by the anticipation of travels to 'foreign lands'.

Although having travelled on overnight services to the West of England the previous month, the familiarity of destinations already known both from having holidayed there over the years with my parents and my SR telephone enquiry job, voyaging north that August night it seemed I was venturing into the unknown. Sure I had studied maps, viewed photographs and read timetables about the cities and towns I was to visit but nothing broadens the mind like actually visiting them in person. Strange dialects, unusual-sounding destinations – it all caused an adolescent 17-year-old some consternation when determining if I was on the correct train/platform to ensure my plans were adhered to. The overnight service down the ECML, specifically advertised for Geordies working away during the week to visit home with cheap tickets, was chock-a-block. This service called at all main stations; the consequential tramping through the open carriages of passengers looking for non-existent seats resulting in very little shut-eye being obtained en route. Upon arrival at Newcastle I was glad of the opportunity to stretch my legs and, albeit a little weary, the two hours there seemed to pass very quickly. Not particularly conversant with the station layout, I fortuitously positioned myself at the north end of the station and was thus able to view both the famed diamond crossing and the goods lines – watching and photographing a plethora of steam locomotive classes only previously seen in *The Observer's Book of Railway Locomotives.*

For those readers interested in football facts, Newcastle's 1964–65 season had yet to kick off. When it did the following Monday they were held to a 1–1 draw at St James' Park by Charlton Athletic.

I had been advised, by those more knowledgeable than I, that Preston was a Mecca for steam activity and so I made my way across the north of England to Carlisle, from where I had by chance selected a steam-hauled Newcastle–Blackpool service to travel south over Shap; Carnforth's 45209 becoming my first of an eventual 289 (so far!) haulages behind one of Stanier's competent Class 5MT workhorses. After arrival into Preston, I went searching for a B&B, luckily finding one within a stone's throw from the station. Then, after depositing my case, I returned to the station in order to complete the final objective of that day – namely travelling over the whole of the Fylde peninsula's railway network.

The first line constructed on the Fylde peninsula, between Preston and Fleetwood, was opened by the Preston & Wyre Joint Railway in 1840. Until the railway was built over Shap this then was the main route for passengers from London to Scotland, utilising a ferry from Fleetwood to Ardrossan. Indeed, Queen Victoria herself travelled this way in 1847. The primary employment for the Fleetwood townsfolk, that was until the Cod Wars with

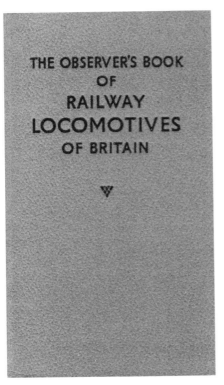

THE OBSERVER'S BOOK
OF
RAILWAY
LOCOMOTIVES
OF BRITAIN

Left: This publication was a present from 'Uncle' Ben for Christmas 1963. He was actually a fellow pharmacist friend of my dad who he met at college when studying medicine. Once a year he ran my dad's shop, staying in our home, allowing us to take an annual break.

Below: This and the following two photographs were taken on Saturday, 22 August 1964. My initial thoughts were, having recently discovered that no print had been developed from it, that it was of my first train over Shap after its arrival into Preston. Upon *Railway Images* expertise being applied it appears to be one of 4-6-0 44947 calling at Preston on a completely unrelated train. Little did I realise then that in just under four years' time I would depart this very platform on Britain's final public steam-hauled passenger train.

Carnforth-allocated Stanier 5MT 45326 about to pass under the Fishergate Road bridge at Preston with a Blackpool-bound service.

Iceland, was the fishing industry – the town's landlubbers being catered for by the 1865-built factory producing the world-famous Fisherman's Friend lozenges. Because the Fleetwood branch was on the Beeching hit list I, with difficulty due to the sparse service, made it a priority to travel over it: one of the thirty-strong class of BR 2MT 2-6-2Ts, 84010, powering that day's trains. It was fortunate that I did because in April 1966 the line was truncated at Wyre Dock – passenger services over the complete line ceasing operation four years later. The line, however, could have a future as not only is there pressure from the local council to reinstate passenger services, the line has been 'mothballed' as far as Burn Naze since 1999. Watch this space.

In 1846 a branch from Poulton-le-Fylde to Blackpool was opened. Renamed Blackpool Talbot Road in 1872, it acquired its final appellation of North in 1932. Eventually enlarged to accommodate sixteen platforms, it was threatened with closure in 1963 but survived – the local council underscoring the fact that the Central station's site was of greater land value. Indeed, in 1911 Blackpool Central was alleged to be *the busiest station in the world*. Although Dr Beeching advocated that Central be retained in preference to the North, money spoke and the council got its way: indeed, a further land grab was made by relocating North station to the site of the former excursion platforms in 1974. The Blackpool & Lytham Railway, first opened in 1863, extended its line eleven years later along the South Fylde coast to Kirkham – renaming its town terminus from Hounds Hill to Central in 1878. The final line in the equation, the Marton direct, was opened in 1903, joining the line to the Central at a newly created Waterloo Road, renamed Blackpool South in 1932.

Blackpool Central was closed in November 1964 – the ground being deemed more financially valuable to the money-strapped BR than its substantial seasonal usage. Naively being more intent on track coverage on the day I returned to Preston via the Marton direct, on a DMU to boot, thus losing out on the only chance I ever had for a run with a Patriot. Carlisle Upperby's 31-year-old 45527 *Southport* together with Newton Heath's 45339 were no doubt returning day trippers to their Lancashire homes having had a glorious day on the beaches and in the funfairs.

The following day, Sunday, 23 August 1964, having spent my *only* night in a B&B in Britain whilst chasing steam, Stanier 2-6-4T 42645 awaits departure time at Preston with the 13.25 for Southport Chapel Street. This West Lancashire Railway-built line via Hoole and Crossens was to close the following month – the 1938-built 4MT Southport-allocated locomotive surviving until July 1965.

All of these lines were *in situ* when visited that day and, by astute planning, travelled over. Although Black 5s dominated most trains that day, I witnessed, but alas failed to acknowledge the significance of, one of the few remaining Patriots, 45527 *Southport*, at Blackpool Central. Although I prioritised a trip over the subsequently closed Marton direct line, now part of the M55, with hindsight I regret snubbing a ride with a Patriot: an opportunity lost forever. I consoled myself with the fact that at least I had visited Blackpool Central, which closed just three months after my visit.

Retrospectively, upon the realisation that overnight train travel was not only cheaper but also enabled greater steam mileages to be gathered, this stopover between clean sheets became the only occasion during four years of travels throughout Britain that I acquiesced to such comfort. That, however, on the first ever night on my own, was not to be known then and snuggling down into the comfortable bed listening to the novelty for me of night-time steam activity resonating from the nearby station, I fell into a fitful sleep.

The following day, a full English breakfast having been consumed, time was spent that Sunday morning at Preston station – the consistency of Stanier tanks on local services and Jintys on shunting duties being broken by Upperby's *Southport*, together with many Black 5s, storming through the station taking day trippers to Blackpool. I wouldn't have known then that, resulting from the contraction of steam services elsewhere in Britain over the coming years, this station was to become a magnet for steam enthusiasts and I was to spend a great many hours festering (to quote modern parlance) in the often forlorn hope that 'required' locomotives would materialise. It was a very hot day and with the train selected in order to make my way via Leeds to Leicester being a DMU, I had no alternative but to suffer and sweat on the two-hour journey via Colne.

Station pilot duties at Preston during 1964 were still in the hands of the elderly Jintys. Here 0-6-0T 3F Hunslet-built 36-year-old 47564 is on carriage-shunting duties. After withdrawal in March 1965 she 'sort of' survived into preservation – being used as spares at the Midland Railway Centre at Butterley!

Colne was originally opened by the Leeds & Bradford Extension Railway, from Skipton, in 1848 becoming, a year later, an end-on station with services operated by the East Lancashire Railway from Blackburn. In its heyday Colne had through services to Yorkshire, Blackpool and London's Euston, but by the 1960s falling passenger numbers saw services truncated at Preston and Skipton – the line north to the latter closing in 1970.

So now, after six hours of travel, I arrived at my father's hometown of Leicester. The first railway into the city was the Leicester & Swannington Railway of 1832 at West Bridge, followed eight years later by the Midland Counties Railway between Derby and Rugby. In the June of 1841 cabinet-maker Thomas Cook put forward an idea to a Leicester temperance meeting that they run an excursion by train to another one based at Loughborough. After receiving the OK from the Midland Railway Company, on 5 July that year a total of 500 persons were conveyed the 12 miles to Loughborough for the princely sum of 1s each – the rest is history.

Initially utilising that route to Rugby, thence via the LNWR (née London & Birmingham Railway) to access London, in 1857 the Midland Railway opened up their direct route via Bedford to Hitchin and the GNR to King's Cross before, in 1868, arriving at their own London terminus of St Pancras. Thus Leicester, further assisted by the arrival of the Great Central in 1899, with its improved transport links was able throughout Queen Victoria's reign to attract a multitude of fleeing European refugees to its wide diversity of industries – a situation very much relevant today.

A newsworthy event in September 2012 was that of Richard III's remains being discovered during an archaeological excavation of a car park – he was then reburied in Leicester cathedral. Sports-wise, Leicester City football club (known as the Foxes) were the unexpected 2016 Premier League winners, having had many mediocre years within the top two divisions of the football league. Earlier that season, Leicester-born *Match of the Day* presenter Gary Lineker had vowed that in the unlikely event of them winning the title he would present the programme in his underwear – a promise fulfilled that September. Meanwhile, another Leicester-born sportsman, Mark Selby (the Jester from Leicester) has been a three times world snooker champion.

With my relatives' family home being located in the Leicester suburb of Evington, sufficient time had to be allowed for any trips out to cope with the likelihood of getting lost amongst the plethora of bus routes operated by the Leicester City bus company. On the Monday I stayed local, firstly viewing Leicester Midland shed (15A) from a conveniently situated road rising sharply adjacent to the depot before going on to Leicester West Bridge. I was fortunate in that on the day of my calling one of the two specially adapted (because of the limited clearance within Glenfield tunnel) BR 2-6-0s was shunting the yard – passenger services having ceased in 1928.

A very hot and sunny Tuesday beckoned, and by now I am certain the reader will have grasped the fact that my manifesto was one of visiting railways 'under the axe'. Hence the destinations of Derby Friargate and Seaton were that day's objective. Expecting a Scot or at the very least steam on the Nottingham service out of Leicester Central, to my abject disappointment, unaware that the LM authorities were utilising spare capacity within a London commuter set, the 08.38 ex Marylebone was a DMU! The forty minutes spent at the fading grandeur of Nottingham Victoria, however, somewhat lifted my mood with examples of previously unseen steam classes, i.e. 9F, BI and O4/8s being witnessed.

Monday, 24 August 1964 and an overview of Leicester Midland shed revealed two of the 580 Fowler 4Fs and a Riddles-designed 9F. Both St Rollox-built 39-year-old 44182, which was withdrawn the following month, and Swindon-built youngster 2-10-0 92089 were home-allocated residents, while 44421 was visiting. The shed closed to steam in June 1966.

These were the remains of the 1893-built Leicester West Bridge station. The line was opened, primarily for coal traffic, in 1832 by the Leicester and Swannington Railway and closed to passengers as early as 1928, with freight lingering on until May 1966.

BR 2MT 78013 is caught shunting at Leicester West Bridge. This is one of two (the other being 78028) examples of that class that had cut down cabs in order to negotiate the height-restricted 1-mile-long Glenfield tunnel.

The 1927 Derby-built 44421 is seen again later in the day at Leicester London Road station with a parcels service. This yellow-striped 4F, although displaying a Leicester smokebox shedplate, was actually allocated to Coalville – being withdrawn that December.

To facilitate the construction of the station I was at that day, 1,300 houses, twenty-four public houses and a church had to be demolished, together with 600,000 cubic yards of sandstone being evacuated from the site. The two owning companies (GCR & GNR) failed to agree on a name, the former naturally favouring Central whilst the latter wanted Joint. The town clerk, highlighting the fact that its official opening day, 24 May 1900, fell on Queen Victoria's birthday, resolved the matter. Constructed in a truly elegant Renaissance style with red-faced bricks and Darley Dale stone and dominated by a 100ft clock tower, the two large island platforms, served by broad wide staircases off an iron footbridge, were both equipped with dining and tearooms. With signal boxes and tunnels at both ends, the entire layout being circumnavigated by passing loops for through freight traffic, the station was, in my eyes a throwback to the times when railway travel was the main transportation throughout the country and as such grand stations akin to this were built to entice prospective customers from all walks of life.

Opposite above: Tuesday, 25 August 1964 saw me visit Nottingham Victoria and is where Annesley's BR 9F 92073 is seen passing through on a northbound freight. This 8-year-old 2-10-0 was transferred to Banbury in June 1965 prior to ending her days at Birkenhead upon that shed's closure in November 1967.

Opposite below: This was the first of three Colwick-allocated locomotives witnessed during my forty-minute stopover at the cathedral of steam, Nottingham Victoria station. The once-thriving parcel business is shown to good effect, B1 4-6-0 61299 being silhouetted in the sunshine awaiting completion of station duties prior to departure.

With the station set in a cutting between two tunnels, the air there always seemed to retain a certain sulphuric content – only being cleared upon a windy day. Here 21-year-old North British-built WD 2-8-0 90259 trundles through with a northbound freight.

Here at an already derelict-looking Derby Friargate station Colwick-allocated Ivatt 2-6-0 43156, a refugee from the M&GN, readies herself for departure with the 13.00 (formed of non-corridor stock) for Nottingham Victoria. The line was to close two weeks later – the Mogul faring little better as it was withdrawn in January 1965.

At Stamford Town, Toton-allocated, Horwich-built 2-8-0 8F 48363 restarts a signal-delayed eastbound freight. In order to take this shot I had prayed for the road not to be cleared before I speed-walked the length of the westbound train I had just alighted from!

Due to service reductions (as detailed in Chapter 3), the scenario I was witnessing on my visit was, however, a very different matter with its train shed roof glazing and the once elegant buildings smoke blackened and filthy, giving the impression that no one cared. Where brickwork had collapsed, improvised sections of corrugated metal sheeting did nothing to dispel the air of neglect. At the north end of the station an LMS Mogul was playing with stock and it was only by chance that, when searching for the 12.05 Derby Friargate departure, I realised it was my train. This was my first run with an example of a LMS Ivatt class known as 'Flying Pigs' – the sobriquet being apparently awarded them by biting footplate sarcasm in that they didn't fly and were pigs to fire! Then followed a most enjoyable forty-minute ride in a four-set non-corridor train over the remaining 18-mile truncated stub of the GNR's Derbyshire and Staffordshire extension, part of which crossed the Erewash valley on the impressive 1,452ft-long Bennerley Viaduct – the complete line closing the following month.

My only shot of an active BR 2MT 2-6-4T was at Seaton, where Wellingborough's 84008 rests having propelled the 16.19 from Stamford Town. This Seaton Flyer became Britain's last rail-motor push-pull-operated service, acquiescing to DMUs in September 1965. Insufficient patronage, however, for these trains, together with those on the connecting cross-country Rugby to Peterborough line, saw both lines close the following June.

Table 56 **Weekdays only**

Rugby and Market Harborough to Stamford and Peterborough

Miles	Miles				A					B SO	C	ThO	MFSO	D SO	SX	SO	SO	SX	E ⊏⊐					
0	—	**RUGBY MIDLAND**	d		06 36		07 25			09 22	09 57			12 33	13 43	13 47			16 50		17 29		19 09	20 53
3½	—	LILBOURNE	d				07 31							12 39							17s35		19s15	20s59
5¼	—	YELVERTOFT & STANFORD PARK	d		06 45		07 35							12 43	13b52						17 39		19 19	21 03
9¼	—	WELFORD & KILWORTH	d		06 53		07 43			09 36	10 09			12 51	14 00	14 04			17 04		17 47		19 27	21 11
12¼	—	THEDDINGWORTH	d		06 59		07 48							12 56	14c04				17e09		17 54		19 33	
14¾	—	LUBENHAM	d		07 04		07 53							13 01	14 09				17e13		17 58		19 38	
17½	—	**MARKET HARBOROUGH**	a		07 10		08 00				10 24			13 07	14 14	14 18			17 20		18 04		19 44	21 24
			d		07 18						10 27			13 12	14 17	14 19			17 22		18 10			21 34
27½	—	ROCKINGHAM	d		07 32						10 38			13 27	14 33				17 36		18 24			
31½	—	SEATON	a		07 39						10 44			13 34	14 43	14 41			17 43		18 31			21 52
—	0	SEATON	d					08 15	09 28			12·15	12 38				14 50	15 15		17 47		18 55		21 54
—	2	MORCOTT	d					08 19	09 32				12 42				14 54	15 19		17 51				
—	3¾	LUFFENHAM	d					08 23	09 37			12 23	12 46				14 58	15 23		17 55		19 03		
—	6½	KETTON & COLLYWESTON	d					08 29	09 43				12 52				15 04	15 29		18 05		19 09		
—	9½	**STAMFORD**	a					08 38	09 52				13 01				15 13	15 38		18 10		19 18		22d11
—	—	SEATON	d		07 40						10 45			13 37	14 44	14 42			17 45		18 33			
34¼	—	WAKERLEY & BARROWDEN	d		07 45									13 42	14 49						18 38			
38¾	—	KING'S CLIFFE	d		07 53						10 56			13 51	14 57				17 56		18 46			
50¾	—	**PETERBOROUGH EAST**	a		08 11						11 12			14 11	15 15	15 09			18 14		19 04			22 34

Weekdays only

Peterborough and Stamford to Market Harborough and Rugby

Miles	Miles										F ⊏⊐	ThO	MFSO		G SX	G SO			H	J SO				
0	—	**PETERBOROUGH EAST**	d				07 05				10 21				13 17	13 17			16 13	17 04		18 18		20 12
12	—	KING'S CLIFFE	d				07 25								13 34	13 34			16 33			18 38		
16¼	—	WAKERLEY & BARROWDEN	d				07 32								13g41	13 41			16 40			18 45		
19¼	—	SEATON	a				07 37				10 52				13 47	13 47			16 45			18 50		20 41
—	0	**STAMFORD**	d					08 55	10 15				13 20				16 19				18 24		20 10	
—	3½	KETTON & COLLYWESTON	d					09 01	10 21				13 26				16f25				18 30		20 16	
—	6	LUFFENHAM	d					09 06	10 26			13 03	13 33				16 31				18 36		20 23	
—	7¾	MORCOTT	d					09 11	10 31			13 07	13 38				16 36				18 41			
—	9¾	SEATON	a					09 17	10 37			13 13	13 44				16 42				18 47		20 31	
—	—	SEATON	d				07 40				10 53				13 48	13 48			16 47			18 53		20 48
23½	—	ROCKINGHAM	d				07 46				10 59				13 54	13 54			16 53			18 59		20 54
33¾	—	**MARKET HARBOROUGH**	a				08 03				11 15				14 09	14 09			17 09	17 56		19 15		21 10
			d	06 25	07 22		08 18				11 18				14 11	14 11			17 14	17 58		19 21		21 18
36	—	LUBENHAM	d	06 29	07 26		08 22									14 16						19 25		
38½	—	THEDDINGWORTH	d	06 34	07 31		08 27															19 30		
41½	—	WELFORD & KILWORTH	d	06 43	07 39		08 34				11 33				14 25	14 25			17 26	18 13		19 40		21 30
45½	—	YELVERTOFT & STANFORD PARK	d	06 49	07 45		08 40									14 31								
47¼	—	LILBOURNE	d	06 53	07 49		08f44																	
51	—	**RUGBY MIDLAND**	a	07 01	07 57		08 52				11 53				14 41	14 41			17 46	18 28		19 55		21 45

MIDLAND RED AND RAILWAYS JOINT MOTOR SERVICES,

RUGBY, WELFORD AND MARKET HARBOROUGH—SUNDAYS

Availability of Rail Tickets by Road

Ordinary single and the outward and return halves of ordinary Return and Services tickets issued by British Railways between Rugby Midland (or beyond) and intermediate stations to Market Harborough (or beyond) or vice versa, are accepted on Midland Omnibus services which leave Rugby Midland station at 15 50 and 19 15 and Market Harborough station at 17 10 and 18 30 on Sundays

Heavy figures denote through carriages; light figures denote connecting services
For general notes see page 11

For complete service between Luffenham and Stamford see Table 124

A Through carriages to March
B 18 June to 3 September. Through carriages Walsall to Yarmouth Vauxhall
C Through carriages Birmingham to Ely
D Through carriages to Ipswich 18 June to 10 September
E Through carriages Birmingham to Yarmouth Vauxhall. ⊏⊐ to Norwich
F Through carriages Yarmouth Vauxhall to Birmingham. ⊏⊐ from Norwich
G Through carriages Ely to Birmingham
H Through carriages from Harwich Town
J 18 June to 3 September. Through carriages Yarmouth Vauxhall to Walsall

b Stops to set down on notice being given at Rugby
c Wednesday only
d Departure time
e Stops at Theddingworth on Fridays only and Lubenham Mondays to Fridays only to set down passengers
f Saturdays only
g Thursdays only
s Stops to set down only

210

Returning to Nottingham, I then caught a DMU to Grantham for a short trip along the ECML to Peterborough en route to Stamford for a ride on the *Seaton Flyer*. This auto train service had, with the Lymington & Swanage branch trains having succumbed to loco-haulage some three months earlier, become Britain's final push-pull operated service. Another representative of the 1953-designed short-lived BR 2MTs, Wellingborough's 84008, propelled me the 9¾ miles through the scenic sparsely populated corner of Britain's smallest county, Rutland, before having to change onto a Peterborough–Rugby service at Seaton en route home to Leicester. It wasn't to last. The 84xxxs allocated for those trains were withdrawn in October 1965 (some transferred *on paper* to Eastleigh for the never-executed plan to replace the aging O2s on the Isle of Wight!), after which DMUs took over, with all lines in the area closing in 1966.

This jaw-dropping panoramic view of Crewe South was taken hanging out of the window while at a signal stop awaiting a platform on Wednesday, 26 August 1964. I had never before seen such a large shed. Over the following three years when approaching Crewe, often during the hours of darkness, upon seeing the welcoming sight of so many steam locomotives surrounded by the seemingly permanent sulphuric haze reflected in the yard lights I knew, as a steam chaser, that whatever the weekend held I was in the right part of the country. Regrettably, upon its closure to steam in November 1967, rows of derelict, rusting hulks awaiting their fate was a common sight.

Normanton's Riddles-designed WD 90254, a long way from home, is at Crewe station awaiting signals for the Stoke branch. This 1943-built 2-8-0 was to end her days at West Hartlepool in February 1967.

One of the sixty-five-strong Riddles-designed 2MT Moguls, Crewe South-allocated 78010, is captured in ex works condition at Derby. Regrettably never catching one in BR revenue-earning service I have subsequently remedied the matter – all three in preservation having been red-lined.

Home-allocated 78061 was in less-favourable condition that day – this 7½-year-old being transferred to Leicester the following month and withdrawn upon that shed's closure to steam in June 1966.

Table 207— LEICESTER AND BURTON-ON-TRENT
WEEKDAYS ONLY

Miles		a.m.	a.m.		a.m.			a.m. (TC to Derby Midland arr. 10.26 p.m)			WSO p.m. (TC to Derby Midland arr. 1.28 p.m. WO, arr. 1.32 p.m. SO)	p.m.	p.m. (TC Derby Midland arr. 6.18 p.m.)	p.m.	p.m.			p.m.
0	**LEICESTER London Road** dep.	5 0	...	...	7 5	...	...	9 10	...	...	12 13	3 48	4 55	5 40	6 15	...	...	9 5
5¾	Kirby Muxloe	.	.	.	7 16	.	.	9 20	.	.	12 23	3 58	5 5	5 51	6 25	.	.	...
8½	Desford	...	...	...	7 21	...	...	9 24	...	...	12 27	4 2	5 9	5 56	6 30	...	...	9 18
12¾	Bagworth & Ellistown	.	.	.	7 30	.	.	9 32	.	.	12 35	4 10	5 17	6 5	6 38	.	.	9 26
16¼	Coalville Town	5 32	5 50	...	7 39	...	...	9 41	...	...	12 44	4 19	5 31	6 17	6 47	...	...	9 35
21	Ashby-de-la-Zouch	.	6 2	.	7 47	.	.	9 48	.	.	12 51	4 27	5 39	6 24	6 54	.	.	9 42
23½	Moira	...	6 8	...	7 51	...	...	9 52	...	...	12 56	4 32	5 43	6 29	6 59	...	...	9 47
26	Gresley	.	6 17	.	7 58	.	.	9 59	.	.	1 3	4 39	5 50	6 35	7 6	.	.	9 54
30¾	**BURTON-ON-TRENT** arr.	...	6 26	...	8 7	...	...	10 7	...	...	1 11	4 47	5 58	6 44	7 16	...	...	10 2

Miles		SX a.m.	SO a.m.	a.m.	WSO a.m.	WSO p.m.	p.m.		SX p.m.			p.m.
0	**BURTON-ON-TRENT** dep.	6 55	7 0	8 17	10 25	1 0	5 25	...	7 50	...	...	9 0
4¾	Gresley	7 5	7 11	8 25	10 33	1 10	5 33	.	8 2	.	.	9 9
7¼	Moira	7 13	7 17	8 30	10 39	1 18	5 39	...	8 10	...	...	9 16
9¾	Ashby-de-la-Zouch	7 19	7 23	8 35	10 44	1 25	5 44	.	8 21	.	.	9 24
14½	Coalville Town	7 30	7 34	8 44	10 54	1 36	5 54	...	8 36	...	...	9 34
18	Bagworth & Ellistown	7 39	7 42	8 52	11 2	1 45	6 2	.	8 45	.	.	9 42
22¼	Desford	7 46	7 49	8 59	11 9	1 52	6 9	...	8 58	...	...	9 50
25	Kirby Muxloe	7 56	7 54	9 3	11 13	1 57	6 13	.	.	.	.	9 55
30¾	**LEICESTER London Road** arr.	8 3	8 5	9 15	11 25	2 10	6 25	...	9 14	...	...	10 6

ƨ—Stops only to pick up passengers.
þ—Stops only to set down passengers.
SO—Saturdays only.
SX—Saturdays excepted.
a—a.m.
p—p.m.

The last timetable of the Burton to Leicester line.

Yet another glorious August day saw me, on the Wednesday, visit Birmingham, Shrewsbury and Crewe. The travel perks associated with BR employment coupled with the energies of youth gave no excuse for teenagers without commitments to explore all the corners of this wonderful land of ours. Using street maps located within Lt Fuller's *Shed Directory*, I negotiated my way from New Street to Snow Hill stations at Birmingham, at the latter witnessing one of the two remaining 81xx Prairie conversion tanks, before progressing onto Shrewsbury. After noting, and vowing to return one day, the many passenger services still in the hands of steam power on the Birkenhead trains, I went on to the axis of the WCML at Crewe, passing by the largest steam shed I had ever seen: Crewe South. Overhead electric, diesels, steam; Crewe had it all and after an hour an awestruck southerner went on his way to Derby and Burton for the final objective of the day – yes you've guessed it, another doomed line; the Burton–Leicester via Coalville line, which closed, to passengers, the following month.

Thursday, 27 August 1964 saw me stay local. The GNR's Leicester Belgrave Road station had last seen regular passenger trains as far back as 1953. Kept open for holidaymaker summer Saturday and excursion traffic to the East Coast resorts of Skegness and Mablethorpe, they too had ceased in September 1962.

During 1965 the remaining freight services over the GC were rerouted away in order to 'prove' the line was not economically viable based on the remaining sparse passenger traffic. Eight-year-old Annesley-allocated BR 9F 2-10-0 92088 interrupted my sunbathing when storming by with a southbound 'windcutter' – a sobriquet given to the Woodford–Annesley fast freights that were once the main revenue earners over the line.

Local trips were made over the remaining two days of my stay. On the Thursday, Leicester Belgrave Road, was visited. Although closed to regular passenger services in 1953, it was still utilised for a further nine years by East Coast resort holiday excursion trains.

On the last day of my stay, the Friday, I made my way across Leicester to a bridge spanning the GC line at Aylestone with the intention of photographing the 'Windcutters' – the famed Annesley–Woodford BR 9F-worked fast freights. This appellation was a nickname awarded these fast freights by enthusiasts – railwaymen simply referring to them as 'runners'. It was a lovely sunny day (weren't they always in our youthful years!) and although witnessing these BR 9F-worked services, in between spells of sunbathing on the embankment, my camera's inferior shutter speed led to just one photograph being of publishable (?) quality – the remainder being just blurred ghost-like apparitions. I had positioned myself near a road over bridge and, although obviously aware of the oncoming train having heard it some distance away, upon it suddenly erupting from under the bridge, in full cry with smoke and steam escaping from seemingly every orifice, the spine-tingling, hair-raising effect it had on me has never been forgotten. It was a living machine, with chimney blasting, cylinders hissing, pistons pumping and rods rotating. If I hadn't already been in awe of the steam locomotive by then I would surely have been converted. Then, after the screeching wheels of the wagons, and the brake van bouncing along at the back had passed, silence returned – the sulphuric aroma of burning coal and smoke lingering in the air becoming the only reminders of what had just passed.

And so to the final day of my weeklong stay with my Leicester relatives – Saturday, 29 August 1964. When changing trains at Market Harborough en route home, Saltley's Stanier 4-6-0 44829 runs light engine through the station.

Stanier 4-6-0 45113 reposes in the sun near her home station of Rugby Midland. This nomadic machine had been reallocated to at least seventeen sheds during her thirty-year career – returning to Rugby on four occasions.

For nearly thirty years Stanier Jubilee 45633 *Aden*, seen here at Bletchley, had worked over WCML metals. This Warrington Dallam locomotive was now, however, in her twilight years – withdrawal coming eleven months later.

Ebbw Junction's 6-year-old 9F 92235, presumably having worked in over the long-since deceased line via Verney Junction from Oxford, rests at Bletchley shed (1E). The shed closed to steam in October 1965 – the 9F faring little better, being withdrawn at Bristol Barrow Road a month later.

Opposite above: With passenger services ceasing the following month, this was yet another line built into my complex itinerary. Derby-built fifty-two-seat single railcar M79990, forming the 14.45 departure out of Buckingham for Bletchley, awaits non-existent passengers.

Opposite below: The last timetable of the Newport Pagnell branch.

able 58	WOLVERTON AND NEWPORT PAGNELL													
	WEEKDAYS ONLY													
Miles					SO	SO		SX	SO	Th FO	Th FX			
		a.m.	a.m.	a.m.	p.m.	p.m.		p.m.	p.m.	p.m.	p.m.	p.m.		
0	WOLVERTON for Stony Stratford dep	7 48	8 33	10 0	12 25	1 13		2 40	2 45	4 42	4 55	5 43	...	...
1½	Bradwell	7 51	8 36	10 3	12 28	1 16	...	2 43	2 48	4 45	4 58	5 46	...	...
2¾	Great Linford	7 55	8 40	10 7	12 32	1 20		2 47	2 52	4 49	5 2	5 51		
4	NEWPORT PAGNELL arr	8 0	8 45	10 12	12 37	1 25	...	2 52	2 57	4 54	5 7	5 56	...	...

Miles					SO	SO	SX	SO				
		a.m.		a.m.	a.m.	a.m.	p.m.	p.m.	p.m.		p.m.	p.m.	p.m.
0	NEWPORT PAGNELL dep	7 15		8 15	8 48	11 40	12 56	1 0	1 30	.	4 0	5 17	6 1
1½	Great Linford	7 18	...	8 18	8 51	11 43	12 59	1 3	1 33	...	4 3	5 20	6 4
2¾	Bradwell	7 24	.	8 23	8 56	11 48	1 4	1 8	1 38	.	4 8	5 25	6 9
4	WOLVERTON for Stony Stratford arr	7 30	...	8 27	9 0	11 52	1 8	1 12	1 42	...	4 12	5 29	6 13

SO—Saturdays only.		**ThFO**—Thursdays and Fridays only.	
SX—Saturdays excepted.		**ThFX**—Thursdays and Fridays excepted.	

Having bid farewell to my hosts on the Saturday, did I go straight home – I don't think so! Two more branch lines required my attention before hitting the metropolis and commuter land I was so used to – both in Buckinghamshire and both closing the following month. Initially surprised at how many of these 'doomed' lines were still steam worked; with an increasing appreciation of railway politics relating to the economics of closure it began to dawn on me that, rather than improve the services in the form of modern stock/regular interval timings to attract potential increased patronage, BR chose to just let such services die on their feet. I was to come across this closure-by-stealth method on many occasions over the next few years – perhaps the most extreme examples being the S & D and ex GCR lines.

Rant over, let's get back to the trip. Having said that, there was an attempt, in the case of the Buckingham branch, to make it pay. Originally running through to Banbury, BR initially dieselised the services west of Buckingham in 1956 before, quoting economics, withdrawal in 1961 – the remaining stub from Verney Junction lingering on until a month after my visit.

The second branch covered that day was that between Wolverton and Newport Pagnell. Opened in 1867, it was originally envisaged that the branch be extended eastwards to Wellingborough, and although some earthworks, and indeed a bridge, had been constructed, the scheme was abandoned in 1871. Known locally as the *Newport Nobby*, Bletchley-allocated Mickey tank 41222 was performing the thirty-minute, 8-mile honours for myself that day, together with the few other passengers aboard.

Condemned to closure within the Beeching report on the last day, the following month, a bucket of water was thrown over a double dressed as the 'good' doctor, reflecting the local's opinions about him. Vociferous cries were always raised whenever a closure was proposed. Petitions were created, placards waved and local newspapers castigated BR – but all was usually to no avail. Everyone wanted a railway station and train service available to them but the majority failed to use them – effectively proving that, financially, Beeching was right!

So that was it. A southerner's appetite had been suitably whetted for further jaunts around the country. My leanings, however, began to veer towards chasing the fast-disappearing steam passenger services – the consequence of which was missing many line closures that were *not* steam operated; the funds of a junior clerk not permitting both to be catered for!

Time Arrive	Time Depart	Station	Traction	Date	Time Arrive	Time Depart	Station	Traction	Date
	23.55	King's Cross	D1532	Fri 21st	16.04	16.19	Stamford Town	84008	Tue 25th
05.41	08.15	Newcastle	D5182	Sat 22nd	16.42	16.47	Seaton	D5014	
09.48	10.45	Carlisle	45209		17.09	17.12	M Harboro	D71	
13.12	14.55	Preston	45096		17.29		Leicester Lon Rd		
		Poulton le Fylde	84010			08.20	Leicester Lon Rd	DMU	Wed 26th
15.42	16.10	Fleetwood	DMU		09.28		Bham New St		
16.25	16.45	Poulton le Fylde	44729			10.24	Bham Snow Hill	D1699	
16.53	17.10	Blackpool North	45096		11.25	12.32	Shrewsbury	D1597	
17.36	17.53	Kirkham & W	44930		13.12	14.20	Crewe	DMU	
18.19	19.32	Blackpool Ctl	DMU		15.39	16.10	Derby Midland	DMU	
19.54		Preston			16.26	17.25	Burton on Trent	DMU	
	13.40	Preston	DMU	Sun 23rd	18.25		Leicester Lon Rd		
15.27	16.10	Leeds City	D98			10.02	Leicester Lon Rd	DMU	Sat 29th
18.48	19.00	Nottingham Mid	DMU		10.22	11.18	M Harboro	D5010	
19.48		Leicester Lon Rd			11.51	12.35	Rugby Midland	D5074	
	10.56	Leicester Ctl	DMU	Tue 25th	13.43	14.10	Bletchley	DMU	
11.27	12.05	Nottingham Vic	43156		14.36	14.45	Buckingham	DMU	
12.44	13.00	Derby Friargate	43156		15.11	16.07	Bletchley	D5081	
13.43	13.50	Nottingham Vic	DMU		16.15	16.55	Wolverton	41222	
14.35	14.51	Grantham	D1525		17.10	17.17	Newport Pagnell	41222	
15.18	15.42	Peterborough N	D5388		17.32	18.17	Wolverton	D222	Laconia
					19.58		Euston		

British Railways
LONDON MIDLAND REGION

Passenger Services

TIMETABLE

LONDON
Euston·St. Pancras·Marylebone·Broad Street

THE MIDLANDS
NORTH WALES
THE NORTH
(including suburban services)

GRATUITOUS

Supplements, giving details of altera-
tions to this timetable are issued free
of charge (see page 4).
See page 3 for special notice.

7 Sept 1964 to 13 June 1965
or until further notice

3

THE GONE COMPLETELY RAILWAY: 1965–66

My next incursion onto LMR metals was undertaken just under a month later, out of Marylebone over the London Extension of the former Great Central Railway. Not initially appreciating what a rich source of new haulage opportunities were available to me so close to home, I should have paid more attention to Herman's Hermit's chart-topping hit at the time 'I'm Into Something Good'.

The majority of Britain's comprehensive railway network was built during the railway mania years of the mid-nineteenth century; new lines constructed after the 1870s being predominately gap-filling branches off main lines to serve more rural towns. One such company was the provincial Manchester, Sheffield & Lincolnshire Railway (MS&LR) created in 1847, which linked the west and east coasts of northern England across the Pennines, and which also had access to London via Retford and the Great Northern Railway. Sir Edward Watkin, who had taken over directorship of the MS&LR in 1864, grew tired of handing over the potentially lucrative London traffic to rivals and, having made several attempts to co-build a London line with other companies, decided to go it alone – having a vision of running through trains from the MS&LR at Manchester, under the streets of London and finally through a Channel tunnel to Paris. Although he was also chairman of two railways over which the proposed trains would travel, the Metropolitan and South Eastern, even he was unable to progress the

The Great Central Railway's coat of arms symbolised the speed and dash of the new organisation. Crowning it all was a locomotive flanked with wings. Beneath that were the elements of the arms of cities served by the company, i.e. Manchester, Sheffield, Lincoln, Leicester and London. In the centre is the winged cap of Mercury, incorporated to give the impression of speed but often disrespectfully described as a bowler hat by its employees. Then follows an adaptation of the City of London arms, with two daggers instead of one (indicative of a warning of a readiness to fight). Most prominent, at the bottom, is the motto – *Forward*. (Steam Railways of Britain: O.S. Nock)

Bill through parliament due to substantial objections by those whose own interests were under threat.

The compromise of completing the 92-mile Annesley to Quainton Road line, which was finally opened for passenger traffic in 1899, received the accolade of being the last complete British mainline constructed. It was indeed a grandiose railway, built to a more generous width as per 1895 Board of Trade regulations, with the exception of the London extension, a ruling gradient of 1 in 176, and including three major city centre stations – Nottingham, Leicester and Marylebone. Seen by rival companies as a loss-maker, the MS&L – became known as the 'Money Sunk & Lost', and when the title was changed (in 1897) to the Great Central Railway – GC – it was mischievously referred to as 'Gone Completely' – signifying the expected losses of the shareholders' investments!

For many years the line, under the auspices of both the LNER and ER, offered fast express trains from Manchester and the Midlands to London including titled trains such as The Master Cutler and The South Yorkshireman. The seeds for its downfall were, however, sown in the 1958 regional boundary changes, when the route was transferred to the LMR. Underscoring a decline in its vital freight traffic, in January 1960 the LMR, viewing the route as a duplicate to 'their' Midland Main Line, withdrew the express passenger services – the accompanying press release stating: 'The express trains were withdrawn not because they were unremunerative in themselves but for reasons for passenger travel as a whole in the territory served' – highlighting an alleged saving of £140,000 per annum together with the expectation (subsequently proving flawed) that existing passengers would use the alternative services into St Pancras. Substituting them with a token three semi-fasts, initially intended to be formed of cross-country DMUs offering refreshment facilities, per day between London and Nottingham, the move led to the matter being highlighted in a House of Commons debate – an opposition Conservative MP stating: 'They (BR) have been closing the line for five years to get the figures to show people are not travelling on it.' The solitary nod to modernisation was in early 1963 when the 08.38 down and 12.25 return went DMU. Later that year, in March, stopping trains over much of the route were withdrawn and many local stations were closed – presaging that better use of the route could be made for parcel and freight traffic!

Opened in 1899, Marylebone was the youngest of London's termini stations. The original proposal for an eight-platform terminus was shelved because of the expense of compulsory purchasing 70 acres of middle-class-owned properties in the St John's Wood, Eyre estate and Lord's Cricket Ground areas in order to gain access to Marylebone itself – the eventual four being the outcome. John Betjeman rightly described the place as having the air of a public library rather than a railway station – it always being one of the quietest of London's termini.

With 1965 being the year I most frequented the station, I found it to be more akin to a suburban terminus with the aforementioned air now saturated with the fumes from Aylesbury and High Wycombe-destined DMUs ticking over. But wait, as if they were unwelcome intruders, over on platform 4, with a wisp of steam at its head, the usually four-vehicle-formed 14.38 and 16.38 Nottingham trains sat quietly waiting for non-existent custom. Seemingly treated as if they were an inconvenience on a suburban scene, upon their withdrawal in 1966 various schemes for diversion of the remaining services into Paddington, BR eying up the profitable land value, culminated in a closure proposal in 1984. Strong opposition from local authorities together with the creation of the Network South East organisation resulted in a resurgence of passenger numbers, and an accompanying two further platforms, with main-line services to Oxford and Birmingham now running.

Table 116 **Weekdays**

London Marylebone to Leicester and Nottingham

Miles			A MX	⌶	B MX	MX				MX				Bus			SO		Bus	K SX ⌶	L ⌶		N SO ⌶
	LONDON MARYLEBONE	d						01 40					03 40			08 38							
9½	HARROW ON THE HILL	d														08 58							
27¾	120 HIGH WYCOMBE	d														*07c45*							
36	120 PRINCES RISBOROUGH	d														*08e12*							
37¾	AYLESBURY	d											05 20			09 31							
59½	BRACKLEY	d											05s46			09 53							
69	WOODFORD HALSE	a											06 02			10 04							
—	WOODFORD HALSE	d				00 12				03 17				07 47		*10t17*			13 17				
80	BANBURY	a				00 33				03 38				08 11		*10t41*			13 41				
	BANBURY	d														*09t25*				14 58	14 58		15 33
—	WOODFORD HALSE	a														*09t49*							
—	WOODFORD HALSE	d			00 17								06 50			10 06							
83½	RUGBY CENTRAL	a			00 38			03 22					07 11			10 24				15 35	15 35		16 13
	RUGBY CENTRAL	d	00 14		00 42			03 23					07 20			10 27	12 30			15 38	15 38		16 16
90	LUTTERWORTH	d											07 31			10 36	12 41						
93¾	ASHBY MAGNA	d											07 40			10 42	12 50						
103	**LEICESTER CENTRAL**	a	00 39		01 07			03 47					07 54			10 55	13 04			16 02	16 02		16 41
	LEICESTER CENTRAL	d	00 51		01 17						07 30		08 00			10 59	13 08			16 06	16 06		16 47
113	LOUGHBOROUGH CENTRAL	a	01 07		01 33						07 44		08 14			11 12	13 22			16 20	16 20		17 03
	LOUGHBOROUGH CENTRAL	d	01 10		01 35						07 45		08 16			11 13	13 23			16 23	16 23		17 05
117½	EAST LEAKE	d									07 54		08 25			11 20	13 32						
126½	**NOTTINGHAM VICTORIA**	a	01 31		01 56						08 10		08 41			11 35	13 49			16 43	16 43		17 26
	NOTTINGHAM VICTORIA	d	01 41		02 10															16 47	16 47		17 30
164½	SHEFFIELD VICTORIA	a	02 57		03 24															18 00	18 00		18 46

Sundays

			SX	SO		SX		Q FO	Q FSX	Q SO		A SX	U SX		A SO	Sundays	Sundays	Sundays A	Sundays	Sundays U	Sundays	Sundays	Sundays	Sundays
LONDON MARYLEBONE	d	14 38		16 38		16 38						21 55			22 45							00 40		
HARROW ON THE HILL	d	14 57		16 57		16 57						*21 22*			22 22							*23y37*		
120 HIGH WYCOMBE	d	*14g15*		*16 52*		*16 59*						22 25										*00 06*		
120 PRINCES RISBOROUGH	d	*14h32*		*17 06*		*17 14*						*22 38*										*00 20*		
AYLESBURY	d	15 38		17 38		17 38						23 04			23 39							01 38		
BRACKLEY	d	16 05		18 05		18 05						23 32			00 04			00 04						
WOODFORD HALSE	a	16 18		18 18		18 18						23 46			00 18			00 18				02 15		
WOODFORD HALSE	d			*18t57*		*18t57*										00 12								03 17
BANBURY	a			*19t21*		*19t21*										00 35								03 38
BANBURY	d	*15t45*		*17t45*		*17t45*		21 16	21 16	21 10			23 50							00 20				
WOODFORD HALSE	a	*16t09*		*18t09*		*18t09*		21 38	21 38	21 32			00 12							00 45				
WOODFORD HALSE	d	16 20		18 20		18 20		21 41	21 41	21 37		23 48	00 17		00 20			00 20		00 47		02 18		
RUGBY CENTRAL	a	16 39		18 39		18 39		22 02	22 02	21 58		00 09	00 38		00 39			00 39		01 08		02 36		
RUGBY CENTRAL	d	16 41	17 20	18 41		18 41		22 09	22 09	22 35		00 14	00 42		00 41			00 41		01 13		02 38		
LUTTERWORTH	d	16 52	17 31	18 52		18 52		22 22		22 18												02 50		
ASHBY MAGNA	d	17 01	17 40	19 01		19 01																		
LEICESTER CENTRAL	a	17 15	17 54	19 15		19 15		22 40	22 40	22 36		00 39	01 07		01 05			01 05		01 38		03 06		
LEICESTER CENTRAL	d	17 19	18 00	19 19		19 24		22 50	22 56	22 43		00 51	01 17		01 10			01 10		01 48		03 16		
LOUGHBOROUGH CENTRAL	a	17 31	18 14	19 31		19 36		23 06	23 06	22 59		01 07	01 33		01 24			01 24		02 04				
LOUGHBOROUGH CENTRAL	d	17 33	18 15	19 33		19 38		23 08	23 08	23 01		01 10	01 35		01 26			01 26		02 07				
EAST LEAKE	d	17 42	18 24	19 42		19 47																		
NOTTINGHAM VICTORIA	a	18 01	18 40	19 58		20 03		23 29	23 29	23 22		01 31	01 56		01 46			01 46		02 28		03 50		
NOTTINGHAM VICTORIA	d							23 43	23 43	23 33		01 41	02 10		01 51			01 51		02 43				
SHEFFIELD VICTORIA	a							00 57	00 57	00 49		02 57	03 24		03 04			03 04		03 58				

Heavy figures denote through carriages; light figures denote connecting services
For general notes see page 11

For complete service between London Marylebone and Aylesbury see Table 120

A Through carriages to Manchester Piccadilly

B Through carriages to York

K 13 June to 2 September. ⌶ and through carriages from Poole to Newcastle

L Until 11 June and from 5 September. ⌶ and through carriages from Poole to York

N 18 June to 3 September. ⌶ and through carriages from Poole to Newcastle

Q Through carriages from Swindon to Sheffield Victoria

U Through carriages from Swindon to York

c On Saturdays dep. High Wycombe 08 08

e On Saturdays dep. Princes Risborough 08 21

g On Saturdays dep. High Wycombe 13 45

h On Saturdays dep. Princes Risborough 14 00

s Stops to set down only

t By omnibus

y Saturday nights

566

able 116 **Weekdays**

Nottingham and Leicester to London Marylebone

		A MX	E MX	G MX						H	J
SHEFFIELD VICTORIA	d	..	00 09	00 45	..	..	..	..	11 37	11 37
NOTTINGHAM VICTORIA	a	..	01 20	01 58	..	..	..	..	12 45	12 45
NOTTINGHAM VICTORIA	d	..	01 33	02 15	07 40	08 15 12 20	..	12 48	12 48
EAST LEAKE	d	..	01 52		07 54	08 29 12 33		13 05	13 05
					08 02	08 37 12 39			
LOUGHBOROUGH CENTRAL	d	..	01 53		08 04	08 38 12 42		13 07	13 07
	a	..	02 08	02 46	08 17	08 49 12 55		13 20	13 20
LEICESTER CENTRAL	d		02 23	03 05	08 20	08 52 13 00		13 23	13 23
ASHBY MAGNA	d				08 36	09 08 13 12			
LUTTERWORTH	d				08 45	09 17 13 20			
	a		02 50		08 55	09 26 13 28		13 48	13 48
RUGBY CENTRAL	d		02 52			09 30 13 30		13 51	13 51
WOODFORD HALSE	a		03 15	03 51		09 50 13 48			
WOODFORD HALSE	d	00 12	03 17	07 47		10 e17	13 17	14 31	14 31
	a	00 33	03 38	08 11		10 e41	13 41		
BANBURY	d					09 e25 12 e30			
WOODFORD HALSE	a					09 e49 12 e54			
WOODFORD HALSE	d			03 56		09 52 13 49			
BRACKLEY	d					10 06 14 01			
AYLESBURY	a			04 e48		10 29 14 27			
120 PRINCES RISBOROUGH	a			07 14		10 54 15 40			
120 HIGH WYCOMBE	a			07 28		11 09 16 e04			
HARROW ON THE HILL	a			05 48		11 09 15 28			
LONDON MARYLEBONE	a					11 25 15 18			

Sundays

		SX	SO	SX	SX	C FSX	D FSO	A	Y	G
SHEFFIELD VICTORIA	d	..		..	..	20 55	20 55		00 09	00 24
NOTTINGHAM VICTORIA	a	..				22 09	22 09		01 20	01 37
NOTTINGHAM VICTORIA	d	17 15	18 15			22 22	22 22		01 33	01 52
EAST LEAKE	d	17 29	18 29			22 41	22 41		01 52	
LOUGHBOROUGH CENTRAL	d	17 37	18 37							
LOUGHBOROUGH CENTRAL	d	17 39	18 39			22 43	22 43		01 53	02 25
	a	17 50	18 52			22 58	22 58		02 08	
LEICESTER CENTRAL	d	17 54	18 55			23 12	23 12		02 23	02 45
ASHBY MAGNA	d	18 10	19 11							
LUTTERWORTH	d	18 19	19 20			23 32			02 50	
	a	18 28	19 30			23 41				
RUGBY CENTRAL	d	18 29				23 47	23 47		02 52	03 33
WOODFORD HALSE	a	18 49				00 10	00 10		03 15	
WOODFORD HALSE	d	18 e57				00 12	00 12	00 12	03 17	
	a	19 e21				00 33	00 e33	00 35	03 38	
BANBURY	d	17 e45		21 10	21 16	23 50				
WOODFORD HALSE	a	18 e09		21 32	21 38	00 12		00 20		
WOODFORD HALSE	d	18 51						00 45		03 41
BRACKLEY	d	19 04								
AYLESBURY	a	19 27								
120 PRINCES RISBOROUGH	a	19 e55								
120 HIGH WYCOMBE	a	20 e57								
HARROW ON THE HILL	a	20 09								05 19
LONDON MARYLEBONE	a	20 25								

Heavy figures denote through carriages; light figures denote connecting services

For general notes see page 11

For complete service between Aylesbury and London Marylebone see Table 120

A Through carriages to Swindon
C Through carriages from York (from 4 July to 1 September through carriages from Scarborough) to Swindon
D Through carriages from York (from 2 July to 3 September through carriages from Scarborough) to Swindon

E Through carriages from York to Swindon
G Through carriages from Manchester Central
H 13 June to 3 September, ㅍ and through carriages from Newcastle to Poole
J Until 11 June and from 5 September, ㅍ and through carriages from York to Poole
Y Through carriages from York to Bristol Temple Meads

b Saturdays excepted
e On Saturdays arr. High Wycombe 16 07
f On Sunday mornings arr. Banbury 00 35
s Stops to set down only
t By omnibus

567

Timetable extracts of the service on offer in the LMR summer 1965 timetable.

Back then, the sparse service on offer resulted in near-empty trains, and always selecting a vacant compartment close to the locomotive, I settled down stopwatch in the left hand and pen in my right, ready to record the ride – after all it would have been repetitive just to look out of the window witnessing the same scenery journey after journey. Off we set climbing through the three tunnels, smoke filling the compartment, it goes without saying in the leading coach through the deliberately opened window, before emerging adjacent to the Metropolitan line racing, and always beating, parallel-running Metropolitan Line trains, which had started out of Baker Street. After briefly calling at Harrow-on-the-Hill, we began to climb into the Chilterns, sharing the line with the aforementioned services from Rickmansworth. Given a clear road, the drivers then let the locomotive off the leash and some ear-shattering ascents of nearly 8 miles of 1 in 105 to Amersham were enjoyed surmounting the summit at MP 31½. Then followed 3 miles of downhill prior to climbing through Great Missenden before descending at breakneck speed into the Vale of Aylesbury.

With water usually being taken at Aylesbury, the station time was often exceeded before we set off along mile after mile of flat, uninhabited countryside. What possessed the Metropolitan Railway to anticipate custom with its 1891 purchase of the Aylesbury and (the never reached) Buckingham Railway is beyond me – perhaps nowadays with the UK population increasing the matter could be revisited. On we ploughed, the many sections of *roaring* rail disrupting speed calculations, out of Buckinghamshire through Oxfordshire (Finmere) to the Northamptonshire town of Brackley. The double whammy of losing both its railway stations within six years will not be remedied in the foreseeable future – the usage of the former GC line trackbed in the vicinity for the proposed HS2 not including any stations nearby. The ruling gradient of 1 in 176 now predominates and, having passed Culworth Junction (for Banbury), we now arrive at what was the axis of the line, 69 miles from London, at Woodford Halse – amply described upon my final visit there, later in this chapter.

Moving on and having travelled through the lengthiest tunnel on the line, that of Catesby, we head down to Rugby Central, after which the WCML is straddled – Rugby Midland station being viewed in the distance. The section we were now traversing had an increased, of sorts, passenger service to Nottingham, the intention of which was to cater for any intrepid commuters brave enough not to suffer lengthy waiting times in between trains.

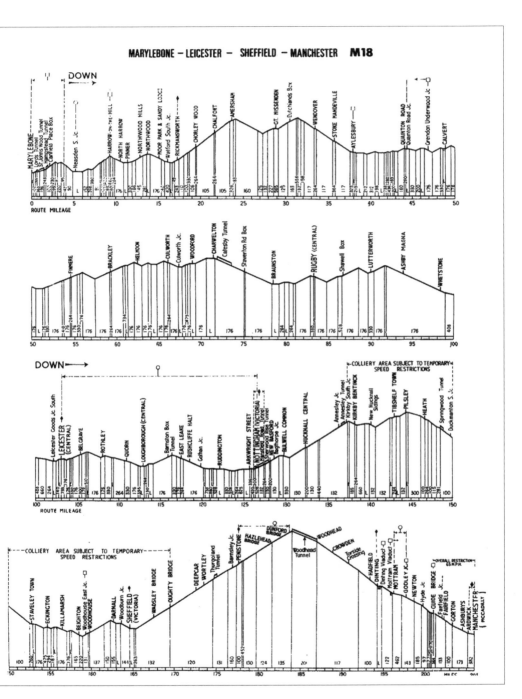

Gradient profile of GC line.

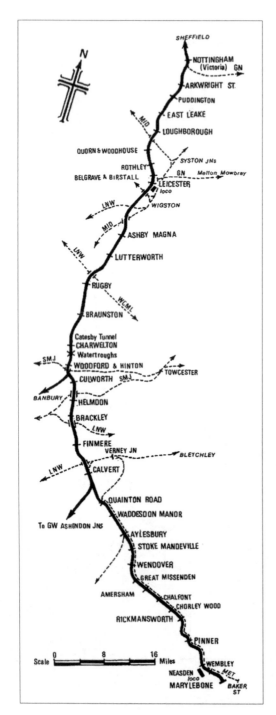

Map of the London extension. (This map originally appeared in issue 180 of *Steam Days* magazine)

If Woodford was the axis of the line as regards freight, Leicester was the passenger equivalent. As mentioned in Chapter 1, I must have, as a school kid, set foot on these platforms before, and during the wait for the southbound train I reminisced as to what locomotives I could have witnessed and, with the obligatory short back and sides and short trousers, what I might have looked like!

Leicester North, built near the site of the closed Belgrave and Birstall station, is nowadays the southern terminus of the highly popular Great Central Railway, the UK's only double-tracked main-line preserved railway. As will be detailed in the following paragraphs, I rarely ventured north of Leicester – returning south on the one evening train to London being the priority.

My self-fashioned pocket-sized GC timetable.

Crewe-built 28-year-old Stanier 5MT 45464 sets forth out of Aylesbury in the gathering gloom of Saturday, 19 March 1966 with the 16.38 Marylebone to Nottingham Victoria. I was adhering to Alternative Plan No. 1 that day and was then to fester in Aylesbury's unheated waiting room for the next two hours.

Rather than carry the bulky LMR timetable with me on my afternoon outings along the line, I fashioned an easy-to-refer-to double-sided pocket timetable card (4in × 3¼in) to carry with me on my increasingly frequent visits over the line. Usually commencing with the 14.38 Marylebone to Nottingham Victoria train, there were three variations of train plans one could use in attempting to obtain runs with as many different locomotives as feasible during those final years of service paucity.

ALTERNATIVE NO. 1

Start out of Marylebone on the 14.38 and, keeping your eyes peeled, you either passed the 16.38 locomotive running light engine en route from Neasden, where it had worked in on the 10.57 parcels ex Nottingham, to Marylebone or at Neasden itself. If it was a required locomotive, i.e. one that I hadn't travelled behind (the number sometimes only just about being discernible through the grime and dirt) then I would alight at Aylesbury, return to Harrow-on-the-Hill on a DMU and catch the 16.38 Marylebone from there. If funds allowed (ticket-wise) I would then go through to Woodford Halse, where after a mere half an hour wait (right time running permitting!) I was able to board the southbound 17.15 ex Nottingham. More often than not I alighted at Aylesbury, where I had the choice of a two-hour wait (for the same train) in a cold, unheated waiting room or returning south immediately on a warm DMU. During the particularly cold winter of 1965–66 needless to say I opted for the latter!

ALTERNATIVE NO. 2

Start out of Marylebone on the 14.38 and, having noted the 16.38 loco-motive en route as *not* being required, continue through to Rugby Central, where, on SX visits only, a 17.20 departure for Nottingham Victoria sat in the down loop. If she was a requirement I alighted and caught her to Ashby

Alternative Plan No. 2 was put into action on Monday, 13 June 1966 when espying a required Banbury 44860 sitting on the stock at Rugby Central in readiness to form the 17.20 stopping service (weren't they all?) for Nottingham Victoria.

Magna (arr 17.40) and whilst awaiting the 17.15 ex Nottingham (dep 18.10) loitered on the island platform. Ashby Magna, together with East Leake, was one of the two local stations 'saved' by the then Minister for Transport, Barbara Castle and, as was the standardised design of all stations along the route, formed of one island platform – the tracks aligned either side to allow widening in the event of continental traffic. Equipped with the customary roofless gents' urinal, this was the only refuge away from an inquisitive porter who, upon espying the solitary passenger alighting, must have wondered as to why he hadn't vacated the station – I was a little wary of the validity of my Weymouth–Perth BR free pass. In the final months, the station becoming unstaffed, I did venture up the steps to the road and, to pass away the wait, strolled along to the bridge over the adjacent newly opened M1 motorway to view the then meagre, compared to nowadays, traffic.

Ashby Magna, a typical island-platform GC line station, is seen from the road bridge later that afternoon – the near empty M1 can be discerned in the background.

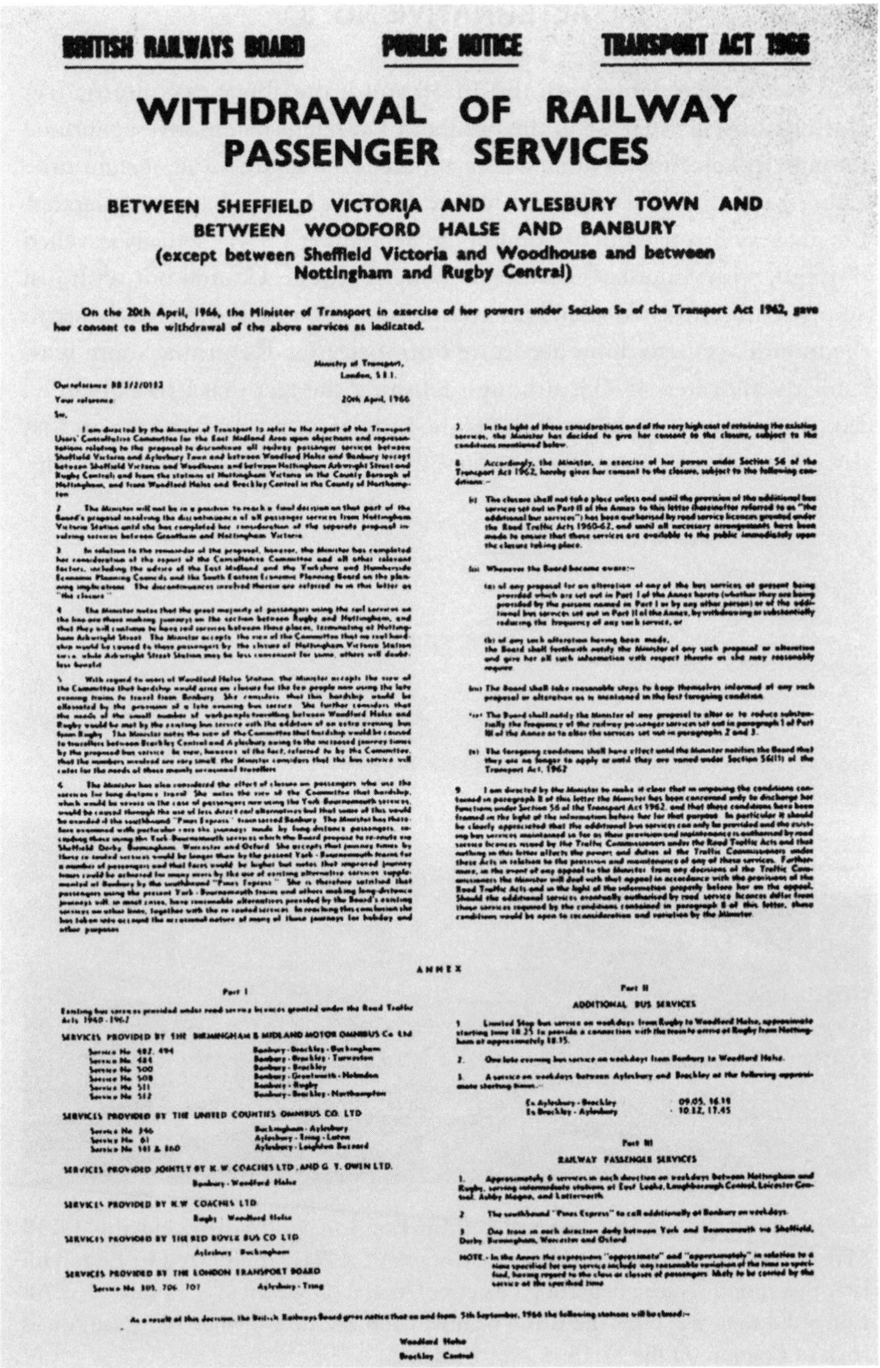

BRITISH RAILWAYS BOARD **PUBLIC NOTICE** **TRANSPORT ACT 1962**

WITHDRAWAL OF RAILWAY PASSENGER SERVICES

BETWEEN SHEFFIELD VICTORIA AND AYLESBURY TOWN AND BETWEEN WOODFORD HALSE AND BANBURY

(except between Sheffield Victoria and Woodhouse and between Nottingham and Rugby Central)

On the 20th April, 1966, the Minister of Transport in exercise of her powers under Section 56 of the Transport Act 1962, gave her consent to the withdrawal of the above services as indicated.

Ministry of Transport,
London, S.W.1.

Our reference BB1/2/0182

Your reference

20th April, 1966

Sir,

[Body of letter — small print, largely illegible]

ANNEX

Part I

Existing bus services provided under road service licences granted under the Road Traffic Acts 1960–1962

SERVICES PROVIDED BY THE BIRMINGHAM & MIDLAND MOTOR OMNIBUS Co Ltd

Service No 482, 494	Banbury - Brackley - Buckingham
Service No 484	Banbury - Brackley - Turweston
Service No 500	Banbury - Brackley
Service No 508	Banbury - Greatworth - Helmdon
Service No 511	Banbury - Rugby
Service No 512	Banbury - Brackley - Northampton

SERVICES PROVIDED BY THE UNITED COUNTIES OMNIBUS CO. LTD

Service No 346	Buckingham - Aylesbury
Service No 61	Aylesbury - Tring - Luton
Service No 101 & 860	Aylesbury - Leighton Buzzard

SERVICES PROVIDED JOINTLY BY K.W. COACHES LTD, AND G.Y. OWEN LTD.

Banbury - Woodford Halse

SERVICES PROVIDED BY K.W. COACHES LTD.

Rugby - Woodford Halse

SERVICES PROVIDED BY THE RED ROVER BUS CO LTD

Aylesbury - Buckingham

SERVICES PROVIDED BY THE LONDON TRANSPORT BOARD

Service No 301, 706, 707 Aylesbury - Tring

Part II

ADDITIONAL BUS SERVICES

1. Limited Stop bus service on weekdays from Rugby to Woodford Halse, approximate starting time 18.25 to provide a connection with the train to arrive at Rugby from Nottingham at approximately 18.15.

2. One late evening bus service on weekdays from Banbury to Woodford Halse.

3. A service on weekdays between Aylesbury and Brackley at the following approximate starting times:

Ex Aylesbury - Brackley	09.05, 16.15
Ex Brackley - Aylesbury	10.12, 17.45

Part III

RAILWAY PASSENGER SERVICES

1. Approximately 6 services in each direction on weekdays between Nottingham and Rugby, serving intermediate stations at East Leake, Loughborough Central, Leicester Central, Ashby Magna, and Lutterworth.

2. The southbound "Pines Express" to call additionally at Banbury on weekdays.

3. One train in each direction daily between York and Bournemouth via Sheffield, Derby, Birmingham, Worcester and Oxford.

NOTE - In the Annex the expressions "approximate" and "approximately" in relation to a time specified for any service include any reasonable variation of the time so specified, having regard to the class or classes of passengers likely to be carried by the service at the specified time

As a result of this decision, the British Railways Board gives notice that on and from 5th September, 1966 the following stations will be closed:-

Woodford Halse
Brackley Central

ALTERNATIVE NO. 3

Start out of Marylebone on the 14.38 and if the above two alternatives failed to assist an increase in the number of different locomotives, continue through to Leicester Central, where a mere forty-minute wait, if right time running was the order of the day, for the 17.15 ex Nottingham was tolerated. On my very first trip out of London (28 September 1964) I actually travelled through, with Annesley's 45450, to Loughborough Central but with just an eight-minute cross-platform connection it was very much a 'heart in the mouth' scenario upon departure from Leicester. Returning south with similarly allocated 45335, although relishing the fact that I had obtained 226 steam miles, I didn't risk the eight-minute, in reality just four on that day, cross-platform connection again – truncating similar out and back trips at Leicester Central.

Having brought me the 103 miles from London whilst working the 14.38 Marylebone to Nottingham Victoria, Annesley's 44717, transferred to Edge Hill later that month, is seen departing Leicester Central on Wednesday, 14 July 1965. All I then did then was cross the island platform and accrue a further 103 steam miles back to London on the 17.15 ex Nottingham.

That same day, Crewe-built, Annesley-allocated sister 44846 was the standby loco at Leicester Central. Upon transfer to Newton Heath she was a regular performer on the Calder Valley-routed 02.10 York to Manchester and worked the final steam departure (03.32 for Halifax) with me aboard out of Leeds Central on Saturday, 29 April 1967.

Saturday, 14 May 1966 and the 14.38 Marylebone to Nottingham Victoria calls at Leicester Central with Colwick's 45190. Transferred to Heaton Mersey the following month, she was withdrawn upon that shed's closure in May 1968. (Alan Hayes)

Now let's turn to the motive-power scene. By the time I *discovered* the GC line in the autumn of 1964, apart from sporadic incursions of B1s, Royal Scots and Standard 5MTs, the motive-power scene was dominated by Stanier Black 5s. It wasn't until mid 1965 that I realised the line could provide rich pickings for a haulage basher such as myself because the foreman at the sheds responsible for providing the locomotives adopted a common user policy by sending out whatever was the fittest and available at the time, i.e. not just from their home shed's allocation. Consequent upon that, I was to collect runs with locomotives allocated from such diverse locations as Aston, Warrington Dallam, Edge Hill and Leeds Holbeck. One by one the servicing points that the GC line locomotives could emanate from/visit were closing to steam – Woodford Halse in June 1965 followed by Bletchley, then in September, Willesden. In an effort to compensate for the decreasing facilities available for steam locomotives working through to the London Extension, eight Britannias (70045–7/50–4) equipped with BR1D enlarged-capacity tenders were transferred to Banbury in October 1965. Taking into consideration their Class 7P rating, they could certainly shift the lightweight trains over the route and the timekeeping improved resulting from their quick acceleration and higher speeds. However, their nemesis was the routine maintenance, which if replacement parts were required had to be dispatched from Crewe or Carlisle, to where the majority of Brits had migrated. Indeed, towards the end of the year the Brits were out of service more than they were in, and in January 1966 they were returned north – the Black 5s regaining their stranglehold on the services. Meanwhile, Annesley had closed and Colwick, transferred from the Eastern Region, had assumed its shed code – changing from 40E to 16B. Twenty-six of Stanier's finest were transferred in, eighteen in December 1965 and eight in February 1966; specifically for the GC-line passenger services. Resulting from their near monopoly from that date until closure, I was to miss but six of them, achieving a respectable 77 per cent (of Colwick's home allocation) success rate!

I was to travel on three overnight services over the line – the first, the Saturday evening 20.25 ex Perth, being a diverted WCML service resulting from electrification work south of Rugby. This short-dated working provided me with, during the summer of 1965, a twelve-hour restful journey home from three Scottish bashes. After Northampton and Blisworth it traversed the somewhat ostentatious flyover at Bletchley, being then routed via Calvert, Grendon Underwood Junction and either Ashendon Junction,

The time is 16.53 on Saturday, 5 June 1965 and Warrington Dallam-allocated 44935 has *just* arrived to work the 16.38 Nottingham Victoria departure out of Marylebone. I was to benefit from the Colwick foreman's propensity to use visiting locomotives, with Black 5s from all over the LMR being caught on the line.

High Wycombe and Wembley Hill or Aylesbury – due into Marylebone at 08.20 on a Sunday morning. Steam hauled to Carlisle, it was then worked by a 'Whistler' (Class 40) over Shap to Crewe, giving way to an AC Electric to Rugby before further Type 4 haulage was collected. On the one occasion it went via Aylesbury I was sufficiently awake to note ex GWR Pannier L95 (formerly BR 5764 and now preserved on the Severn Valley Railway) on an engineering train.

Another convenient way of returning south after steam chasing 'oop north' was the 22.50 Manchester Central to Marylebone service, on which I was to travel on six occasions. With my scant knowledge of Mancunian railway routes, I did question the logic of a train allegedly destined for London leaving Manchester heading west. All became clear as it circumnavigated a myriad of junctions (including the wonderfully named Throstle Nest) before then making its way eastwards, relinquishing its Trafford Park locomotive at Guide Bridge for an EM2 DC Electric (Class 76/7) through the 3-mile long Woodhead tunnel to Sheffield. The fun was only just starting because, fully

Replacing a non–available Brit on the 1D35 (14.38) departure out of Marylebone's platform 4 on Monday, 13 December 1965 was Tylseley–allocated 44859.

The clean air act of 1956 had consigned the obnoxious yellow smog-ridden days of London to history. There were still, however, a great many foggy days and on one of them, Saturday, 23 October 1965, former Scottish Brit 70050 *Firth of Clyde* (at just 12 years old she became the shortest-lived Brit when withdrawn) awaits departure time at Marylebone with the 14.38 for Nottingham Victoria.

expecting this three-vehicle train (two coaches, one van), having been taken over at Sheffield by a Type 3 (Class 37) 'Tractor', to hand over to a Type 2 (Class 24) somewhere en route, what should take us forward from Leicester Central but a *tender-first* Black 5! This steam bonus (I was to learn that the locomotive duty involved had worked the 22.45 down from Marylebone and was en route home to Banbury) was to take me the 34 miles non-stop (the *only* service over the line *not* calling at Rugby Central) to Woodford Halse, before handing over to a 'Splutterbug' for the final 69 miles into Marylebone. It was a struggle to stay awake for the number of the locomotive taking over at the Leicester departure of 02.45 but documentation was paramount in recording the fast-disappearing steam scene. Having said that, I did on one occasion miss the changeover and had to rely on the guard's accuracy within his journal at Marylebone. Arrival there was at 05.06 and, with no night buses and the underground yet to commence running, a not unpleasant dawn walk along the deserted streets of Park Lane and Grosvenor Road to Victoria for my 06.08 Kent-bound EMU was the norm.

Upon the closure of Annesley, excepting the four-month inconsistent tenure of Banbury-based Brits, Colwick took over the responsibility of the remaining GC-line passenger services. Here, at Marylebone, Stanier 4-6-0 44825 readies herself for departure on Saturday, 19 March 1966 with the 14.38 for Nottingham Victoria – she becoming, certainly in my travels, an annoyingly regular performer on them. Selected, and superficially cleaned, for the final 17.15 Nottingham–Marylebone train she was failed prior to departure – being replaced with a filthy, but competent, 44984.

Date	Man Ctl to Guide Bdg	Guide Bdg to Sheff Vic	Sheff Vic to Leic Ctl	Leic Ctl to W Halse	W Halse to Marylebone
16/10/65	42066(9E)	27005	D6746	44869(2D)	D5085
02/04/66	D5200	26051	D6747	44811(16B)	D5087
14/05/66	45220(9E)	27000	D6798	45288(16B)	D5007
21/05/66[2]	D5274	27000	D5856+D6754	44811(16B)	D5092
18/06/66	45239(9E)	27001	D1547	44941(16B)	D5077
25/06/66	44851(9E)	26051	D6752	44984(16B)	D5086

[2]   On 21 May 1966 the train was combined from Sheffield to Nottingham with the 22.20 (SO) York to Oxford because of a shortage of guards – D6754 working forward from Nottingham alone.

The section of the ex-GC line north from Nottingham Victoria was traversed by a mere four services per day (16.47, 23.43, 01.41 and 02.10), of which just one, the 19.15 Swindon to Sheffield, was steam operated. With eight days to go before closure, on Friday, 26 August 1966, I departed Paddington on the 18.10 for Banbury – connecting into the Swindon train there. A Hymeck Type 4 (Class 35), D7009, took me to Leicester Central where, rather than the excepted Colwick Black 5, Tyseley's 44865 was the power that night for the 61 miles of the by then tortuously speed-restricted passage via Annesley, Tibshelf and Staveley – depositing me at Sheffield Victoria at 00.51. This neatly, after a few minutes' walk, fed me into the 02.00 Jubilee-hauled Leeds departure from Sheffield Midland on which, by alighting at Normanton at 03.00, connected into the famed Calder Valley mail train services so favoured by haulage bashers back then. Reading this back nowadays I wonder at the sanity of these nocturnal outings – but then again it was fast disappearing and just had to be done!

Perhaps resulting from the influx of Stanier 4-6-0s at Colwick, there weren't enough smokebox shedplates to go around! Replatformed on Maundy Thursday in 1966 because of being formed of *five* vehicles, 31-year-old 45190 awaits departure time with the 14.38 for Nottingham Victoria.

In the thirty-three minutes I spent at Nottingham Victoria on Friday, 7 May 1965 I was able to take these four shots (others too poor to be published!). Former Parkeston Quay, now Colwick-allocated, B1 61232 sits at the head of a southbound parcels train.

Similarly allocated sister 61299 passes through light engine: the grandiose former refreshment room serving as an atmospheric backdrop. She was to spend her entire seventeen years working GC-line trains.

My only sighting of a Robinson-designed 7F 2-8-0 Class O4/8. Colwick's 63675 is held at signals whilst working a southbound freight – this 49-year-old veteran being withdrawn the following January.

At the head of my 126-mile journey to London was Bletchley's 4-6-0 44909. She was working that day's 1B97, the 17.15 Nottingham Victoria to Marylebone, and was, after the GC was closed, transferred to Rose Grove.

The most frequented train I was to travel on was the notoriously poor timekeeping 17.15 Nottingham Victoria to Marylebone – due in London at 20.25. On the second occasion of catching it (7 May 1965) I had deliberately travelled north on the Poole–York (34097 *Holsworthy* to Oxford, 6947 *Helmingham Hall* to Banbury and D6817 forward) in order to cover the entire route south of Nottingham with steam. The half-hour connection at Victoria passed very quickly with a plethora of locomotives from various classes passing through this now sadly neglected cathedral of steam. Bletchley-allocated Black 5MT 44909 was the power that evening for the 126½-mile journey – a respectable mere twelve minutes late into London. Although often frustrated at the prospect of missing my EMU train home into Kent resulting from the late running, it was with a certain sense of superiority, usually being the sole occupant of a compartment, that upon overtaking a parallel-running underground train south of Harrow I looked upon the open-mouthed passengers gazing out from their crowded cattle truck!

Above left: Noted dead in the sidings at Aylesbury in July 1965 (the very month she was withdrawn) was Willesden's 45379. Forty-five years later she was brought back to life at the Mid Hants and she is seen running round her train at Alresford.

Above right: A celebratory poster depicting the event on Friday, 10 September 2010.

Unlike the 14.38 and 16.38 departures out of Marylebone, which were usually (excepting one occasion when the 14.38 was a four-set suburban non-corridor) formed of four BR Mark 1 vehicles, the 17.15 ex Nottingham was often a mishmash of ex-LMS/LNER/GE vehicles, usually six, and one van. The poor condition of the locomotives often led to loss of time and a phone call requesting a replacement en route was sometimes made. On two occasions when I was aboard, the Banbury foreman sent a spare locomotive to Culworth Junction to work it forward – 45211 vice 44985 on 19 February 1966 (forty-seven-minute delay) and 45426 vice 44835 on 27 May 1966 (fifty-three-minute delay). With watering facilities at Marylebone often 'dry', extended time at Aylesbury to replenish the locomotive's reserves was par for the course. I can still remember the feeling of exhilaration as, having departed Aylesbury, we set off up the gradients towards London. Barking away at the front whilst climbing through the picturesque Chilterns on a summer evening, a Black 5 was somewhat different from the effeminate Bulleid's exhaust beat I was more used to on my SR travels. Although some good speeds were sometimes recorded south of Amersham, the severe restriction through Rickmansworth station (25mph) plus integration with Metropolitan Line services (the operators of which viewed the Nottingham train as an interloper) often thwarted any attempt to make up time – and if nothing else had delayed the train we often sat in Lord's tunnel awaiting a platform at Marylebone!

So, as always noting any deviations to the norm, what did I witness that was different on my forays over the line? In July 1965, Willesden's 44763, whilst working the 14.38, was held at Woodford for twenty minutes before crawling through the 2,997-yard Catesby tunnel[3] because of a broken rail. Never having experienced travelling through such a lengthy tunnel at a slow pace, I leant out of the carriage window drinking in the unique aroma associated with soot-encrusted walls, only to get unexpectedly soaked with water cascading from the tunnel roof! Looking back through my notebooks whilst researching for this book, it was with a sense of satisfaction that I seemed to have caught a run with every locomotive observed during those journeys – even if I had to wait forty-five years; the now-preserved 45379 being viewed dead in Aylesbury goods yard the

---

[3] Catesby tunnel was initially planned as a cutting but its existence was due entirely to the owner of the Catesby estate not wanting unsightly trains blotting his landscape.

Stanier 4-6-0 Aston's 45322 slakes her thirst at Aylesbury whilst working the 14.38 Marylebone to Nottingham Victoria on Friday 13 August.

following week. In August that year, and after visiting Feltham shed in order to photograph the remaining S15s at close quarters, I was, later that day, refused entry at Southall. Having taken half-day leave I wasn't going to waste it and so joined Aston's 45322 at Harrow on the 14.38 ex Marylebone – returning to London from Aylesbury over the then-required track via Princes Risborough.

During autumn 1965 further delays were often encountered at Woodford awaiting the bus connection ex Banbury – the trains were sometimes sent forward without the bus having arrived! The race was now on for 'foreign' Black 5s before the allocation of six Brits, which were expected to monopolise the services. October 1965 certainly saw the Brits arrive in force, and when approaching Aylesbury on one occasion whilst leaning out of the first carriage window behind Brit 70046 *Anzac* wondering what on earth was the noise coming from the loco, I discovered I was witnessing my first steam locomotive equipped with an automatic coal pusher – getting drenched in the process. November saw a B1 work the 14.38 but not, alas, with me aboard – I travelled on it the following Monday – with a borrowed/loaned Crewe South 70024 *Venus*.

As for speeds, the normal maximums were in the mid 60s – but with stop-watch in hand you were always hopeful for the unexpected. Northbound, the racing sections were down Wendover and Finmere banks, whilst south-bound it was between Quainton Road and Aylesbury, together with the descent through Chorleywood. Selective highlights were Brit 52 covering the 28 miles between Harrow and Aylesbury in thirty-four minutes with a 15mph PWS on the climb through Chorleywood followed by a maximum speed of 77mph down Wendover bank – weeks later Black 5 45267 with the usual four coaches achieving 80mph at the same location. On another occasion 45288 attained 74mph approaching Calvert, whilst southbound I recorded 44825 at 75mph and Brit 54 with 73mph through Chorley Wood.

So the above were some of the out-of-course running I witnessed. Summarising extracts out of *The Railway World* magazine, it appears that the Colwick foreman was often predisposed to dispatching any of his B1s out on the 08.15 ex Nottingham/14.38 return but never when I was around. The southbound Neasden parcels train was also a frequent late runner – the result being a DL 'having to be found' for the 16.38. One day in that November

Another one-time Aston-allocated locomotive, BR 7P 4-6-2 70046 *Anzac*, was also captured at Aylesbury working the same train. The day was Saturday, 9 October 1965, midway through her short stay (three months) at Banbury.

both Brits 70046 and 70052 were failed at Marylebone – the 14.38 being cancelled and the 16.38 formed of eight vehicles with a DL. Failures en route were common – a delay of three-and-a-half hours at Woodford Halse awaiting a replacement locomotive from Banbury perhaps being the worst.

Another factor not assisting timekeeping occurred in December 1965. The water column at the south end of Rugby Central station was temporary taken out use, thus requiring locomotives needing water having to call additionally at Rugby Goods Loop. Indeed, water columns throughout the London extension were gradually falling into disrepair – trains often having to call at Great Missenden for replenishment.

Returning to my travels, by February 1966 the Brits had gone – I have to say I somewhat selfishly welcomed their disappearance as it could only enhance the total number of different locomotive catches! As if to emphasise that, one day in March I caught three required Black 5s, one of which gave me 86mph down Wendover bank on the 16.38. Any old stock was often put out for the 17.15 ex Nottingham and later that month I was swinging along at the rear in a Gresley non-corridor – SC87195E for coaching-stock devotees. On Maundy Thursday the authorities, perhaps expecting increased custom, strengthened the 14.38 to *five* vehicles, causing it to be replatformed to platform 3 – indeed there were at least two persons per compartment! Throughout the majority of my journeys over the line I was usually the only enthusiast – the run-down Black 5s and erratic timekeeping not glamorous enough to entice them away from London's other steam terminal of Waterloo. There was, however, during the final months an increase in them; offsetting the reduced patronage of 'normal' customers – the latter perhaps assuming the line had already closed.

In May 1966 Barbara Castle (Labour's manifesto promise of ending the rail closures if elected being completely reneged upon) authorised the GC closure, highlighting a £900,000 per annum saving – the train's small number of regular passengers *being adequately catered for* by replacement bus services. Indeed, the busiest train that ran over the route was the Inter Regional York–Bournemouth – the majority of those passengers being through travellers. The last months of the line's existence was beset by failures – railwaymen, as always, doing their best with the equipment provided and even though their future employment was in doubt they often pulled out all the stops to get passengers to their destinations.

On 29 July Colwick turned out their 8F 48193 for the 10.57 parcels, which, because of late running, would never have made the 16.38 return

– a 'spare' 45426 being found in time. On the same day the 17.15 ex Nottingham Class 5MT failed at Culworth Junction – with Banbury's 9F 92227 taking the train forward. On 21 August the 14.38 failed at Brackley Central, a DL coming down from Aylesbury propelling it to Culworth, from where Banbury sent out Saltley's 9F 92223 to work forward.

My own personal final day trip out of Marylebone was on Tuesday, 23 August 1966 when, having presented myself for the 14.38 departure, I observed the subsequently preserved Hull Dairycoates B1 61306 simmering in the sidings at Marylebone, having suffered hot bearings on her tender whilst working in on the 08.15 ex Nottingham. Dismayed at the replacement power, D5008, to fill in time prior to the 16.38 I travelled to Harrow, passing en route Banbury's 9F 92228 heading for Marylebone! Buoyed with excitement, sure enough upon my return to London she was in position on the 16.38, having, I found out later, worked south on the 10.57 vans ex Nottingham. A mediocre run was suffered, due to four separate speed restrictions over the Chilterns, before an exhilarating 74mph down Finmere bank approaching Brackley Central followed by 68mph at Culworth Junction.

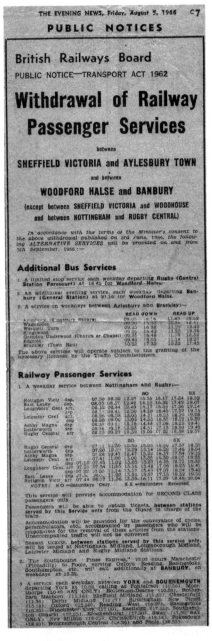

The 5 August 1966 public announcement of the closure courtesy of the *London Evening News*.

Hull Dairycoates-allocated Thompson B1 61306, having been declared a failure with hot bearings, rests at Marylebone on Tuesday, 23 August 1966. Although obviously miffed at not collecting a run with her then, the matter was remedied thirteen months later when the Low Moor foreman dispatched her to work the final steam-hauled Yorkshire Pullman – with me aboard. She is now one of the two preserved B1s.

The LCGB Great Central Rail Tour is seen arriving at Harrow-on-the Hill with Merchant Navy 35030 *Elder Dempster Lines* in charge. The Bulleid Pacific had started out of Waterloo at 09.00 and was to work the tour to and from Nottingham, returning it into Marylebone at 21.37 that night and thus becoming the final steam locomotive-worked passenger train into Marylebone. (Keith Lawrence)

Marylebone later that same day and an uncared-for Tyseley-allocated 45292 has been turned in readiness to work the final 1D37 – the 16.38 departure for Nottingham Victoria. Despite appearances she was to survive a further fourteen months calling in at Stoke before ending her days at Birkenhead. (Keith Lawrence)

I alighted that evening at Woodford Halse and, during the short time there, I stood on the island platform, surveyed what remained of this once important axis of the GC. Woodford Halse was an unassuming Northamptonshire village prior to the arrival of the GC's 'London Extension'. The population, housed in rows of terraces, peaked, in 1931, at 1,700. It was once an important hub for freight traffic and extensive marshalling yards, constructed as recently as the Second World War and provided for the millions of wagons dealt with each year. In June 1965, following the deliberate diversion of parcels and express freight via alternative (often lengthier) routes, the famed 'Windcutters' were withdrawn – in one final calculated bid by the LMR to kill off the line.

Back to that evening, and in charge of the 17.15 ex Nottingham that night was Colwick regular 45288 and, although five minutes late ex Woodford courtesy of a max of 75mph en route, we were right time at Harrow. Extra station time there dealing with parcel traffic, however, thwarted an on-time appearance into Marylebone – arriving there at 20.27. The Colwick foreman must have been short of fit Black 5s that week because the following day (I read about) he sent out his Standard 4MT 76089 for the 17.20 Rugby–Nottingham and five days later he dispatched his 8F 48617 south on the parcels/16.38 working!

I didn't participate in the final day's activities, Saturday, 3 September, as I was on a five-night bash of WCML services. In the final fortnight three locomotives had been failed upon arrival into Marylebone – they being unceremoniously removed to Banbury in the early hours of the last Saturday. On that last day 44872 (2D) started out on the 08.15 before failing at Aylesbury, D5089 working forward after an hour's delay. The 08.38 Marylebone–Nottingham and 12.25 return trains were strengthened to eight-car DMUs. Merchant Navy 35030 *Elder Dempster Lines* worked the LCGB Great Central rail tour, 45292 (2A) worked the 10.57 parcels and 16.38 return and 45267 (16B) worked the 07.40 Nottingham to Rugby and 12.30 return. D5000 worked the 14.38, much to the disappointment of many, and Colwick's 44984 worked the *eight*-coach 17.15 Nottingham – 44825 having been bulled up but failed with injector trouble. The very last steam departure out of Marylebone was that night's 22.45 departure, which was not only well laden with enthusiasts but was witnessed by a great many at the lineside and stations en route. Three overnight services used steam locomotives that final Sunday morning, 44847, 44858 & 44984 all being Colwick allocated.

On, and from the following day, Monday, 5 September, the withdrawal of passenger services between Aylesbury Town/Banbury and Rugby Central and north of Nottingham Victoria was enacted – the BR objective for complete closure being thwarted by various local opposition groups. What stations remained open were destaffed – the guards selling tickets on the trains. The six-trains-per-day DMU service from Rugby Central to Nottingham Victoria was, similar to the S & D scenario played out earlier that year, merely a stopgap to the inevitable. In July 1967 the Grantham trains were diverted to Nottingham Midland, followed by the truncating of the Rugby services at the reopened Arkwright Street station, ¾ mile short, that September thus allowing Nottingham Victoria, at a mere 67 years old, to be closed to passengers. Eventually the through lines, having remained open to freight a further eight months, were closed and the site was sold, falling victim to the inevitable residential/commercial redevelopment, albeit incorporating the station clock tower. The services lingered on, described by some as 'the living death', until finally, after two and a half years of deliberate neglect, decline and retrenchment BR won the day – the complete closure coming in May 1969. If only the increased rail patronage now being enjoyed throughout Britain could have been foreseen back then – the route being a prime candidate for conversion to the proposed HS2.

Statistically, having travelled the line on thirty-three occasions I caught forty-six different locomotives, amounting to 4,335 miles. The line may have gone completely but, for those who had the privilege of travelling over it, it will never be forgotten.

Date	14.38 Marylebone Nott Victoria	16.38 Marylebone Nott Victoria	17.20 (SX) Ruby Central Nott Victoria	17.15 Nott Victoria Marylebone
Formation	4 coaches	4 coaches	3 coaches	6 coaches + 1 van
Mon 28/09/64	45450(16B)			45335 (16B)
Fri 07/05/65				44909 (1E)
Sat 05/06/65		44935 (8B)		44814 (1G)
Fri 09/07/65	44763 (1A)			45299 (1A)
Wed 14/07/65	44717 (16B)		*45134 (1H)*	45308 (1H)
Fri 13/08/65		45322 (2J)		
Mon 27/09/65	44863 (8A)	*70046 (2D)*	44665 (16B)	44763 (1A)
Sat 02/10/65	70054 (2D)	*70051 (2D)*		70052 (2D)
Sat 09/10/65	70046 (2D)			70052 (2D)
Sat 23/10/65	70050 (2D)			45454 (2D)
Mon 25/10/65	70046 (2D)		44663 (2A)	70054 (2D)
Mon 29/11/65	44965 (2B)	70024 (5B)		
Mon 13/12/65	44859 (2A)	45349 (2A)		
Sat 18/12/65	70052 (2D)	45446 (5B)		70046 (2D)
Sat 12/02/66	45454 (2D)			44661 (2A)
Sat 19/02/66	44920 (16B)	45222 (2D)		45211 (55A)
Sat 05/03/66	45324 (16B)	45267 (16B)		45333 (16B)
Sat 19/03/66	44825 (16B)	45464 (16B)		44936 (16B)
Thu 07/04/66	45190 (16B)	*44825 (16B)*	*45222 (2D)*	45426 (16B)
Mon 18/04/66	45190 (16B)	*45222 (2D)*	44835 (16B)	45288 (16B)
Sat 07/05/66	44941 (16B)	*45190 (16B)*		45288 (16B)
Fri 27/05/66	44825 (16B)	44936 (16B)	*45349 (2A)*	44835 (16B) 45426 (16B)
Mon 13/06/66	45283 (2B)	*44941 (16B)*	44860 (2D)	44825 (16B)
Tue 19/07/66	44847 (16B)	*44920 (16B)*	*45222 (2D)*	44941 (16B)
Tue 23/08/66	D5008	92228 (2D)		45222 (2D)

Locomotives in italics indicate seen but not travelled with.

1A – Willesden: 1E- Bletchley: 1G – Woodford Halse: 1H – Northampton: 2A – Tyseley: 2B – Oxley: 2D – Banbury: 2E – Saltley: 2J – Aston: 5B – Crewe South: 8A – Edge Hill: 8B – Warrington Dallam: 16B Annesley (until 03/01/66) then Colwick: 55A – Holbeck.

4

THE ELECTRIC EFFECT: 1966

The WCML electrification, arguably the largest infrastructure and modernisation project undertaking for Britain's railways in decades, was to be fully implemented in April 1966. The Crewe to Manchester route had gone live in 1960, followed by the Liverpool branch two years later. Although some through trains had begun electrically operated south of Crewe from November 1965, a completely revised and fully electrified train service was to commence on 18 April 1966. This was to have severe ramifications within the motive-power scene throughout the North-West, with displaced DLs – predominantly Type 4 English Electrics (Class 40), being redeployed on former steam-operated services.

Indeed, steam was now in full retreat. The steam locomotive represented, in BR management's eyes, a symbol of a past life and did not fit in with the image they wished to portray. The locos, together with unprofitable lines, were to be dispensed with ASAP. At the beginning of 1965 there were 4,990 steam locomotives in Britain. Now, exactly one year later, numbers had dwindled to 3,003. Upon appreciating the severity of the changes, courtesy of the office copy of *The Railway World* magazine, I formulated a four-night, 1,600-mile itinerary, to be undertaken just weeks prior to the end of the winter timetable, in particular focusing on services that were to be dieselised or withdrawn. It was a daunting prospect. I had never before spent more than two nights out on the railway system and even then they were in the comfort of warm compartments to and from Scotland. Was I going to succumb to sleep without warning – missing stations I should have alighted at? Would I possess the stamina to last the course or return home earlier than anticipated with my tail between my legs having failed to accomplish all of my plans? Were my parents concerned at their 19-year-old son being exposed to the flotsam of sometimes over-inebriated nightlife that searched out a place to put their head down while sheltering from the cold? If they were I don't recall them expressing any reservations – perhaps convincing themselves that, unlike a minority of teenagers of the time who were dabbling in flower-power hallucinatory drugs or drinking, I was participating in the risk-adverse hobby of trainspotting. Personally, the adrenalin and excitement of the possibilities that awaited me were all that I was concerned about.

With the commencement date of Wednesday, 30 March having been selected, perhaps a summary of non-railway related news events can be slotted in here. The following day's General Election saw Harold Wilson's Labour Government increase its majority from the previous election held a mere seventeen months earlier from five (which had been reduced to two resulting from by-election defeats) to ninety-eight. That month had seen a great many protest marches throughout the USA against involvement in the Vietnam War, while at home Pickles the dog had recovered the stolen World Cup football trophy wrapped in newspaper in a south London garden. Musically, the Walker Brothers' 'The Sun Ain't Gonna Shine Anymore' was holding the top spot, inadvertently appropriate, as the reader will find out.

I headed north that cold and wintry night out of the building site that was allegedly Euston station. Very much castigated by both the press and notables such as John Betjeman and Michael Palin, the latter describing it as 'one of the nastiest concrete boxes in London: devoid of any decorative merit', it was the demolition of the celebrated Doric Arch by the builders Taylor Woodrow that attracted the most criticism. More concerned with locating the departure platform of my 22.35 Whitehaven train, I was unaware of the politics of the situation, only vaguely recalling briefly loitering in the great hall, at the centre of which was a statue of the father of the railways: George Stephenson. This train conveyed seating accommodation only, a following 23.15 Euston to Workington Main catering for sleeping-car users.

The 141 miles of railway between Crewe and Carlisle were constructed in a piecemeal fashion during the years 1832 to 1846 by a fusion of companies. They were the Grand Junction Railway, the North Union Railway, the Lancaster and Preston Junction Railway and the Lancaster and Carlisle Railway – each being eventually absorbed into the all-conquering London & North Western Railway. The myriad of lines, particularly in the Warrington and Wigan areas were, to a southerner like me, of a bewildering complexity and it was only after a great many visits to the area that a smidgeon of understanding of all the routes was gained. With Hest Bank being the only sighting of the coast from which the derivation of sobriquet West *Coast* Main Line (WCML) is acquired, perhaps the greatest engineering feat of the line is the 35 miles from Carnforth to the 916ft-high summit at Shap. All but four of the 20 miles of railway from Carnforth to Grayrigg are uphill, with gradients ranging between 1 in 111 and 1 in 173, and while the line from Grayrigg to Tebay is relatively level, it was followed by 5 miles at 1 in 75. In the opposite direction, the northerly approach to Shap from Carlisle is 30 miles long, with gradients varying between 1 in 131 and 1 in 228 to Penrith, and then mainly at 1 in 125 to Shap summit. The ½-mile-long cutting at Shap summit is cut through solid rock and is up to 60ft in depth. The scenic Cumbrian mountains, together with the necessity to avoid large estates en route, were always going to put the WCML at a disadvantage to the almost flat, straight racing track of the ECML with respect to the Scottish-destined traveller but, selfishly, with the often necessary banking requirements of Grayrigg and Shap it was nectar to a steam follower.

Returning to my journey, although anticipating that the train would be steam worked north of Crewe, I was somewhat surprised, upon arriving into Carnforth at 04.18, when the 12A-allocated Stanier 5MT 44900 relinquished the train to Brit 70025 *Western Star* for the 28½-mile journey along the north coastline of Morecambe Bay to Barrow. The scenic delights of this line, due to the pre-dawn darkness, could not be witnessed by myself that visit – the matter not being remedied until my first daylight trip over the route some nineteen months hence. Indeed, having reversed at Barrow with Crewe South's 45494 taking us forward at 05.30, it wasn't until departure from Seascale, at 06.35, that snow-laden clouds could be seen threateningly on the point of releasing their potentially travel-disruptive contents.

The 311-mile journey from London arrived into Whitehaven Bransty a mere five minutes late at 07.30 and, with nothing much to hang around for, I continued northwards to Workington on a connecting Carlisle-bound DMU. Shed bashing, so prevalent amongst a great many gricers, was never a priority for me. However, with more than an hour's wait for my connection, I thought why not. As always, following instructions as detailed in my ever-present Lt Aidan Fuller's *Shed Directory*,[4] the five-minute walk to 12D was easily undertaken. Seemingly deserted of personnel, I bunked the shed without trouble. The pungent miasmic sulphuric haze always associated with any cathedrals of steam (admittedly this one not much bigger than a pulpit) will always stay with me. The detritus of a working shed, the dirty environment, the piles of coal, the ash pit: we all knew it was never going to last. You had to drink in the atmosphere before it was all gone forever. Common sense saw us avoid danger. Moving locomotives, hazardous walking conditions – today's health and safety jobsworths would have blown a gasket. As for the locomotives themselves, you noted their numbers and took photographs of them knowing full well that the likelihood of ever seeing them again was nothing short of nil. Bureaucracy had ordained a death sentence on them.

31/03/66	12D Workington at 08.00
In steam	43006, 43008, 43073, 45424 (10A), 45494 (5B), 46424, 46432, 46491 & 47612
Dead	46452 & 46485
Withdrawn	44160
Diesels	D5705

Returning to the station, I then caught the 09.25 Cockermouth, Keswick and Penrith-routed DMU to Carlisle. This line, opened between Workington and Cockermouth in 1847, was eventually extended west, including the impressive twelve-arched Mosedale viaduct, to Penrith in 1865, and was without doubt one of the most scenic lines I travelled over. It was no wonder lifelong Cumbrian resident poet William Wordsworth, who strongly objected to the railway encroaching on 'his terrain', eulogised over the Lake District's splendid landscape. It was also author Beatrix Potter's adopted homeland, the farm at Near Sawry being where so many of her iconic animal tales were penned. Staying with my family at Windermere in the 1990s, I was fortunate enough to stumble across a minibus tour, specially arranged for Japanese students (both writers being a predominate part of their English thesis), which visited both establishments.

---

[4] Lieutenant Aiden Fuller (1920–73) was a chartered accountant by profession having served in the RAF during the Second World War. A lifelong steam enthusiast, his first directory was published in 1947 – Ian Allan taking over in 1961. Although giving precise directions on how to access the sheds, the following cautioning caveat was also included within it: 'This directory in no way gives authority to visit the sheds – the compiler will not be held responsible for any detention.'

Just six (three at Crewe Works and three at Barrow) of the original 580-strong class of Fowler 0-6-0 4Fs remained on BR's books at the beginning on 1966. Here, at Workington shed on Thursday, 31 March 1966, home-based 44160, having been withdrawn four months earlier, awaits dispatch to the breaker's yard.

Kingmoor-allocated Stanier 5MT 44982, working a northbound freight, is kept waiting in the goods loop adjacent to Workington shed for the passage of a passenger train.

Ivatt Mogul 46432, having spent the majority of her seventeen years here at Workington, was transferred the following month to Springs Branch (Wigan). I was to obtain a 'shunt' with her at 2 a.m. one morning that September – thus qualifying for a red-line entry in my *ABC*!

Thirty-seven-year-old Jinty, Fowler 0-6-0T 3F 47612, is seen on shunting duties at Workington. Just eighty-three of the original 417 were in service at the beginning of 1966.

British Railways Board

Public Notice---Transport Act, 1962

Withdrawal of Railway Passenger Services between

WORKINGTON-PENRIT

BRITISH RAILWAYS BOARD.   PUBLIC NOTICE – TRANSPORT ACT 1962

Withdrawal of Passenger Train Services
BETWEEN WORKINGTON AND KESWICK

The London Midland Region of British Railways announce that arrangements to withdraw the Passenger Train Service between Workington and Keswick and to close the undermentioned stations have been approved by the Minister of Transport under powers conferred by the Transport Act 1962:

BRIGHAM, COCKERMOUTH, BRAITHWAITE, BASSENTHWAITE LAKE

ON AND FROM MONDAY, 18th APRIL, 1966.

Alternative facilities by Road Transport, operated by Cumberland Motor Services Limited, will be available as intimated in previous public notices.

ANNEX

PART I

Existing Bus Services provided under road service licences granted under the Road Traffic Acts, 1960-62

Services operated by Cumberland Motor Services Ltd.

Services operated jointly by Cumberland Motor Services Ltd. and Ribble Motor Services Ltd.

Service operated by Messrs. Tittorington (Mr. E. Tittorington

PART II

ADDITIONAL BUS SERVICES

Services between Workington and Keswick via Brigham, Cockermouth, Bassenthwaite and Braithwaite

In view of the Minister's decision, Th London Midland Region will withdraw th Passenger Train Services concerned on date shortly to be announced

British Rail | London Midland Region

January, 1966.   BR. 35014

H.A. I.

The line, whilst running through the heart of what became the Lake District National Park encircled by numerous mountains, was however destined to close, west of Keswick, within weeks of my visit – the transport minister of the day, Barbara Castle, citing poor all-year patronage. It was, as many other branch lines during the 1960s, a victim of the motorcar, with visiting holidaymakers and locals alike preferring the ease of road transport. The remaining section between Keswick and Penrith eventually succumbed to closure as late as 1972.

After spending five-and-a-half hours visiting both Kingmoor and Upperby sheds at Carlisle, I headed south-east over the Pennines on the 16.37 all-stations steam-operated service to Bradford via Ais Gill. Having entered the North Eastern Region of BR at Skipton at 19.31 hours that night, I was to spend the following twenty-odd hours shuttling between Leeds, Sheffield and Bradford. As the services over the 'Little North Western' were being dieselised the following month, the next day I station hopped between Leeds, Skipton and Hellifield before finally returning to LMR metals: arriving into Morecambe Promenade at 20.18 on the Friday evening.

The route via Lancaster Green Ayre was first opened in 1848 and was electrified west of Lancaster in 1908. By 1952 the overhead line equipment (OLE) and stock had become life expired and was temporary replaced by steam traction whilst the system was upgraded. The same reasoning used to condemn the Woodhead route, i.e. non-standardisation with OLE systems elsewhere on BR, had seen its demise two months earlier – my train having to take the longer alternative line via Carnforth. I now headed south to Crewe, first catching a DMU to Lancaster Castle and changing there onto a London-bound service disappointingly hauled by a Brush Type 4. It was a bitterly cold night, snow had begun falling thickly and the heaven-sent warmth of Crewe's all-night buffet together with its hot cooked meals was most welcome.

Out of all my travels perhaps it was this one I spent the most time at Crewe on and so a brief résumé on the town is opportune. Crewe was, before the Grand Junction Railway decided to position its main works there in the late 1830s, just a sleepy hamlet barely mustering seventy inhabitants. Crewe station itself was opened in 1837 and with the expansion of the works in 1871 the population increased to 40,000. The LNWR, the Grand Junction Railways' successor, became the town's benefactor, with land purchased/donated for a park, doctor's surgery, cheese market and a clothing factory. The Crewe station I was to frequent so often during the 1960s had been substantially rebuilt between 1896 and 1907 to its present day twelve-platform size, the eight through ones being ¼-mile long. The increasing freight traffic was catered for in 1901 with the opening of the alternative Independent Lines. Electrification of the WCML north of Weaver Junction (1974) and track simplification (1985) to allow 80mph through running have little changed the impressive structure.

My next objective was the Windermere branch and the train I was intending to travel there on, the 23.15 ex Euston, was yet another service set to be discontinued in the forthcoming timetable change. When, however, the preceding Workington train arrived, and having double-checked the timetable to ascertain that both trains called at Wigan en route north, I boarded it to collect a run with Green Ayre-allocated 44761. I needn't have bothered because with the locomotive lasting until April 1968 I was to catch further runs with her in the Manchester area – but you never knew back then which locomotives were to be withdrawn or when. They were becoming dispensable and any defect, sometimes as minor as a broken floorboard in the cab, if requiring financial expenditure, could result in condemnation.

After an hour's wait on the windswept northbound platform at Wigan North Western, the 03.23 for Windermere rolled in, a mere eight minutes late, with Brit 28 *Royal Star* at its head. Securing a warm compartment eventually, after thawing out, sleep overcame me. This was, after all, my third night out. I didn't note where or when we were delayed en route, I believe Shap was temporarily blocked by snow, but a 100-minute late arrival into Windermere, at 07.33, certainly reduced the waiting time for the first train back out, the 08.10 for Manchester.

This 10¼-mile branch, opened throughout in 1847 by the Kendal & Windermere Railway, was leased in perpetuity to the Lancaster & Carlisle Railway in 1858 before being absorbed into the L&NWR the following year. Windermere station (actually located in the village of Birthwaite) boasted, at the time of my visit, four platforms, an overall roof and a turntable. Reduced to a single platform in 1973, the line was truncated in 1986 – the former train shed being incorporated into a supermarket.

Although the 08.10 departed a mere six minutes late, a commendable quick turnaround for the Brit, delays over the WCML resulted in a twenty-eight-minute-late arrival at Preston. Services were in disarray because of the weather and a derailment at Skew Bridge, and caught up in all this was double-chimneyed Jubilee 45596 *Bahamas* on a Lakes & Fells Rail Tour. Deliberately homing in on services that were to be discontinued in the forthcoming timetable change, I spent the next ten hours between Preston and Crewe, using Wigan as the pivotal station. Regrettably, I didn't take any photographs whilst waiting around at the stations, perhaps because I wouldn't take my frozen hands out of my pockets. Calling it a day, upon catching Type 4 D268 on a supposedly steam-worked train ex Blackpool South, I headed into Manchester for that night's bed home – the 22.50 Manchester Central to Marylebone.

Had I finished my steam travels that weekend – I think not! The LCGB had organised a 245-mile Wilts and Hants Rail Tour utilising two of the soon-to-be-withdrawn SR Moguls and a Q1. I eventually arrived home on the Sunday at 20.30 after exactly four days and nights of continuous travel. What an adventure! Congratulating myself at having survived such a length of time on the railway network, I subsequently surmised that the outing was a taster to whet the appetite for a great many further, often lengthier, jaunts in search of steam.

All services I travelled on north of Crewe on that trip were affected by the timetable change on 18 April that year. On the Cumbrian Coast route the overnight through train from London was truncated at Barrow, sleeping-car passengers getting no further north than Preston. The Workington to Keswick via Cockermouth line was closed. The all-stations Ais Gill-routed services to Bradford were truncated at Skipton and became DMU operated – Holbeck's Jubilee 45660 *Rooke* working the final southbound on the 16th. The steam-train services over The Little North Western (Skipton–Morecambe) were turned over to DMUs. The Windermere branch lost its overnight through service from London. Most of the trains caught during the Saturday daytime were discontinued, leaving just a handful of all-year steam workings over the WCML.

Summer, however, was on the horizon and, as detailed in the following chapter, the short-dated wavy-lined entries in Table 50 of the 648-page LMR timetable were to provide rich pickings for a steam-hungry haulage basher.

5

SUPER SUMMER SATURDAYS: 1966

Does everyone consider the summers of their youth to have had better weather than the present day ones? They would be correct in the case of 1966. With air-conditioning as yet to be conceived, the only option was to retreat indoors to watch on your newly purchased or rented colour TV shows such as *Till Death Us Do Part*, *The Man from U.N.C.L.E.* or Emma Peel's leather ensemble in *The Avengers*. As for fashions, the 'mod' movement (if I have to be labelled, I was a sideboard-furnished, DA-hairstyled teddy boy) with its associated turtle-necked jumpers was in full swing.

Musically, the Beatles' celebrity status had taken a hit following John Lennon's 'we're more popular than Jesus' remark, with Americans in particular starting a 'burn your Beatles albums' crusade. But there were plenty of other chart-topping songs around such as 'Hanky Panky' by Tommy James and The Shondells, 'Wild Thing' by The Troggs, 'You Don't Have to Say You Love Me' by Dusty Springfield, 'Paint It Black' by the Rolling Stones, 'Pied Piper' by Crispian St Peters and 'Summer in the City' by The Lovin' Spoonful, to name a few. We could all listen to those songs, some of which were broadcast from Swinging Radio England's boat moored in the North Sea, on our transistor radios with their single earpiece and plastic dial – if the usually abysmal reception would allow it.

In 1966 it was a very busy summer for steam enthusiasts such as myself. Indeed, every Saturday from mid February until the end of the year, strangely barring

London Midland Region Timetable

London (Euston, St. Pancras, Marylebone, Broad Street)
The Midlands
North Wales
The North
including suburban services

Passenger Services

18 April 1966
to 5 March 1967

Price 3s. 0d.

one in early June (a parental request to stay around for distant relatives visiting perhaps?), saw me chasing steam somewhere in the country – thus quantifying the fact that, at 35,553 miles, it was to be my highest steam mileage year ever.

A pre-emptive visit to the WCML with Alan, a subsequent lifelong friend and proofreader of this tome, was undertaken in mid May travelling down on a train that was to be frequented a fair number of occasions – the 23.45 Barrow departure out of Euston. With an arrival time into Preston of 03.45 this, allowing for late running, effortlessly connected into the 05.35 Preston to Crewe stopper: a train we *hoped* was steam powered. It was all very hit and miss, with no certainty being guaranteed. On that occasion, however, the waiting time was cut to a mere twenty-five minutes because an ailing Brush Type 4 (D1852) that had taken over the London train at Crewe was unable to restart the train out of Wigan NW northwards up the incline. After twenty-five minutes an unidentified Black 5 gave us a shove, only for us to come to a complete stand, for thirty-five minutes, at Rylands Sidings before presumably the same locomotive returned and assisted us forward to Standish Junction. Here a Control-arranged locomotive came on the front and took us the 13 miles to Preston. Upon alighting we were delighted to discover that Springs Branch-allocated 8F 48319 was our rescuer – she becoming my only 8F haulage on a timetabled passenger train. On that visit, having returned the 51 miles on the aforementioned stopper, we headed over to the steam-drenched Chester area, eventually returning home on the overnight GC-line train out of Manchester.

Meanwhile, Bolton had received twelve displaced former WR-allocated BR Standard 5MTs that April but, with no booked passenger work, what chance was there that a haulage basher was ever likely to come across them. Often noted on parcels or freight, these Brunswick green-liveried machines were annoyingly untouchable.

The wages of a BR junior clerk (£235 pa + £10 London weighting allowance) were such that costly expeditions on rail tours were, for the first years of my travels, beyond my financial means. Into 1966, and having obtained promotion (thus receiving the giddying amount of £310 pa), I was able to afford participating on a selected few: the criteria being motive power I was not able to travel with on scheduled services – the first of these being the LCGB-organised Fellsman on Saturday, 4 June that year.

This 657-mile tour (305 miles in steam) started out of Euston at a respectable time of 08.26, being taken forward from Liverpool's Lime Street station with an ultra-clean Brit 4 *William Shakespeare*. The proposed usage of Stockport-allocated locomotives such as her enticed my participation on the tour – 9B having lost all passenger duties that April. After the unique Stephenson link Black 5MT 44767 had been placed on the front at Carnforth a speed of 87½mph was attained between Calthwaite and Southwaite stations en route to Carlisle.

After just crossing over the border into Scotland to Quintinshill, of the two Jubilees returning us to Crewe one of them just *had* to be the *only* Jub I'd already had a run with, namely 45593 *Kolhapur*! At least the other was the now-preserved double-chimneyed 45596 *Bahamas*.

We sat at Crewe for some time and, having learnt that the overhead wires were down on the main line, we were (eventually) DL-hauled via Bescot – arriving 203 minutes late into London. Taking on board this unexpected turn of events, and rather than wait nearly six hours for my Kent-bound EMU home, I walked across London and caught the 03.15 Southampton-bound (diverted via the Guildford New line and Pompey direct due to Bournemouth line electrification works) Paper train out of Waterloo for a top up of steam mileage!

THE LOCOMOTIVE CLUB OF GREAT BRITAIN

★

Membership Card

The Locomotive Club of Great Britain (LCGB) membership card. This entitled members to a reduction of fares on the rail tours together with trade price railway-orientated books such as Colin Gifford's 63s (315p) *Decline of Steam*.

A crowded scene at Liverpool Lime Street on Saturday, 4 June 1966 as Stockport-allocated Brit 70004 *William Shakespeare* prepares to take the LCGB Fellsman rail tour forward the 135 miles to Scotland. This former *Golden Arrow* locomotive, which had been paraded at the London's South Bank during 1951 Festival of Britain exhibition, was, prior to *Oliver Cromwell*'s reign, a regular rail-tour participant before being withdrawn during the mass Britannia cull of December 1967 at Kingmoor.

Opposite above: Enticed onto the tour with the promise of Stockport-allocated Jubilees, what should be turned out but Holbeck's 45593 *Kolhapur* – a locomotive that had already taken me over Beattock the previous year! Jostling with the tour's participants during the water stop at Blackburn, this was the best shot I could obtain!

Opposite below: Also seen at the Blackburn water stop is the subsequently preserved North British-built 4–6–0 double-chimneyed Jubilee 45596 *Bahamas*. A Stockport-allocated (since July 1962) locomotive rarely seen on passenger work, capturing a run with her just weeks before withdrawal made the very long day worthwhile.

British Railways Board (M)

The Locomotive Club of Great Britain
THE FELLSMAN RAIL TOUR
SATURDAY, 4th JUNE, 1966

Euston, Crewe, Liverpool (Lime Street),
St. Helens (Shaw Street), Wigan, Shap
Summit, Carlisle, Gretna Junction, Ais
Gill, Hellifield, Blackburn, Wigan,
Crewe, Euston

SECOND CLASS   For conditions see over

0275   0275

THE LOCOMOTIVE CLUB
OF GREAT BRITAIN

ITINERARY OF

THE

FELLSMAN

RAIL TOUR

SATURDAY 4th JUNE 1966

The 18 June heralded the commencement of a great many short-dated services, depicted within Table 50 with a wavy line throughout the timing column coercing the reader to refer to the letter at the column head detailing precisely which dates the train was running. My original well-thumbed, torn, disintegrating LMR timetable, having been constantly referred to and stuffed into my attaché case didn't survive the years and I had to, in order to attain accuracy within this book, buy one on eBay. At £9.99 I considered it good value.

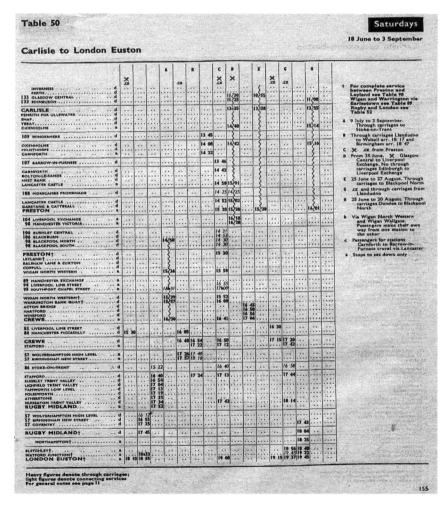

Timetable extract of a page showing an example of the wavy-lined entries so prevalent on a summer Saturday.

The early part of that summer was spent concentrating on obtaining runs with the remaining nine NER-allocated Jubilees. On Saturday, 25 June, while the Beatles topped the charts with 'Paperback Writer', I was with Paul and having used the aforementioned 05.35 Preston starter and a flying visit to Chester as an aperitif, we doubled back to Preston en route to Blackpool for the 13.25 for Bradford/Leeds. At the beginning of that summer we were unsure which trains were steam worked and which weren't, and to this end, having alighted at Kirkham with the intention to hop on and off several mid-morning Manchester–Blackpool workings, what did we get – a succession of DMU-operated trains, that's what! Oh well, at least the Bradford train turned up trumps with Wakefield's 45694 *Bellerophon* in charge. Eventually filtering back to the LMR, my first occasion of travelling on the Belfast Boat Express rewarded me with haulage with Carnforth's 'pet' 45025. Returning home via the GC-routed 22.50 ex Manchester one final time, although the mileages weren't high a very healthy twelve required locomotives were red-lined upon arrival home.

Saturday, 25 June 1966 and the summer services were in full swing. With resources stretched, visiting locomotives from freight depots were often purloined for usage such as seen here at Preston. Speke Junction's 45223, withdrawn that December, departs with a Morecambe service.

The train central to our plans that day was the 13.25 Blackpool North to Bradford/ Leeds. It was the second day of its running that year and Wakefield's Jubilee 45694 *Bellerophon* was the power. Lady Luck was with us that day and, whilst it had been worked the previous Saturday by B1 61013 *Topi*, the majority of sightings of the train throughout that summer were of a nondescript Black 5MT.

In that July the sixth National Jazz and Blues Festival was held at Windsor – it being the precursor of the Isle of Wight, Glastonbury and Woodstock counterparts. Its line-up in that year moved from being blues and jazz to bands such as The Who, the Small Faces and the Yardbirds featuring Jimmy Page and Jeff Beck, not to mention the first unveiling of a trio with as yet no name comprising Eric, Ginger and Jack. Some of the top hits that summer were The Kinks' 'Sunny Afternoon', George Fame and The Blue Flames' 'Getaway' and Chris Farlowe's 'Out of Time'.

Film-wise, *Who's Afraid of Virginia Woolf, Alfie* and *Born Free* took record box-office receipts. Football, and Liverpool were that year's First Division champions with Manchester City winning the second, while Everton beat Sheffield Wednesday 3-2 at Wembley to win the FA Cup. Then there was England's 4-2 world cup win against West Germany. It was an achievement that gave the whole country a mad celebratory feel-good factor for a few weeks – and why not. It might not ever happen again.

On the 23rd of that month, having fortunately successfully completed my Jubilee hunt culminating in a ride with *Kolhapur* over Ais Gill on that day's Birmingham–Glasgow train, I turned my attention to the WCML – and what better way to start than with a required Brit over Shap, 70032 *Tennyson* on a Dundee–Blackpool service, to Preston. This catch was quickly followed up with all of 4 miles to Leyland with Stanier 4MT 42546 on a Wigan local. Then, after a return trip to Lancaster, which included an exhilarating 82mph with Brit 25, I headed for Manchester, collecting a run with a Patricroft Caprotti on the 01.00 Wigan portion en route home. Eight further catches had fallen into my hands that visit, with a higher than usual steam mileage of 338½.

I was addicted. Preston was the place to be. With valid travel tickets/passes to cover all contingencies, all one had to do was wait for required locomotives to put in an appearance. The reader has to appreciate that at the time it was trial and error/hit and miss with no definitive documentation to guide us. Sure, the details eventually appeared in magazines such as *The Railway World* and *LCGB Bulletin* but they were after the event and some of the short-dated services had even ceased running by then! The only method to monitor all the arrivals and departures was by constantly patrolling the platforms. It was certainly one method of keeping fit because whenever a wisp of steam appeared in the distance we had to race over the bridge or through the subway on the off-chance it was a requirement, thus necessitating the need to board. Whenever a 'not required' locomotive turned up, boos/whistling/ jeering emanated from us, with cheering/clapping being awarded to the one that was required. Indeed, some of the habitually appearing locomotives acquired nicknames not able to be printed here! The south end of the station with its four-tracked vista offered an excellent opportunity to test one's eyesight and recognition skills of the differing classes of locomotives as they approached – those getting it wrong being ridiculed. To quote radio DJ Kenny Everett 'it was all done in the best possible taste' and the banter was all part of the friendly rivalry so prevalent amongst us.

A brief synopsis of steam-worked departures out of Preston available to us chasers between the hours of 05.35 to 23.45, as extracted from my tattered travel-worn notebooks, reveals there were nine for Wigan, six for Manchester, three for Liverpool, eight for Blackpool and ten for Lancaster and beyond. That was without any reliefs or Control-arranged extras so frequently run to Blackpool, Morecambe and Barrow to cope with the overwhelming demand.

Having caught a Fairburn tank out of Preston to Leyland on a Wigan stopping service on Saturday, 30 July 1966 during the short wait for a returning DMU, two Black 5MT services sped through the then overhead-wire-free station. The first, Crewe South's 44844, races through with a northbound train – a mere two weeks later I was to catch her substituting for a Brit on the 06.10 ex Blackpool South.

Initially named Golden Hill when opened by the North Union Railway in 1838, this is another scene at Leyland the same day. Long-term Carnforth resident 44709 storms through with the 14.35 Barrow to Manchester Victoria.

The regularly published *Ian Allan Locoshed* mini books were, to a haulage basher such as myself, an essential 'Bible'. Always held in readiness upon sighting a distant wisp of steam, they were constantly referred to, and resulting from them being stuffed in coat or trouser pockets, they were, to avoid full disintegration, often held together by sellotape. Here are the front covers of the July 1965, January 1966 and January 1968 issues.

Trains caught obviously depended on one's personal requirements and, having trawled through my notebooks, it appears that when at Preston in mid-morning a semi-regular sequential pattern of connectional trains starting with the 10.47 Barrow departure was travelled upon. Having taken this to Carnforth, after a twenty-minute wait I headed south to Lancaster, changing onto a Preston-bound train before once again returning to Lancaster, where, having arrived at 14.54, the usual yield of four locomotives were red-lined.

Although often briefly visiting Carnforth, at the time I failed to acknowledge the significance of it being the location of the 1945 film *Brief Encounter* starring Celia Johnson and Trevor Howard. Filming sequences centred on the refreshment room (albeit many being imaged at the Denham studio) and the recording was restricted to the night hours so as not to disturb train operations. A great many train services in the area fell victim to the Beeching-inspired cuts to such an extent that the main-line platforms closed in 1970 – the station buildings falling into disuse and neglect. More recently (2003) both the Carnforth Station Heritage Centre together with the Brief Encounter Refreshment Room organisations have opened and both are now thriving tourist attractions.

On an unrecorded Saturday in August 1966, Kingmoor's 45363 trundles through Lancaster Castle with a northbound freight. This Armstrong-Whitworth-built 29-year-old was withdrawn that October – but not before I caught her on a Preston portion.

Another scene at Lancaster Castle sees Lostock Hall's 45450 arriving with a lengthy southbound parcels train.

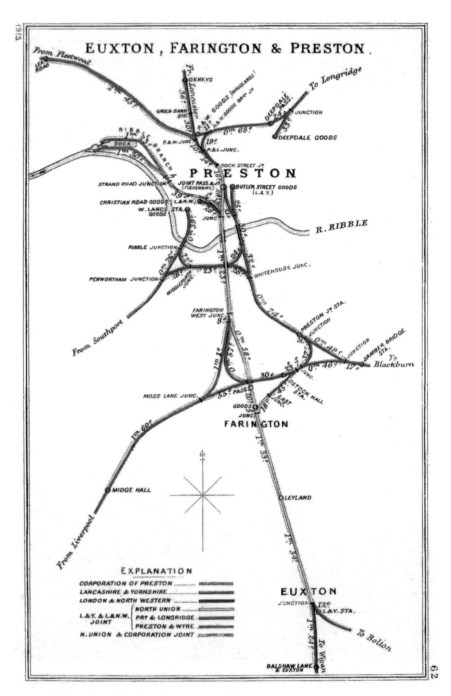

A 1913 Railway Clearing house map of Preston.

Then was the, to me, confusingly unique scene when witnessing Blackpool-bound services departing southbound. With my geographic knowledge of railway routes gradually becoming clearer, I eventually comprehended that they negotiated a loop via Lostock Hall and Farington Junctions prior to then storming non-stop through Preston some fifteen minutes later.

So for the remaining Saturdays of that summer I was to be seen rushing around like some demented lunatic hopping on and off trains, often making minus-minute connections (due to late running) at a wide range of stations within the LMR's Preston division. This was where it was all happening. After all, the WR had dispensed with steam that March, I had caught all of SR's main-line locomotives and, having blitzed the NER earlier that summer, the greatest source of required locomotives were here at work in Lancashire.

The one August Saturday I was absent from the area was spent in Scotland – the sparse steam services available finally yielding a much-desired run with a Gresley V2. With SR steam mileages being sated after work each weekday evening, I, and many of my like-minded colleagues, were to be found departing north out of Euston every Friday filled with hope, the anticipation of many new catches in our hearts. Whilst most of the travel out of Euston (to Preston) was on the 23.45 departure, when it became known that there was a 2 a.m. southbound steam service originating from Carlisle, the earlier 20.20 *Highlander* was used.

If we were flush with annual leave or took compensatory time off in lieu of overtime worked then *all* of a Friday could be booked off and nearly 200 miles of steam travel aboard the 13.27 Manchester Victoria to Edinburgh Waverley was imbibed upon. What was so attractive about this train? Well I would respectfully suggest the prospect of scratching six locomotives in one hit was a good enough incentive. Newton Heath sent out a Black 5 for the 30-odd miles to Preston, where the portion was put on the back of the same timed departure out of Liverpool Exchange – itself usually powered by a Kingmoor Brit. Exchanging Brits at Carlisle, a four-coach portion for Edinburgh was detached at Carstairs – a St Margarets Black 5 working that. The other two locomotives involved were the bankers at Shap and Beattock – the heavy thirteen-vehicle train proving too much for the usually run-down Brits. Poor timekeeping often led to several late arrivals into Edinburgh – but never enough to miss the 23.55 back to Birmingham – it being the aforementioned early morning Brit-worked departure out of Carlisle. Simples!

Sunday, 17 July 1966 saw me alight of off my 'normal' service home to London at Crewe at the ungodly hour of 4 a.m. – en route to Leicester for a family meet-up. During the three-hour wait for the first Derby-bound train I came across 38-year-old Vulcan Foundry-built Jinty 47482 simmering quietly to herself in a bay at the south end of the station.

Week after week the numbers caught went into double figures, peaking at fifty-one in August.[5] When transferring them neatly at home into various books the associated euphoria felt akin to a beneficial blood transfusion! Whilst most services were monopolised by Black 5MTs and Brits, representatives from other classes such as Flying Pigs (Ivatt 2-6-0s) together with Stanier/Fairburn tanks and Standard 4 & 5MTs weren't uncommon.

Did we – there were a hard-core bunch of us amounting to about two dozen – all travel around together similar to pack animals hunting our prey? With all of us having differing requirements, I think not. If there was a gap in steam services then perhaps a pint or two was imbibed in Preston's refreshment room but with information exchanged we all took off in different directions or just waited … and waited.

---

[5] This figure was only ever bettered once – fifty-two in February 1968 whilst on a pan-European trip.

Looking through my records, perhaps the most prolific train I used was the aforementioned 10.47 Preston to Barrow. The Brit working this train then returned south with the 13.46 to Crewe and, although only taking it to Lancaster, one could effectively ignore the 15.30 southbound departure out of Preston as being already known about. Indeed, with experience certain balancing, i.e. out and back diagrams, could be identified and dealt with according to needs – subject, as ever, to failures!

To list all the catches, detail the trains travelled on, the stations visited, and the length of festering whilst awaiting 'requirements' to turn up, would probably lead any reviewer to describe the book as merely a list of statistics and dates – so I won't! Perhaps, however, I can be allowed to highlight a couple of oddities before progressing to the overnight adventures.

On the second Saturday in August, having visited Scotland earlier that day, I was at Carlisle in the late afternoon ready to board the 14.00 Glasgow to Liverpool train. Brought in by Brit 5, I couldn't believe it when Upperby dispatched Patricroft's Caprotti 73128, which limped into the station oozing with steam leaking out of every orifice and adorned with a coating of rust around her cylinders. The driver refused to take her over Shap with the fifteen coaches that the Brit had arrived with, so two were taken off. You have to give credit to the miracles performed by the footplate staff back then with the equipment

Saturday, 17 September 1966 and Crewe Works-allocated Fowler 4F 0-6-0 44525, just days away from withdrawal, shuffles around carrying out her mundane tasks – no doubt oblivious to the fact that she had become the final survivor of her class.

they were provided with, i.e. run-down, worn-out steam locomotives proba-bly long past their overhaul dates – often receiving 'please explain' notes from the Divisional Manager's Office when losing time en route. On this occasion Penrith was reached in thirty-five minutes – the Standard maxing at 42mph. It was an opportunity such as this, Alan reminded me, during which it was essential to 'window hang' in order to drink in the atmosphere of the sheer power and noise associated with a steam locomotive being worked hard. The Caprotti certainly struggled up the 10 miles of 1 in 125, the speed dropping as low as 23½mph at Harrisons Sidings. With Shap Summit being breasted at 32½mph, we then tore through Tebay at 78½mph. Upon reaching Preston a commendable mere twenty-eight minutes late, having lost just ten minutes on the schedule, the driver understandably declared her a failure – a replacement Black 5 ex Lostock Hall taking the train forward.

Come 19.00 the choices became somewhat limited. It was too late to return to London each Saturday so to kill the hours prior to the overnight journey home there were Brit-booked 18.25 and 21.45 departures ex Crewe or the 20.45 Blackpool portion out of Preston. If taking the latter that, unlike the 1967 timetable, *didn't* call at Kirkham (readers will realise the significance of that in Chapter 9), dependent on timekeeping we could make St Annes-on-Sea or Lytham St Annes before doubling back to Kirkham for the 21.55 Edge Hill-resourced Blackpool North to Liverpool Exchange service.

Whereas our northern friends then disappeared off to their homes and warm beds, the choice for us southerners after arriving into Preston was then either the 23.45 departure for Liverpool Lime Street, which could be taken to Wigan and travelled on if required, or the 23.17 DMU for Manchester in order to connect into the 01.00 sleepers for Wigan. I am unsure as to the reason for the 23.45 Preston's existence. Usually formed of three LMS vehicles, I was frequently the only passenger on board – a fact that may have contributed to its disappearance from the public timetable in January 1967. Calling at Wigan 00.06–00.13, St Helens Shaw Street 00.39–00.42 and arriv-ing into Liverpool Lime Street at the godforsaken hour of 01.02, no wonder no one else was aboard. As mentioned, the train was only travelled on if the locomotive was a requirement and to that effect, with the locomotive *in situ* on the train in the south bay platforms at least by 23.00, it was the forty-five minutes of wonderfully warm steam-heated sauna in which sleep deprivation often caught up with me. Awoken by the train's movement, it was a further twenty-minute struggle to stay awake and not miss the Wigan call. Reports published in *The Railway World* early in 1967 indicated that one of the two remaining Stanier 5MT Crabs, Springs Branch-allocated 42968 (which I copped in August 1966 at Lostock Hall shed looking as if it had been stored) had sometimes worked the train. Fortunately preserved, I was able to red-line her whilst attending a Steam on the Met event in May 1998.

Why, one might ask, did all roads lead to Wigan? Well, for us Southern-based contingent of chasers not wishing to arrive into London at the unearthly hour of 02.40 on the Barrow kippers (22.40 off Preston), the next London-bound train from Lancashire was the 02.53 from Wigan. This train, 1M12, the 21.15 ex Perth, arrived into the smoke at the far more convivial time of 06.20. Although more frequently than not I walked across the deserted streets of London to Blackfriars for my 07.49 Kent-bound EMU home, there were several instances when the lure of an extra 216 steam miles to/from Bournemouth or an SR-based rail tour were partaken of.

The 23.45 ex Preston arrived into Wigan at six minutes past midnight, thus awarding us a potential near three-hour 'fester'. At least by travelling via Manchester on the 01.00 sleepers, with an arrival time into Wigan of 01.36, the waiting time was reduced somewhat. More time was occupied if the shunt, to attach the portion to the rear off the 00.45 Liverpool–Scotland train, was steam worked, which meant staying aboard for another steam haulage – *any* movement was a haulage!

It would be a demoralising exercise to calculate how many hours of my life I spent/wasted/festered in Wigan's waiting room – the erratic timekeeping of the homeward-bound overnight Anglo–Scottish sleepers not assisting matters. As there were up to a dozen of us most Sunday mornings, the majority on at least their second night out, time was passed, amongst those managing to stay awake, by the playing of a redundant piano somewhat incongruously placed there. Often with no coal for the fire we sat/laid around on the cold wooden benches – too tired to even boast/brag about that weekend's catches. The walls of this establishment became, over the remaining months of steam, embellished with the type of graffiti only comprehensible to like-minded chasers: locomotive names, numbers and nicknames both of the locos themselves and fellow enthusiasts. This was the downside of our hobby for sure but each week we were back in the area in hope of more requirements being scratched in our crumpled, soot-stained, dog-eared, well-thumbed, torn *ABCs*. Eventually, upon hearing the ringing of a bell – the signalman's warning to station staff of the London train's arrival, we rubbed our bleary eyes, woke those still asleep,

Some of the tickets regularly proffered to the sleeping car attendant upon departure from Wigan.

staggered through the subway onto the up platform and made a beeline for empty compartments. The eagle-eyed sleeping car attendant (just the two – alternatingly fortnightly), having observed this bunch of youths swarming aboard his train, would quickly home in on us, slam open the compartment doors and demand to see our tickets. It was only after this, he having viewed the tattered, well-used BR free passes with suspicion accompanied by the predicable, 'Haven't I see this ticket before?/No, but you might have seen me', scenario, did we pull down the blinds, dim the lights (or take them out of the ceiling if the dimmer failed), discard our shoes and stretch out, two per compartment, falling into a deep sleep – usually our first lengthy respite since leaving for work on the Friday morning!

6

THE 109-HOUR
MARATHON: 1966

This five-and-a-half-day marathon, my lengthiest to date (little did I envisage far longer European bashes in 1968 and '69) was undertaken because many of the short-dated summer services running over the WCML were finishing that weekend. Sure I had caught upwards of sixty required locomotives during the preceding four weeks but, as any haulage basher will tell you, whenever the likelihood of further catches were in the offing then every effort must be made. There was urgency about the scene: the chase was on – to catch a run with something endangered before it was gone. There was nothing we could do to halt the march of progress. They could be consigned to the scrapheap prior to next visiting the area. How would that look when fellow conspirators bragged, 'How an earth did you miss that one – it was common as …?' Besides which, discounting the obvious dominance of Stanier's workhorses, there were *still* eight Brits that had, as yet, escaped my clutches.

As can be seen from my notebook extract overleaf, I didn't just confine this visit purely to the WCML, after all variety is the spice of life. I commenced on the Wednesday with the early-morning Calder Valley circuit. Positioning myself predominantly at Bradford during daylight hours on that first day, I departed for the LMR on the York–Aberystwyth TPO well satisfied with four Fairburns, one B1 and a Black 5, all receiving fresh red-lined entries in my ever-present *Locoshed* book. The jukeboxes at the station cafeterias

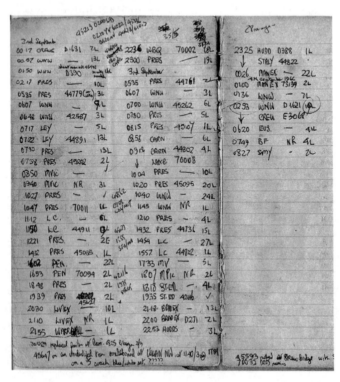

were blasting out The Beatles' double-sided *Yellow Submarine/Eleanor Rigby*. A few days earlier they played their final concert at Candlestick Park, San Francisco, before concentrating on recording.

It was now Thursday, 1 September and the 01.00 Scottish sleeper departure out of the long-gone Exchange station had Patricroft's 73011 at its head – a locomotive caught whilst working a North Wales service earlier that year. Upon arrival at Wigan, however, instead of the normal DSL placing us onto the rear of the Liverpool train the honours that morning went to Springs Branch-allocated Ivatt 2MT 46432. A further surprise was that instead of the usual Gateshead Peak DL, which was a diagrammed fill-in move off a Trans-Pennine working from Liverpool to Preston and return, Kingmoor's 70053 *Moray Firth* was standing in for the Peak's failure and took me forward the 15 miles to Preston. So, at 02.20, I had arrived at the location at which I was to spend a considerable number of hours – the minus-four-star-rated Preston waiting room. At least it wasn't all that cold and the need to rouse oneself every half hour or so to activate the cord-operated wall-mounted heater in an attempt to keep warm didn't arise.

Sleep deprivation must have finally caught up with me because the next 'move' was the southbound 07.00 departure. The majority of WCML services were now monopolised by a diet of Black 5s and Brits, and although they were usually sourced from a regular number of depots, every now and then a stray from outside the area broke the mould. The 06.10 Blackpool South to Euston, normally a Crewe South Brit, was that morning powered by Holyhead's 45247 – no doubt borrowed by the 5B foreman for the previous evening's 19.05 ex Euston. After alighting at Warrington, I headed west to Chester, spending the remainder of the day on the steam-saturated services between Shrewsbury and Birkenhead. I eventually wended my way to the welcoming all-night buffet/waiting room at Crewe for a hot meal – the first in thirty-six hours – of sausages and chips, which was hungrily wolfed down.

By default, whilst travelling between steam services, I was to collect runs with consecutive-numbered Brush Type 4s D1837–1861 – all being given the allocation DO5 (LMR's Stoke Division). Just before 1 a.m. on the morning of Friday, 2 September, the similarly allocated D1631 deposited me at Wigan and, having seen the Manchester sleeper portion shunt being steam worked (again), jumped aboard only to find out, when the locomotive was sighted, that it was the same LMS Mogul as twenty-four hours earlier – but

It's Friday, 2 September 1966 and at Preston the 10.47 for Barrow had former ER-allocated 70011 *Hotspur* working the train that day. As part of a 5B Brit duty she would return to Crewe with the 13.46 Barrow to Euston.

it might not have been! After a three-hour fester at Preston, the 05.35 Crewe stopper, a regular train for ex works locomotives running in, turned up with a pristine Warrington Dallam 44779 in charge. Taking her to Wigan, I then returned to Preston, the predestined axis of my travels, changing trains at Leyland en route.

A fairly respectable day reaping runs with several requirements culminated in what became the highlight of the entire visit. By mid July I had cleared all of the NER-allocated Jubilees, resulting in there being just one left in Britain to catch a run with: LMR's Bank Hall-allocated 45627 *Sierra Leone*. There were many unfounded rumours circulating amongst the enthusiast fraternity on the pre-internet method of communication: the bush telegraph. Having been sent out on the 09.00 portion just once that May she had become unfit for passenger use; she was frequently booked out but failed for several of the Preston portions – of which were unsubstantiated! She had, however, been witnessed on that day's 12.27 Liverpool Exchange to Blackpool North. Would she adhere to the roster and work the 19.00 return?[6] The relief upon the faces of the many waiting bashers upon her easing slowly into the East Lancs platform had to be seen to be believed. My only remaining required Jubilee in Britain was red-lined in my book with gusto! After creeping past Lostock Hall shed and a six-minute signal stand at Moss Lane Junction, at least she achieved a max of 75mph with her seven-vehicle train through Rufford. *Sierra Leone* was withdrawn eight days later. After then catching a DMU across to Wigan Wallgate, a short walk to the nearby North Western station led to 15¼ miles with *Geoffrey Chaucer* on the 19.05 ex Euston north to Preston.

Of the 267 line closures that year the largest of them all, the ex GC, was to be enacted that Saturday, 3 September. At Preston, however, it was only the possibility of further anticipated required catches that saw me through another six-hour fester in the waiting room. Was it all worth it? Looking back through my records and notebooks I'm glad I did it. It was all part of history. Fatigue was now seriously kicking in and I was beginning to doubt my sanity. I must have travelled to Wigan on the 05.35 with a non-required loco to placate the boredom.

Then followed a day of head-spinning timetable consultation – never knowing from which direction my 'requirements' were coming from. Come the afternoon and after an hour's wait at Lancaster, and upon arrival of an extremely common Newton Heath 44802, I called it a day and went through with her to Manchester. I felt I had exhausted both myself and what was available on the WCML, and just for the sheer change and novelty value I headed south to Stockport in order to catch a run on the once-a-day Bradford departure. I had frequently caught this train in from Halifax but never all the way over the Pennines. Low Moor's Fairburn 42116 was in charge that evening and I have to admit to fitfully drifting off to sleep to the blissful sound of the lively tank's exhaust during the near two-hour journey. The first 8 miles of this train's route was, in 1966, traversed by about eighteen DMUs per day but

---

[6] Information gleaned many years later revealed that it was known amongst the local enthusiast fraternity that this was to be *Sierra Leone's* last working – and it was externally cleaned by the Unofficial Volunteer Birkenhead Steam Cleaning Gang – making a change from their usual diet of Crabs, tanks and 9Fs.

In the gathering gloom the LM's sole-surviving Jubilee, Bank Hall's 45627 *Sierra Leone,* comes to a stand in Preston's East Lancs platforms with the 19.00 Blackpool North to Liverpool Exchange. Transferred from the Midlands in 1962, this 31-year-old Crewe-built locomotive was withdrawn just eight days later.

45627 / 7 coaches		
PRESTON	0.00	
WHITEHOUSE STH JCN.	2.49	28½
TODD LANE	4.34.	28.
LOSTOCK HALL	849	21
MOSS LANE JCN.	1324	
MOSS LANE sigs.	1420 / 20.16	
MIDGE HALL	2305	53/60½
LITTLEWOODS	2445	68.
RUFFORD	2545	70½.
RUFFORD	2747	75.
BURSCOUGH JCN ATH	2947	64
BURSCOUGH JCN.	3050	—
ORMSKIRK.	535	40
AUGHTON PARK.	250	41
TOWN GREEN	356.	55
MAGHULL	624	75
OLD ROAN	744	·
AINTREE SEFTON ARMS	956	18
ORRELL PARK	1150.	44
WALTON JCN	1250	41
KIRKDALE	1452	29
SANDBACH	1637	42
LIVERPOOL EX.	2004	

from 1992 the bare minimum, to avoid costly closure procedures, of a single train, the 09.22 (FO) Stockport to Stalybridge, has operated. Returning into Manchester one final time, both the Stalybridge portion and the Wigan sleepers provided me with two further needs – a fitting finale to the trip.

Statistically the outing wasn't groundbreaking. A total mileage of 1,642, only 976 of which were steam, reaped forty-eight runs with forty-three different locomotives – only twenty-eight sating my needs. Even so, if considered alongside the increasing number of blanked-out entries (denoting withdrawals), the unlined entries within my *Locoshed* book were getting less and less. It could have been so much different. I might have not been so lucky – or it could have been better. Much as many enthusiasts would like to, you can't turn back the clock and I was grateful for what I did achieve.

It's Saturday, 3 September 1966 and an unusually clean Brit, 70032 (Lord) *Tennyson*, waits at Preston to take the Euston to Aberdeen Granite City rail tour forward to Carlisle. She had spent her entire career within the LMR and was to be withdrawn at Kingmoor in September 1967.

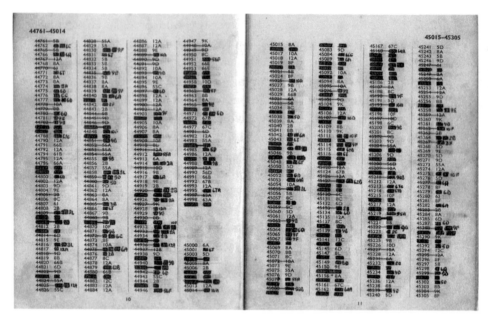

Here are two pages extracted out of the autumn 1965 issue of the *Locoshed Book*, in this example depicting the Stanier 5MTs, with inked amendments up until September 1966 – thus highlighting the extraordinarily fast pace of withdrawals and transfers within the steam fleet.

Locomotive stock changes

THIS list is correct to the following dates: LMR, December 3, 1966; ER, December 3, 1966; NER, December 3, 1966; ScR, November 26, 1966; SR, December 12, 1966.

MOTIVE POWER DEPOT CHANGES

New Code: HM-Healey Mills. The following Depots closed to steam from the dates shown: Machynlleth (6F) and Holyhead (6J) from December 12; Barrow (12C) from December 12, 1966.

NEW LOCOMOTIVES

2,750 h.p. Diesel-electric Co-Co: D1105/6-50A; D1953-WL; D1954-WL, then to D16 and back to WL; D1955-WL, then to D16; 1,250 h.p. Diesel electric Bo-Bo: D7661/2/3/4-D01; 1,000 h.p. Diesel-electric Bo-Bo: D8160/73/5/6/7-D16.

LOCOMOTIVES REALLOCATED

London Midland Region: W/E November 12: 42233/5/67/87, 42574-NER; 42587-8H; 44661, 45051/2-6D; 44663, 44865-2B; 44762/76-6C; 44825, 44936-12A; 44858-8L; 45222-9D; 45267-8F; 45292-5D; 45349-5B; 48025661-2B; 48045, 48119/24-8A; 48167-8G; 48170, 48201-9B; 48214/82-9H; 48253, 48632/69/97-6C; 48304-8E; 48380-9K; 48384-10A; 48393-10D; 48600-8L; 48620-9D; 48678-8F; 48763-9E; 75027-10G; 76051/75-8C; 78013/28/44/55-9K; 78020/1-10D; 78036-6D; 92002, 92223-2E; 92087, 92118/28, 92131/2-8H; 92151/2-8H; D1954-D16; D2219/35-8H; D2903/4/5/6-5A; D3098, D3181, D3247/90, D3467-5A; D3446/7 8/9/50/2/73/5/82-16A; D3686-9D; D5243/5-

D16; D5283-ML; 12038-8C; 12050/1/81/98-9D; 12052/5-5A; 12097-8F.

W/E November 19: 46503/16-8E; 47279/89-8G; 75026-10G; 78062-9K; D1624-D16; D1954-WL; D2058/9-12C; D3202-12D; D5239/46-D16; D5405/12-D14.

W/E November 26: 43119-12E; D1625-D16; D3412-12C.

W/E December 3: 42656/63-9E; 47293-10G; 48085, 48375, 48522-5D; D1955-D16; D7650-D16.

Eastern Region: W/E November 26: D1532-40B; D5828-31B; D5861-32A; D8208-30A; D8242-40B.

W/E December 3: D208-32B; D8023/53/4/5-30A.

North Eastern Region: 4 weeks ending December 3: 42233/5/67/87, 42574-56A; 42177, 44693/5, 44990, 45208-56F; 44826/96, 44943, 45562, 45647-55A; 48076, 48664-55D; 61173-50A; 61115/89, 61309/88-56A; 65804-N, Blyth-S. Blyth; 65865/85-52F; 65869/92-52G; 90061, 90116-51C; 90112, 90370-52G; 92201/30/65, 92135/50, 92215-56A; D243, D348/56/97-HM; D2231/69-SR; D3652/3/6/8-55A; D6835/6-50B; D6860/2/3/4/5-50A, then to HM; D6861-50A.

Scottish Region: 9 weeks ending November 26: 42691-64A; 42789/95, 42803-66B; 44703-65A; 44722, 44879-63A; 45161, 45365-66E; 45167-66E, then to 66B; 45213, 45319, 45423/67/90/2-62C; 61029-62C; 61072, 61180, 61340/54-62B; 61140, 61342-66B; 64569, 64602/11/20/3-62B; 73146-66B; 73149/50/3-65J; 76004, 76114-66F; D2436/43-67C; D2736/7/72/3-65A; D3005/6/7/8/9, D3198, D3200/2/10/83/6, D3410/2, D3530/1,

D3736/40/1, D3897-LMR; D3209/14, D3926-67C; D3533-65A, then to 66C; D3536, D3898/9, D3900/1/3/4-65A; D3537/8/9-65F; D5050/1/2/3/4/5/6-65A; D5063/7/70-64B; D6821-NER; D6857/9-64B; D7598/9, D7600/1-65A; D8031/3/4-66A; D8032-64B.

Southern Region: Period ending December 12: D2231/69-NER; D6551-70D; D6577-73C.

LOCOMOTIVES WITHDRAWN

4646/96, 9774, 41202/4/7/20/9/33/4/44/51/86, 41304, 42069, 42115/28, 42664/91, 42782, 42919, 43009/22/40/79/95, 43103/32/3, 44712/4/20/3/4/62, 44847, 44941/52/84, 45029/51/3, 45127/54/62/8, 45217/24/89, 45309/29/32/72, 45408/32/51/69/73, 46405/28, 46512/7, 47273, 47314/67, 47444/72, 47533/90, 47603/59/67/71/3/5, 48083, 48113/9/42/48600/41/51/62/3/72/86, 60530, 60813/24/68, 60955/76, 61017/22/32, 61303/7/8/30/50, 62028, 63377, 64570, 64618/23, 65267, 65319, 65815, 65903/9/12/4/5/7/8/20/1/2/5, 70054, 73072/99, 73145, 75050/79, 76004/21/47/74/6/8, 78018/9/36/46/59/61/4, 80028/92/3, 80126, 90044/78, 90090, 90441, 90534/47, 90723/31, 92063/4, 92116/24/55, 92231/9, D3122/3/4/6, 12022.

DIESEL UNITS

Withdrawn: MSB50285, MSB50611; MC79509/10; MS79150/1/2/3, TBS79326/7; TS79402; Railbus 79958/9/67/8/74/9.

LOCOMOTIVES RECLASSIFIED

D5593, D5610/62, D5813 from 12/2 to 14/2.

An example of the necessary documentation one had to cope with on a monthly basis. (*Railway World*, February 1967)

7

MANCUNIAN MEANDERINGS: 1966–67

Manchester, together with the neighbouring city of Liverpool, was where it was all happening during the 1960s. With football clubs from both cities riding high in the First Division together with domination in the pop music charts by Manchester's The Hollies and Liverpool's Beatles, Cilla Black and Gerry and the Pacemakers the 'Northern Powerhouse' (to quote modern parlance) was the place to be. One of my personal favourite TV shows was *The Wheeltappers* and *Shunters Social Club*, which featured comedians such as Bernard Manning, Frank Carson and Norman Collier – all being kept in order by the bell-ringing Colin Crompton.

A native of Manchester is a Mancunian and a sprinkling of luminaries who qualify are as follows: comedian Les Dawson, cricketer Michael Atherton, TV presenter Judy Finnigan, singer/songwriter Mick Hucknall, Prime Minister David Lloyd George, suffragette Emmeline Pankhurst and actor John Thaw.

Manchester, which throughout the 1960s had a justifiable reputation for abysmal dull and wet weather, received its city status in 1853 and became connected to the Irish Sea courtesy of the Manchester Ship Canal in 1894. With its cotton and heavy industries booming, Manchester soon acquired its ranking of Britain's second most populous city. Targeted by the Luftwaffe in the Second World War, the largest blitz in December 1940 destroyed a huge part of its historic city centre, killing 376 people and damaging

30,000 houses. The city was also often referred to as the other Fleet Street – editions of *The Manchester Guardian*, *Daily Telegraph*, *Daily Express*, *Daily Mirror* and *Sporting Chronicle* being printed there. By the 1960s the Port of Manchester had become the UK's third largest but as it was unable to deal with the increasingly gargantuan container ships it was to eventually close in 1982. With the once traditional industries declining through either recession or cheaper importation, a regeneration programme involving the conversion of disused mills into apartments and shopping centres was begun in the 1980s running concurrently with the construction of the Metrolink, the Manchester Arena and the rebranding of the port as Salford Quays. With the 2002 Commonwealth Games being held there Manchester has deservedly regained its unofficial accreditation of being Britain's second city. Whether the BBC's HQ being moved from London to Salford assisted the attainment is a matter of conjecture!

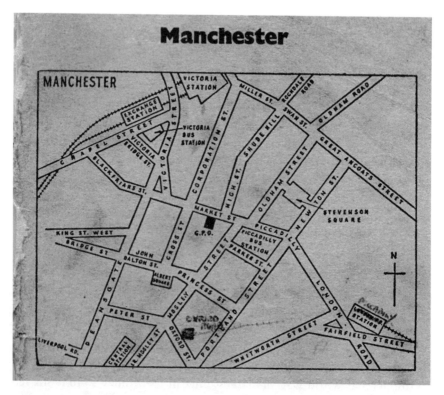

The city of Manchester street map. (Lt Fuller's *Shed Directory*)

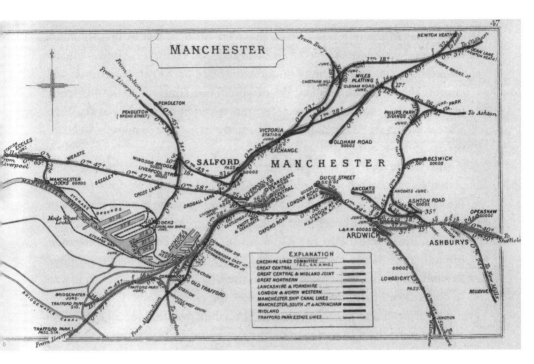

A 1910 Railway Clearing House map of Manchester's railways.

Having initially concentrated my travels over routes threatened with closure under the Beeching axe, it wasn't until October 1965 that I made my first visit to Manchester. This was a big 'foreign city' to a teenager from the smoke, so armed with a street map, courtesy of Lt Fuller's *Shed Directory*, I undertook what was to become the first of numerous walks across the city from one terminus to another – in this case between Manchester's Oxford Road and Central stations. There was no Metro in those days but as regards safety I can honestly say that at no time did I feel threatened or worried about possible consequences of such actions – just as well, however, my parents were unaware of such nocturnal activities! Perhaps it was the naivety of youth, which saw me escape any problems that in today's society are only too common. The sometimes unsavoury clientele that wander the same environment today lead me to realise how fortunate I was not only to have experienced the ability to walk the streets safely but also, taking into consideration the purpose of the mission, to travel throughout Britain by steam-hauled trains irrespective of what hours they operated.

Analysis of my notebooks from those far-off days reveals that the most frequented walk was that between Piccadilly and Victoria stations – usually having come direct from my London workplace on a Friday afternoon and crossing for the evening Belfast Boat Express. I had fine-tuned this particular walk to an art – an example being having arrived into Piccadilly at 20.39 on a late-running service and speed-walking in a mere sixteen minutes to board the 20.55 BBE out of Victoria.

Another walk that was undertaken with increasing regularity was completely on railway property – along the lengthy connecting platform between the Victoria and Exchange stations. Depending upon how many nights I, or more usually we, had been travelling, the walk from the 00.05 arrival from Preston into Victoria for the 01.00 Wigan portion out of the Exchange, carefully negotiating the then frenzied activities of porters loading colossal amounts of parcels or newspapers from the BRUTEs[7] deliberately (?) placed to obstruct our path, always seemed to get longer each time.

The atmosphere at each Manchester termini was different. The clinical cleanliness of the then newly rebuilt Piccadilly (née London Road) was at odds with the drab, doomed Central station. Then there was the windswept joint station of Exchange/Victoria with its aforementioned activity of mails, parcels and papers. Each station had its share of human flotsam – either sleeping off excessive drink or adopting a waiting room as a residence until being moved on. Without doubt, by following my hobby of chasing the steam locomotive throughout Britain my eyes were opened to other people's way of life. Travel broadens the mind and the thoroughly enjoyable pastime of those years is now firmly filed in the section of memories marked 'life's experiences'.

I have a theory, and that is that the railway hierarchy obviously didn't want the dirty, environmentally unfriendly, polluting steam locomotives on show to the public during normal hours and so colluded with the train planning/locomotive rostering departments to ensure that most steam passenger trains were operated in the dead of night! This in turn discouraged, in their eyes, those tiresome steam-locomotive followers who congregated at platform ends performing number-taking duties. At the time of restructuring and modernisation throughout British Rail (ways) the steam locomotive and its attendant

---

[7] BRUTE stood for British Railways Universal Trolley Equipment and they were in use from 1964 to the late 1980s. They were designed for use on both station platforms and for carrying freight on trains.

enthusiasts were unwanted blots on the landscape, which they didn't want to be seen. As will be noted later in the book, the majority of the final few steam-hauled passenger trains in or out of Manchester operated between 00.30 and 06.30. Our hobby, by default, had turned us into nocturnal animals!

In reality, of course, with the regular daytime passenger services on most secondary lines being in the hands of the diesel multiple units, it was only the mails/papers/parcel traffic that prolonged steam's final workings over many routes. The 1936 LMS publicity film *Night Mail* perfectly epitomises the night-time activity that was about in the 1960s and which I witnessed. With Britten's music and Auden's words it accurately portrays the work performed during the night hours. The delivery and collection of mail, the lorries arriving with freshly printed papers ready for loading into a fusion of vanfits and parcel vans, the shared companionship amongst the workers with their good-natured banter being thrown around. Then there were the often-solitary passenger, who, having missed the last train, huddled in a foetal position on a platform bench in an attempt to stave off the cold.

Nowadays, albeit somewhat older, there is no way that I would even attempt to take on such activity involving so much time spent away from the comfort of a warm bed under a roof. It would have been so much easier to have just spotted but the sheer exhilaration of travelling behind as many different steam locomotives as possible became seriously addictive – consequently turning us into night owls. Overnight travels were thus spent either actually on trains or in platform waiting rooms, which back then were usually free from vandalism and graffiti attacks, and some of them had the luxury of heating. To stay in bed-and-breakfast accommodation would have meant missing out on considerable steam activity as well as increasing the costs far beyond a junior clerk's financial means.

On my trips, sometimes accompanied, sometimes not, because the number of steam services was continually contracting, I nearly always met like-minded haulage bashers, with whom competitive catches, i.e. locomotives 'needed' by others, and the latest news was exchanged. Information in that pre-mobile phone and internet age was always by word of mouth. Events such as shed closures, locomotive transfers, and the inexorable change of steam services going diesel kept us all on our toes. However sad today's youths might think the railway enthusiast, at least we caused no problems to anyone else, occupying the somewhat traumatic hormone-induced years with a hobby encompassing surprising educational benefits such as geography and the origins of locomotive names.

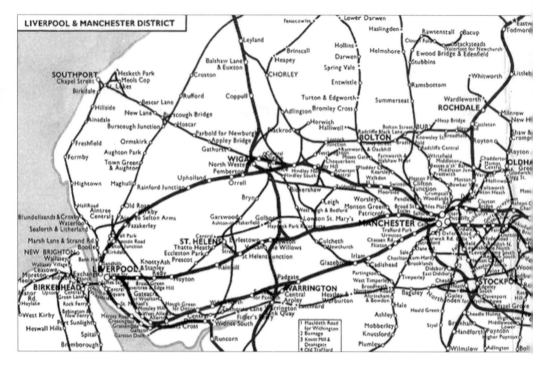

A 1966 map of Manchester and Liverpool railways. (Creative Commons License – mickeyashworth)

So may I now be permitted to take the reader on a tour of Manchester's railway stations? I will start with Manchester's first railway station, Liverpool Road, and progress clockwise around the city. Liverpool Road, opened in 1830, was the two-platform Manchester terminus of the world's first inter-city passenger railway on which timetabled services were hauled by steam locomotives and is the world's oldest surviving terminal railway station. A mere fourteen years later, with the line from Liverpool being extended to Victoria to join the Manchester & Leeds Railway, it was closed. The site is now the Museum of Science and Industry, its main-line link having been severed in connection with the Ordsall Curve project linking Victoria and Piccadilly stations. Comprising 300m of new track between Castlefield and Deal Street Junctions and opened in December 2017, the route includes a futuristically designed asymmetric bridge, which locals have dubbed akin to 'half a tennis racket'.

Before moving on to Victoria one mustn't forget the Exchange station, which was opened by the LNWR in 1884; this five-platform station allowing the LNWR to vacate the congested L&YR Victoria site. Platforms 1 and 2 were bays, the others being through roads. In 1929, platform 3 was extended eastwards to meet Victoria's 11, thus creating a 2,194ft three-train-length platform – at the time Europe's longest. The station was severely damaged in the Luftwaffe blitz of December 1940 – part of the roof never being replaced. After various passenger service reductions during the 1960s, what ones remained were diverted to Victoria in 1969 and the station was closed – although it continued to deal with newspaper traffic into the 1980s. In 2015 the final remnants were razed to the ground in connection with the Manchester–Preston electrification works.

The most frequented train I was *ever* to use on LMR metals departed the Exchange station at 01.00 hours. This was the overnight sleeper to Scotland, which had one BSK within its formation. Departing from platform 1 (occupancy was available from 23.00), Patricroft shed provided the power as far as Wigan North Western, where the station pilot would propel it onto the rear of the Peak DL-worked 00.45 Liverpool Lime Street to Glasgow/Edinburgh train. Mainly resulting from it being pitch black, but also factoring in tiredness, I am unsure of the route, which I am sure varied, that was taken by this train, although I do recall, however, on one occasion hanging out of the window to ascertain what the delay was and noting both Parkside and Golborne Junction signal boxes.

With steam heating having been provided for at least two hours, the overly warm compartments saw many an enthusiast nod off – others shaking the miscreants awake upon arrival at Wigan. The problem when alone was that there was no one else to perform the honours and on one occasion, as detailed in Chapter 10, I ended up at Carlisle. I also learnt never to enter a locomotive in my notebook until it actually moved – it wasn't unknown for the steam locomotive, having heated the train, coming off at the last minute to hand over to a DL! Fortunately, out of the forty-eight occasions that I travelled on this train, only six were not steam-powered. Although Patricroft shed usually sent out one of its Standard 5MTs, either normal or Caprotti versions, there were many occasions when a Black 5 (often Liverpool area allocated) was supplied. For a short period during 1967, on Mondays the train was part of a Kingmoor Brit duty. More often than not the same locomotive, having visited Springs Branch shed in order to turn, would work the balancing 05.45 ex Wigan – but, as always in those uncertain times, that wasn't always the case. You couldn't guarantee anything back then!

We began blitzing the aforementioned 01.00 Exchange departure during the summer of 1966 and, at some point soon after, became intrigued, whilst walking the lengthy connecting platform off of the 00.05 arrival at Victoria, as to a two-coach steam-hauled passenger service arriving there at about half past midnight. Perusal of LM's maroon timetable revealed it to be a portion off of the 21.50 York to Shrewsbury TPO – having been detached at Stalybridge, a town that straddles the Lancashire–Cheshire border. Previously unaware of the existence of the train, it fortuitously turned out to be steam worked on Sunday mornings only – the very night we haulage bashers most needed it! I have often wondered over the years why this was and only recently learnt that on all other mornings an assisting DL was placed on the front of the TPO at Leeds, detached at Stalybridge, worked the portion into Manchester and returned to the NER on a paper train. Facebook has its usages! This train thus became a useful link after an NER bash. Any Black or Standard 5MT from various sheds was liable to be turned out – uniquely working the portion tender first. I can still place the wonderfully surreal 8-mile journey in my mind as, undertaking the necessary window-hanging vocation, the train threaded its way high over the illuminated Mancunian suburbs – on one occasion maxing at 52mph en route. It wasn't always steam – of the eleven occasions aboard a regrettable two were DLs – but there was the 01.00 to look forward to wasn't there?

The North Wales services out of Manchester Exchange were usually in the capable hands of Patricroft-allocated Standard 5MTs. With the exception of the 'Club' trains (07.40 Llandudno–Manchester and 16.30 return, which retained steam for a further three months) they were dieselised in October 1966.[8] Although catching quite a few runs on them in the Warrington/Chester/Llandudno area my only incursion into the Exchange on one was in July 1966. George, a fellow Scottish enthusiast – with whom I was with for at least twenty-four hours that particular bash – and I had

---

[8]   These particular 'Club' trains were ones that, when operated by the LNWR, conveyed special eight-wheeled carriages (available only to members) furnished with leather-padded armchairs for personal individual use, being provided for the many magnates of the Manchester cotton industry who resided in the North Wales coastal resorts.

Table 89

Huddersfield and Manchester to Wigan and Liverpool

	B	A				C	D
NEWCASTLE .. .. .. d							
HULL .. d							
LEEDS CITY .. .. .. d						07 22	
BRADFORD EXCHANGE d							
HALIFAX .. .. d							
HUDDERSFIELD d						07 55	
LONGWOOD .. d							
GOLCAR d							
SLAITHWAITE .. .. d							
MARSDEN d							
DIGGLE .. .. d							
SADDLEWORTH d						08 15	
GREENFIELD .. d						08 18	
MOSSLEY d						08 22	
STALYBRIDGE .. .. a						08 27	
d	00 12				07 30	08 29	
ASHTON CHARLESTOWN .. d					07 33	08 32	
DROYLSDEN d							
CLAYTON BRIDGE .. d							
PARK d					07 40		
MILES PLATTING d					07 42	08 40	
MANCHESTER VICTORIA a					07 47	08 44	
d							
MANCHESTER EXCHANGE .. a	00 26						
d		01 00					
ECCLES d							
PATRICROFT .. .. d							
MONTON GREEN .. .. d							
WORSLEY d							
TYLDESLEY .. .. a							
d							
LEIGH .. .. .. d							
WIGAN NORTH WESTERN .. a		01 36					
d							
NEWTON-LE-WILLOWS d							
EARLESTOWN .. .. d							
WARRINGTON BANK QUAY a			08 18	08 37			
d							
EARLESTOWN d			08a27	08a47			
ST. HELENS JUNCTION .. a							
d							
ST. HELENS SHAW STREET .. a							
RAINHILL d							
HUYTON .. .. d						09 33	
ROBY d							
BROAD GREEN .. .. d							
EDGE HILL d						09 39	
LIVERPOOL LIME STREET .. a						09 44	

Heavy figures denote through carriages; light figures denote connecting services
For general notes see page 11

For local train service between Wigan North Western and Liverpool Lime Street see Table 94

A and through carriages Manchester to Glasgow Central. Through carriages Manchester to Edinburgh

B Through train from York

C 19 June to 4 September. Through train Crewe to Blackpool North

D 19 June to 4 September

Timetable extract (1966) depicting the regularly travelled upon Sunday morning 00.12 Stalybridge and 01.00 Manchester Exchange trains.

The date was Saturday, 25 June 1966 and Carnforth's 'pet' 45025 powers the Belfast Boat Express away from her Bolton Trinity Street stop.

With the Exchange station in the background, Agecroft-allocated Stanier 8F 48666 is captured running LE through Manchester Victoria on Friday, 1 July 1966. This Brighton-built 22-year-old, having spent the majority of her life in the Midlands, was withdrawn from Rose Grove at the very end – in August 1968.

travelled west on the 09.15 Leeds–Llandudno with 45562 *Alberta* and, having negotiated a myriad of freight lines in the Warrington area, was running sufficiently late to make us bale out at Rhyl. The reason being the need to return ASAP to the NER in order to connect into the 18.10 Sheffield Midland to Bradford: the outward working having been seen that morning with a required 45581, *Bihar & Orissa*. To facilitate this we caught the 13.15 Llandudno to Manchester Exchange prior to dashing over to Manchester Piccadilly for an AM2-worked service to Sheffield Victoria. Standard 5MT 73006 took us into Exchange that day and blow me if she didn't take us out again at 01.00 the following morning!

If the Brits' final resting place was Kingmoor, the BR Standard 5MTs' was Patricroft. With numbers peaking at forty-two (during 1966), they had migrated from all parts of the LMR: displacement usually through shed closures. Seemingly hibernating from passenger trains during the day, we battle-hardened haulage bashers *had* to become night owls if requiring runs with them – the Wigan portions being the only all-week trains they powered. If I hadn't have bashed these two portions my red-linings would have been that much poorer.

And finally one mustn't overlook the enthusiasts' favourite FO working – that of the 17.34 Manchester Exchange to York. During 1966 reported observations that were subsequently published in the railway press show locomotives such as 45627 *Sierra Leone* (29 April), 45593 *Kholapur* (7 October) and 45562 *Alberta* (28 October) as having worked it.

With annual leave days at a premium I wasn't on it on as many occasions as I would have liked, just five in fact, the first being the last occasion it was routed via Standedge (2 June 1967) and although by that date the train was rostered for a Kingmoor Brit it was, as was more usual, a 12A Black 5MT. I forget the usual size of the train but it was deemed necessary for it to be banked to up to Miles Platting – part of which was 1 in 47. Memorably leaning out of a window whilst passing Victoria station, the sight and sound of the train, with the two locomotives opening up, definitely made the commuters look up from their evening papers in bewilderment.

From 9 June 1967 (70035 *Rudyard Kipling*) it was retired to start at 17.47 and run via the Calder Valley, and although three of my four further travels on it yielded the inevitable Stanier 4-6-0, at least on my November visit I had 76 miles of Brit 51 *Firth of Forth* haulage – the very final steam working on this train, on 29 December that year, being in the hands of sister *Oliver Cromwell*.

The same day saw sister 48636 of Patricroft heading a westbound freight past Manchester Victoria.

On Sunday, 27 August 1967 Standard 4-6-0 73000 is seen at Manchester Victoria having worked the portion detached at Wigan NW off the overnight Glasgow–Liverpool train. On all other days this train would have terminated at the Exchange station but with no Sunday shift rostered, Victoria it had to be. This nomadic prototype Standard 5MT, which showcased alongside *The Duke* (71000) at the 1954 Rolling Stock Exhibition at Willesden, was withdrawn at Patricroft, her fourteenth shed, in March 1968.

The location was Manchester Victoria and the date Friday, 1 December 1967. Kingmoor's 45259 has arrived with 1J42, the 12.17 portion (off the 08.25 Glasgow–Liverpool) from Preston, whilst Newton Heath's 44890 is held at signals on the adjacent goods line. I was aboard 45259's train and we had had a near two-minute stop at Salford to regain steam pressure – the whistle having stuck in the open position.

Moving onto Victoria: opened in 1844, the single lengthy 852ft platform was initially jointly used by both the MLR for its services east to Leeds and the Liverpool & Manchester Railway for its westward-bound services. By the late nineteenth century six separate companies were using the station and reconstruction shortly afterwards by the L&YR in 1909 awarded the site with the seventeen platforms that I was to encounter in my travels. With the bay platforms at the eastern end being the preserve of suburban DMUs and Bury-line EMUs, it was only because the Calder Valley night mail trains utilised the adjacent through platform that I was to frequent that part of the station. Separated by through running lines from the Exchange station, it was platforms 12 to 17, those that dealt with services from the west, that saw my greater usage.

The station received Grade II listed-building status in 1988 for its period features and Edwardian neo-Baroque facade, booking hall, glass dome, tiled map of the Lancashire and Yorkshire Railway together with a memorial for servicemen who did not return after the First World War. During the 1990s, following the transfer of some services to the Metrolink and the construction of the Manchester Arena, the number of platforms were drastically reduced to just six. Having received the dubious accolade, in November 2009, of Britain's worst Category B (Regional Interchange) station, Network Rail has subsequently rebuilt it citing anticipated increased patronage in connection with both the Ordsall curve services from Piccadilly and Metrolink.

The train I frequented the most *into* Manchester Victoria was the 6 a.m. arrival – the 02.10 ex York. I was aboard this Calder Valley-routed train on twenty-five occasions. When the North Eastern Region was awash with steam I used to alight, together with literally hordes of other ferroequinologists,[9] off of this service at Hebden Bridge, merely crossing the platform to return east twenty-three minutes later with the opposite way 04.25 ex Victoria. As steam ebbed away on the NER it became purposeless to return east and so I stayed aboard, and having arriving into Victoria at 6 a.m., the LMR was at my mercy. I either headed for steam-saturated Preston or, during the final months, the 09.00 Liverpool Exchange portion. With the NER losing all of its home allocation of steam in October 1967, it was truly astonishing that this train remained steam worked (9D Black 5 forward from Halifax) right through until May 1968 – no doubt to the annoyance of the NER authorities.

Although the majority of my visitations into/out of Victoria with steam emanated off of the Bolton route, i.e. Preston portions, Blackpool, Morecambe and Barrow services together with the Belfast Boat Express, there were still, until January 1967, a number of peak-hour departures to Southport, Blackpool and Windermere. I also occasionally travelled on some of the short-dated Summer Saturday East Coast-bound services that utilised the Standedge route over the Pennines, most of which remained the preserve of steam. Then there were frequent relief, control and Wakes

---

[9]   A ferroequinologist is a person who pursues or is interested in the study of the Iron Horse.

weeks extras.[10] We became proficient in scrutinising each week's LMR STNs for supplementary services that, taking into consideration where the ECS for them originated from, were likely candidates for steam haulage.

Then there was the Hope Valley route, via Chinley and Edale, surmounting the Pennines to Sheffield, over which some of the local services remained steam until January 1967. The train I frequented most, during the summer of 1966, was the 22.55 FO Victoria to Yarmouth Vauxhall. This ran for a mere six weeks each year and accessed the route having threaded its way via the tortuously slow myriad of lines via Phillips Park Nos 1 and 2, Ashburys and Bellevue, arriving into Sheffield Midland at 00.29 – not inconveniently connecting into the 2 a.m. Calder Valley mail train scenario! On one Friday in July 1967 this train started back at Accrington in connection with the town's Wakes week and having boarded the train at Chorley an unexpected locomotive exchange, from Springs Branch's 44761 to Edge Hill's 45039, was enacted at Victoria en route. Both this and the balancing 16.59 return working were Newton Heath-crewed – the latter affording a wonderful daylight steam-hauled journey over the undulating route through the scenic Pennines.

The only occasion I had to use the Victoria waiting room was early one Saturday morning in June 1967 when, having spent the Friday evening on SR services and not leaving London until 21.25, I arrived into Piccadilly at 01.28. Perhaps the connections from the south were late but, whatever the reason, having missed the 01.00 out of the Exchange I made my way over to Victoria and festered there for two and half hours in order to catch Newton Heath's 44822 on the 04.25 York departure. After alighting at the once principal centre of the flannel trade, Rochdale, a further hour was spent, on a fortunately warm summer's morning, waiting for the 02.10 ex York, which turned up with a required 45083. I reasoned that the wait was worthwhile as I was never to have 45083 again – she was withdrawn that December.

---

[10] The Wakes weeks were a holiday period in parts of England and Scotland. Originally a religious celebration or feast, the tradition of the Wakes weeks evolved into a [initially unpaid] secular holiday, particularly in the north-west of England during the Industrial Revolution. Between June and September each year each Lancashire town, on a coordinated rotational basis, effectively closed down – the factory and mill owners using the opportunity to undertake annual maintenance. This annual exodus was to prove too much for the regular train service to cope with and specials to a variety of coastal destinations were the norm.

It's 5 a.m. on the morning of Friday, 2 June 1967 and Newton Heath's 44822 gets into her stride upon departing Rochdale with the 04.25 Manchester Victoria to York – which she would work as far as Normanton.

Temporarily interrupting the tour of Manchester's terminus stations (there being no other suitable place within the book to detail it) I participated in two rail tours that started at or travelled through Manchester's Victoria station. The first on Saturday, 26 November 1966, was the Manchester Rail Travel Societies organised Three Counties Special. This tour was postponed from 12 November for operational reasons – of which I didn't make a note of or didn't know.

With the tour not starting out of Manchester until 10 a.m., I took the opportunity of a pre-dawn aperitif of the 06.10 Blackpool and Belfast Boat Express trains beforehand, wonderfully reaping the reward of Brit 51 and Carnforth-allocated 45373 – *both required*.

Saturday, 26 November 1966 and one of two remaining Trafford Park-allocated Stanier tanks, 42644, is at Manchester Victoria with the 10.00 four-vehicle Three Counties Tour. This 28-year-old 2-6-4T had arrived from Wigan (L&Y) at 9E two years previously and was withdrawn in March 1967.

Notwithstanding the appalling rain-plagued conditions, I yomped across the River Irwell at Bacup and took this shot of 42644 running around its train. Bacup was to lose its passenger services the following week.

Two elderly tank locomotives undertook the 22-mile leg of the tour, from Bury Bolton Street to Stockport. Preparing to work the tour forward are 67-year-old Vulcan Foundry-built Johnson 3F 0-6-0T 47202 and the younger (at a mere 40 years old) Fowler-designed 47363. While the former was withdrawn at Newton Heath the following month, the Fowler, although also withdrawn at 9D, was reinstated in February 1967 and dispatched to Westhouses for a further eight months. Leading a somewhat charmed life, she survived into preservation and can be found nowadays at the Severn Valley Railway.

Opposite above: Spending the first thirteen of her twenty years at the Welsh shed of Tredegar, Crewe-built, Ivatt-designed 2-6-2T 41204, one of Stockport's four remaining Mickeys, prepares to take the tour forward from Stockport Edgeley to Manchester Central (via Buxton and Millers Dale). It was probably her final revenue-earning train – she being withdrawn the following week.

Opposite below: One of three remaining J94s, Buxton-allocated 68006, is seen in the dying light of a damp November afternoon at Millers Dale – having 'towed; the tour the 5½ miles from Buxton itself. She was withdrawn the following May. (Alan Hayes)

I was primarily aboard this tour for the tank haulages – there being by that date (excepting the sporadic use of Lostock Hall's meagre allocation being *very* occasionally put out on the Blackpool portions) no tank-operated passenger services throughout the LMR. Geographically the tour was, to me, an eye-opener as to the complexity of routes within the Greater Manchester and Peak District railway network. Initially heading east over what is now a Metrolink via Oldham to Rochdale, the train then turned westwards and journeyed over a route closed by BR in 1970 but is now (from Heywood) under the auspices of the East Lancashire Railway preservation organisation. Having travelled through Bury, we now headed north via Rawtenstall to Bacup, a town reached by the East Lancashire Railway in 1852. The line north of Rawtenstall was to close a week later – services south thereof ceasing in 1972. Stanier 4MT 42644, having run round at Bacup, then retraced her route to Bury, where the two Jintys, 47202 and 47383, took over for the trip via Molyneux Brow (which nowadays forms part of the Irwell Sculpture Trail) to Manchester Victoria. Pausing briefly for crew-change purposes, we then travelled via the Ashton Moss Junctions to Stockport Edgeley. Here Mickey tank 41204 took over for the journey to Buxton, where one of the three remaining J94s, 68006, was coupled onto the rear. The rear became the front and the J94 took the train the 5½ miles to Millers Dale – the Ivatt having to remain on the train due to the lack of vacuum brakes on 68006. After a further reversal, the remaining 30 miles from Millers Dale (closed 1968) via Cheadle Heath (closed 1967) to Manchester Central (closed 1969) was once again in the hands of the Ivatt.

The weather was rainy and freezing, and after temporarily losing my way amongst the myriad Manchester city streets in my bid to locate Piccadilly station, I headed for Crewe – en route home? No way – I was making the most of my last visit to the area that year and although *Firth of Forth* powered that evening's 18.25 Crewe to Barrow. at least the capture of two required Edge Hill Black 5s on the 20.45 and 23.45 departures out of Preston made the stay out worth it. Nine new – not bad for a November visit to the area!

The second tour, held on Sunday, 16 April 1967, was the Epsom Railway Society's Mercian. The attraction in this instance was the usage of three preserved locomotives: Viscount Garnock's K4 3442 *The Great Marquess* between Stockport and Leeds, the embryonic K&WVR's Mickey tank 41241 and Alan Pegler's 4472 *Flying Scotsman* into London's King's Cross. It had been planned that a trip over K&WVR metals would take place but the necessary Light Railway Order had yet to be granted – the result being that

THREE COUNTIES SPECIAL

Train Reporting No. IT55.

Position		Booked T	Actual T
00	Manchester Vic	1000	..10.01
1½	Miles Platting	1005	..10.07
2½	Thorpe's Bdg Jcn	1008	..10.09
4¾	Hollinwood	1016	..10.13½
7½	Oldham Mumps	1025	..10.19½
14¼	Roc hdale E.Jcn	1040	..10.32
14¾	Rochdale	1042	..10.33
16½	Castleton E.Jcn	1047	..10.40
21¾	Bury K. Street	1056	..10.42
22	Bury South Jcn	1058	..10.55
22	Bury South Jcn	1106	...✓..
22¼	Bury B. Street	1107	10.55..11.05
26¼	Ramsbottom	1114	..11.15
27	Stubbins Jcn	1115	...✓..
27	Stubbins Jc n	1120	..11.16½
34¼	Bacup	1142	..11.41
34¼	Bacup	1210	..12.10
41½	Stubbins Jcn	1232	...12.26
42¼	Ramsbottom	1233	...12.27
46½	Bury B.Street	1240	....12.36
46½	Bury B.Street	1255	..12.54
48½	Radcliffe N. Jcn	1259	..12.57½
52¼	Clifton Jcn	1306	..13.03½
54½	Windsor Bdge No 3	1310	..13.08
55¾	Windsor Bdge No.1	1312	..13.10
57	Manchester Vic	1315	13.15

Position		Booked T	Actual T
58½	Miles Platting	1320	..13.20
61½	Droylsden	1327	..13.28
62¼	Ashton Moss Jcn	1331	..13.33
64	Denton Junction	1333	..13.34½
67½	Heaton Norris Jcn	1342	..13.41½
68½	Stockport Edgeley	1345	..13.49
68½	Stockport Edgeley	1405	..14.03
69	Edgeley Junction	1408	...14.06
75¼	Disley	1423	..14.25
88	Buxton	1454	..14.44
88	Buxton	1510	..15.04½
88¼	Buxton No 1	1513	..✓..
88¼	Buxton No.1	1523	..✓..
88½	Buxton East	1525	..✓..
93½	Miller's Dale	1535	...15.22½
93½	Miller's Dale	1552	..16.08
98	Peak Forest	1604	..16.20
101¾	Chapel-E-L-Frith	1612	..16.25½
103¼	Chinley North Jcn	1614	..16.27½
103¾	Chinley	1616	..16.29½
106	New Mills S.Jcn	1620	..16.32½
115½	Cheadle Heath	1629	..16.43
120	Chorlton Jcn	1637	..16.48
122	Throstle Nest Jcn	1641	..16.52
123½	Manchester Central	1645	..16.59

Stock :- Coach A(SO) ?B(SO),C(SO),D(BSK)

Sunday, 16 April 1967 and The Mercian rail tour is seen soon after arrival into Blackburn. The preserved K4 3442 *The Great Marquess*, which was working the tour from Stockport to Leeds, had been assisted on the 13¾ gradient-strewn miles from Bolton (via Entwhistle) by 29-year-old 9K-allocated 4-6-0 45377. The tour organisers, in an attempt to attract haulage bashers such as myself, regularly requested Bolton-allocated locomotives fully aware that, by that date, the shed had no booked passenger work.

we were all bussed from Keighley to/from Haworth, where a shunt along what was available took place with the Mickey tank. An added bonus was the ability to 'cab' the 91-year-old L&YR 2F 0-6-0 Ironclad No. 957 – a locomotive that was to achieve celebrity status by starring in the 1970 film *The Railway Children*. Although the itinerary showed that we were booked to run via Leeds City and change locomotives at Wakefield, in reality the changeover between the K4 and the A3 actually took place at the soon-to-be-closed Leeds Central. Another two classes of steam locomotives scratched!

Returning to the theme of this chapter, we now move to the south of the city to Manchester's Piccadilly station. Opened as Store Street in 1842 adjacent to London Road (after which it was renamed in 1847) overcrowding in the 1860s, not assisted by the fractious relationship between the separate companies using it, resulted in the first of many rebuilds – comprising of a subsequently listed train shed with four spans. A further four platforms, now totalling fourteen, were added in 1910 when the adjacent Mayfield station was opened. Even after nationalisation in 1948 segregation *still* applied, with the ER and LMR services being divided by iron railings on platform 5. Renamed Piccadilly in 1960 in connection with WCML electrification (during which the First World War memorial to the loss of railwaymen was removed; rededicated by Michael Portillo in 2016) yet another rebuild, in 2001–02, took place in order to welcome the crowds attending the 2002 Commonwealth Games. I personally found the station, with its somewhat cramped concourse, a draughty and uninspiring establishment. Although I considered it too clean to entertain steam trains, as the next paragraph explains there was one, run in the dead of night, perhaps to avoid detection, which continued to operate into 1968.

The steam-operated service out of Manchester Piccadilly referred to was the 01.17 departure to Cleethorpes. This newspaper/mails service departed from a non-electrified platform adjacent to an access road within the station's confines and was rostered for a Trafford Park-allocated locomotive. 9Es locomotives were, as far as I was concerned, as rare as hen's teeth on passenger work and so I regularly monitored the Saturday-morning departure, even walking to/from Victoria if necessary. In those far-off days you went wherever your requirements took you and I never even considered how I would return into Manchester from its first (unadvertised) locomotive changing stop of Guide Bridge. Completely ignorant as to any buses that might be running during the early hours, I can only assume that a four-hour fester on a presumably closed station was the only answer. Taking all that into consideration, I secretly

Epsom Railway Society

L.N.E.R. Preservation Tour

We would like to take this opportunity of thanking everyone for supporting us in joining this tour. We hope that you will have a most enjoyable day.

Unfortunately, we heard very recently that the M.O.T. and British Railways have decided that a passenger-train may not be run for us on the Keighley and Worth Valley Railway as the Light Railway Order still has not been granted. However, a fleet of buses will take all passengers to Haworth where they may visit the extensive railway museum. It is hoped that there will be engines in steam, probably including the L.N.E.R. N2 which the Gresley Society own and very kindly gave us permission to use if we had run a train.

If you would like to visit the Brontë Museum, please inform one of the Society officials who will be wearing a badge.

The timings for the train are appended and we have provided a space for inserting the actual times.

We have tried to keep our fare as low as possible on this trip, but unfortunately costs have risen very steeply since our last tour and we find we have not been able quite to cover costs. We have given the matter much thought and decided that rather than have us cancel the tour for a matter of a few pounds, most of you would prefer to give us an extra donation of....5.....shillings.

We apologize sincerely for asking this, but would make it quite clear that you are under no obligation whatever to make this donation. We are sure however that you would not want us to have to stand this loss personally.

May we again wish you a most enjoyable and interesting day.

A. SHOOTER   P. G. THOMPSON   G. D. N. MILLER

An accompanying leaflet detailing an appeal for further funding together with the apology in being unable to travel over the K&WVR.

hoped that the power on each occasion, whenever not supplanted by a pesky 'Splutterbug' or Peak DL, would already have a red-lined entry in my *ABC* and sure enough over a period of months during 1967 they were.

On 7 October 1967, however, 9E's 44929 was *in situ*. Decision time had arrived. Whilst en route to Guide Bridge, I reasoned that taking into consideration the scarcity of daytime steam services over WCML metals by that date, i.e. nothing guaranteed until the evening Preston portions, I might as well make a day of it covering railway routes yet to be visited by myself – and so I stayed aboard. EM2 Co-Co 27001 *Ariadne* took over at Guide Bridge, powering the train through the Woodhead tunnel to Penistone, being substituted there by Brush Type 2 D5859 for the remainder of the journey across the moonlit flat Lincolnshire countryside. As it was the first night I didn't feel the need to sleep and thoroughly enjoyed the ride enhanced, perhaps, by viewing the then extensive well-lit marshalling yards at Wath as we passed by. Some 105½ miles later, and following an on-time arrival of 05.37 at Cleethorpes, I wandered the pre-dawn streets in an eventually successful quest to find a café serving breakfast. I then took the 06.55 King's Cross D1533-worked departure via the ex GNR route to Peterborough, changing there onto a Birmingham-bound train that, at Nuneaton, enabled me to return to the North-West in good time for the evening's Preston portions – learning that I hadn't missed anything during the day.

And so in completing the circuit of Mancunian terminals we come to Manchester Central. Opened in 1880 by the Cheshire Lines Committee as a replacement for the inadequate Trade Hall station, the six-platform above-street-level terminus was provided with a magnificent single train shed that was 550ft long, with a span of 210ft and a height of 90ft – a further three platforms being added in 1907 due to increased patronage. It was the Midland Railway's access to the city and indeed was the departure point for the famed Midland Pullman. Its usage, although of considerable convenience for diverted/additional trains during the WCML electrification work, was severely dented with the closure of the former Midland Railway Millers Dale route in July 1968, and following the diversion of the former CLC-line trains to Oxford Road/Piccadilly closure came in May 1969. For over a decade the Grade II listed building fell into a dilapidated state, was damaged by fire and ended up somewhat predictably as a car park. The property was acquired by Greater Manchester Council and in 1982 work began on converting in to the Greater Manchester Exhibition and Conference Centre, or G-Mex.

With the Black 5MT having been detached, an adoring crowd surrounds *The Great Marquess* while she slakes her thirst.

It was subsequently renamed Manchester Central in honour of its railway history – the undercroft being converted into a car park serving the Centre and Bridgewater Hall.

Other than the six occasions, as detailed in Chapter 3, on which I travelled out of this station on the 22.50 Marylebone departure, just two other loco-hauled visitations were made – they being the aforementioned Mickey on a November 1966 rail tour and my only daytime visit with Peak D124 on a Derby departure in October 1967. There were also several other instances when, having arrived into Liverpool Exchange on the 21.23 Preston portion, I walked across to Lime Street and travelled on the former CLC line into the Central station, then walked over to the Exchange for the 01.00 Wigan departure (this hobby of mine certainly required a heavy usage of Shanks's pony!). I was regrettably completely unaware that rush-hour steam services to Cheadle Heath, Liverpool and Buxton ran until January 1967. A single 17.22 departure for Buxton even remained steam for a further three months, as told in fellow enthusiast Ray Trader's excellent *Tales of a 1960's Steam Traveller* – a Christmas 2016 present.

8

THE BRIT AWARDS: 1966–67

The title of this chapter does not, of course, refer to the pop music industry's self-congratulatory glitzy feast of backslapping held in February each year – the British Record Industry Trust (BRIT) awards. *These* Brit awards were attained under far more onerous conditions involving time, effort and determination, and were given only to followers of the BR Standard Britannia 4-6-2s. Those recipients undertook the mission, sometimes enduring perilous travelling conditions often during very unsocial hours, to travel with as many examples as feasible prior to their premature annihilation. I was one of them.

With the Duchesses, Patriots and Scots all having been withdrawn during the years prior to my appearance on the scene, the most prestigious 'namers' remaining, ones that certainly achieved a cult following, were the BR Class 7 4-6-2 Britannias.

The immediate post-war years were a time of austerity and economic deprivation, and with the necessary large financial investment for the war-damaged railway systems rebuild never going to happen, the Standard locomotive classes were constructed with cost being uppermost in mind. They were designed to meet the requirements of the times, i.e. cheap to build, able to work economically, convenient to drive and fire, to cover greater mileages between major overhauls and easy to service and repair.

The Britannia design was the first of the new BR Standard classes, being constructed at Crewe between January 1951 and September 1954. While they were no more powerful than various multi-cylinder locomotives of the four pre-nationalisation companies, they were a far more practical machine with their two cylinders, sturdy frame, large boiler and wide firebox. Various weight-saving measures also resulted in increased route availability for a 'Pacific'-type locomotive intended for use throughout the BR system.

The result, in my opinion, was a handsome, high-running-plated distinctive machine that, whenever espied approaching with a service I was about to board, was most aesthetically pleasing. Originally envisaged to have a working life of nearly forty years, the 1955 Modernisation Plan spelt the early death knell of the class – the first withdrawal being 70007 in June 1965 and the last, 70013, in August 1968.

Initially allocated throughout BR, they had, by my first catch in May 1965, all migrated to the London Midland Region. Although the majority were allocated to sheds working services on the WCML north of Crewe, there were pockets elsewhere – Oxley (2B), Holyhead (6J) and Newton Heath (9D) all having a handful. Another pocket of them were to be found at Stockport Edgeley (9B): their usage on the York TPO not being known by myself until the dieselisation of the said train in April 1966.

The extraordinary variety in the names that were conferred on the class often led me to look up the origin of the person/location depicted on the smoke deflectors of these inspirational machines – thus improving upon a somewhat lacklustre secondary-modern education. Back then I had to refer to my parents' encyclopaedia or visit the local library. Today's generation has it so much easier by just using the search engine on their mobile phone! They started off, in February 1951, with *Britannia* (taken off Jubilee 45700, which was renamed *Amethyst* eight months later), celebrating the Festival of Britain, followed by *Lord Hurcomb*, the first chairman of the then recently created British Transport Commission. Following in the list were the names of famous British writers of the past from *Geoffrey Chaucer* to *Robert Burns,* and then next in the sequence came famous names from British history. 'Star' class names were used for some of the WR allocated batch: 70017–29. British poets had a look in for the next six before British military celebrities took over several members of the next batch with *Lord Rowallan* included as a tribute to the Scout movement. Then came the oddities of *Anzac* and *The Territorial Army 1908–1958*, being separated by the never named 70047.

The final six, destined for Scottish services, were sympathetically named after various Scottish firths, by default resulting in a widening of my geographical appreciation of the British Isles.

Toward the end, with pilfering rife amongst souvenir hunters, makeshift substitute variations were fabricated, i.e. 70010 *Owen Glendower* became adorned with green nameplates showing the variation of *Owain Glendwyr* (one side only!) and both 70031 *Byron* and 70032 *Tennyson* names were prefixed with *Lord*. Many others had their names highlighted in white on blue backgrounds. Who would have thought trainspotting and education went hand in hand!

Throughout the various chapters within this book the occasional catches of these machines are mentioned. The objective here is to deal with the Brits as a separate entity detailing, numerically, how many I caught – or more negatively, missed! At the time, with only *The Railway World's* motive power miscellany column detailing, well after the event, shed reallocations and withdrawals, there was often a sense of disillusionment that hoped-for catches, without us knowing, had already met their fate. Research, conducted for the purpose of this book, revealed that I was never going to catch runs with all fifty-five members of the class – a fact I was blissfully ignorant

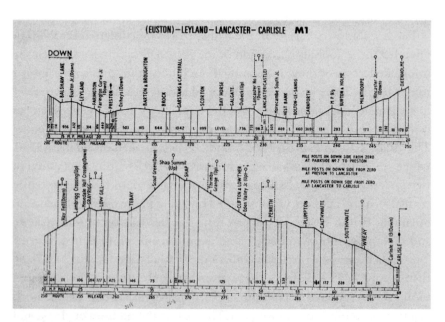

Gradient profile of WCML from Leyland to Carlisle.

B.R. STEAM LOCOMOTIVES
Nos. 70000-92250

7P6F **4-6-2**

Introduced 1951. Designed at Derby.

Weight
Locomotive: 94 tons 4 cwt

Boiler pressure
250 lb sq in

Cylinders
(O) 20" × 28"

Driving wheel diameter
6' 2"

Tractive effort
32,150 lb

Valve gear
Walschaerts (piston valves)

70000	*Britannia*
70001	*Lord Hurcomb*
70002	*Geoffrey Chaucer*
70003	*John Bunyan*
70004	*William Shakespeare*
70005	*John Milton*
70006	*Robert Burns*
[redacted]	
70008	*Black Prince*
70009	*Alfred the Great*
70010	*Owen Glendower*
70011	*Hotspur*
70012	*John of Gaunt*
70013	*Oliver Cromwell*
70014	*Iron Duke*
70015	*Apollo*
70016	*Ariel*
70017	*Arrow*
[redacted]	
70019	*Lightning*
70020	*Mercury*
70021	*Morning Star*
70022	*Tornado*
70023	*Venus*
70024	*Vulcan*
70025	*Western Star*
70026	*Polar Star*
70027	*Rising Star*
70028	*Royal Star*
70029	*Shooting Star*
70030	*William Wordsworth*
70031	*Byron*
70032	*Tennyson*
70033	*Charles Dickens*
70034	*Thomas Hardy*
70035	*Rudyard Kipling*
70036	*Boadicea*
70037	*Hereward the Wake*
70038	*Robin Hood*
70039	*Sir Christopher Wren*
70040	*Clive of India*
70041	*Sir John Moore*
70042	*Lord Roberts*
[redacted]	
70044	*Earl Haig*
70045	*Lord Rowallan*
70046	*Anzac*
70047	
70048	*The Territorial Army 1908–1958*
70049	*Solway Firth*
70050	*Firth of Clyde*
70051	*Firth of Forth*
70052	*Firth of Tay*
70053	*Moray Firth*
70054	*Dornoch Firth*

TOTAL: [redacted] 52

Combined volume extract – depicting the first three Brits having been withdrawn.

On Saturday, 25 June 1966 70005 *John Milton*, the first ever Brit I had a run with in May 1965 (in Scotland), awaits departure time at Preston with the 10.47 for Barrow.

of at the time. We haulage bashers always naively lived in hope that a require-ment would miraculously appear, or that the desired locomotive missed on the outward leg would materialise on its booked return working.

During 1965 I made several visits to Scotland, being rewarded with runs behind 70002 *Geoffrey Chaucer*, 70005 *John Milton*, 70020 *Mercury*, 70033 *Charles Dickens* and 70052 *Firth of Tay* in the process. The first two were while they were working north out of Carlisle, the others on overnight Anglo–Scottish services over Shap. Then the short-lived (three months) allo-cation of Brits to Banbury for usage on the GC-line services resulted in the red-lining of 70024 *Venus*, 70046 *Anzac*, 70050 *Firth of Clyde* and 70054 *Dornoch Firth*. I had, however, missed 70007 *Coeur-de-Lion* and 70043 *Lord Kitchener*, these having being withdrawn that June and August respectively.

Into 1966, and with a running total of nine, a blitz, as detailed in Chapter 3, that April, deliberately planned knowing many services were to be diesel-ised or withdrawn in that summer's timetable (commencing on 18 April),

Saturday, 13 August 1966 sees Brit 23 *Venus* at Lancaster Castle whilst working the 16.10 Euston to Barrow. She was then Crewe South-allocated, but when 5B lost its Class 1 trains to diesel haulage the following March, she was transferred to Kingmoor. (Alan Hayes)

Former WR Brit 70027 *Rising Star* calls at Preston for a crew change whilst working a Heysham to Haverfordwest pigeon special on Friday, 2 June 1967.

Crewe South-allocated 70028 *Royal Star*, the locomotive that had taken me overnight to Windermere through the snow five months earlier, attacks the 1 in 101 climb out of Preston on Saturday, 20 August 1966 with the 13.27 Liverpool Exchange to Glasgow Central/Edinburgh Waverley.

On Saturday, 20 August 1966 a visit to Lancaster rewarded me with a shot of 70040 *Clive of India* when calling there on a northbound parcels service.

rewarded me with a further five – namely former WR-allocated 70023 *Venus*, 70025 *Western Star*, 70027 *Rising Star* and 70028 *Royal Star*, together with ex Norwich 70040 *Clive of India*.

The Stockport-allocated 70004 *William Shakespeare* was caught working The Fellsman rail tour on 4 June. Although four more fell into my hands that July – 70017 *Arrow*, 70022 *Tornado*, 70031 *Byron* and 70032 *Tennyson* – I felt as if I was swimming against the tide because withdrawals were gathering pace with 70000 *Britannia*, 70019 *Lightning* and 70030 *William Wordsworth* all heading off for the cutter's torch that spring. Statistically there was still some way to go, having had nineteen with thirty-one more available.

Often thwarted by Black 5MT substitutions for a non-fit Brit, it was equally frustrating to learn from other chasers (afterwards!) that a certain locomotive that was very much required by me, but not them, had been seen heading into Scotland or venturing along the North Wales coast route. You couldn't be everywhere at the same time. Decisions had to be made often on the spur of the moment, not always with the best results. Another miss was Brit 18: whilst I was festering at Preston in the early hours in late June, she tantalisingly sneaked through (having been checked by signals) on

Always an LMR-allocated locomotive, Brit 70045 *Lord Rowallan*, now at Kingmoor, prepares to take 1S62 11.40 (relief) Birmingham New Street to Edinburgh Waverley the 141 miles from Crewe to Carlisle. The date was Whit Saturday, 27 May 1967 and she was part of my 1,170-mile steam bash on that weekend. Note the nemeses of Brush Type 4s lurking in the background.

Brit 10 *Owen Glendower* receives some attention from some of my fellow travellers whilst calling at Lancaster Castle on Saturday, 26 August 1967 whilst working 1A33, the 08.10 Barrow to Euston. This scene perfectly depicts an example of an individual haulage basher's requirement. Clackers (seen 'caressing' the Brit) and I had both travelled on that morning's 02.22 out of Carlisle and were reunited later that day on the evening Blackpool portion – he having caught this his last Brit and I mine (see page 161). (Alan Hayes)

the 23.55 Edinburgh–Birmingham. I was sorely tempted to run alongside and jump aboard but the combination of a vociferous 'stand away' from the guard combined with possible physical damage to myself made me have second thoughts.

August 1966 turned out to the high point of Brit catches with a grand total of nine (yes nine!) being ensnared. It would/should have been ten but 70048 *The Territorial Army 1908–1948*, working that particular day's 10.47 Preston to Barrow (Saturday, 20th), was rejected in favour of sister 70049 *Solway Firth* on a simultaneously timed southbound departure – the reasoning being that she was rostered to return south later in the day on the 13.46 ex Barrow. However, she was failed at Barrow, being substituted with Carnforth's 45014! At least the two occasions I was aboard the 10.47 departure that month gave me runs with the nameless 70047 and 70053 *Moray Firth*. No. 70047 was one of five catches on the first Saturday that month – the others being 70006 *Robert Burns*, 70012 *John of Gaunt*, 70045 *Lord Rowallan* and 70013 *Oliver Cromwell*. The last catch was courtesy of Deno, one of my colleagues, who upon seeing one of *his* final five required Brits, *Oliver Cromwell*, working 1S80 the 13.15 Euston to Glasgow, booked non-stop Crewe to Carlisle, being checked through the speed restricted (20mph) Preston station awaiting signal clearance, ran through the subway in case it stopped. Some of our colleagues were already on board and 'helpfully' opened a door for him to jump aboard – which he successfully and safely accomplished. The guard, however, had witnessed the incident and applied the emergency brake, bringing the train to halt. Whilst both he and the platform staff admonished the culprit, a good many of us sneaked aboard the rear coach. An act of stupidity but beneficial to all!

That August saw me ensnare both 70010 *Owen Glendower* and 70038 *Robin Hood* but lose out on withdrawal victim 70001 *Lord Hurcomb*. Although four more fell into my clutches that September, namely 70008 *Black Prince*, 70009 *Alfred the Great*, 70011 *Hotspur* and 70029 *Shooting Star*, the successes over the past few weeks were somewhat negated with news of three further withdrawals – 70036 *Boadicea*, 70037 *Hereward the Wake* and 70044 *Earl Haig*. The only benefits of all the above were the statistics – I'd now caught thirty-two Brits, which meant only thirteen more to go!

During the late autumn and winter months that year, with the Bournemouth electrification dates having been affirmed, I selfishly, to the obvious detriment of Brit chasing, concentrated on my home patch's ever-decreasing steam services. The impending cessation of the through Paddington to Birkenhead services in March 1967, however, kick-started my return 'oop north'. The preceding four consecutive Saturdays saw me bashing the Chester steam scene and, with services winding down for the day, I, together with a great many other enthusiasts, headed to Crewe on the two-car DMU 17.55 Chester departure. Due to arrive into Crewe at 18.26, without waiting for the train to come to a stand, doors opened and what can only be described as a 'collective of gricers' made the dash for the 18.25 Brit-worked Barrow departure. The fact that it was a minus one-minute connection time there didn't worry us; we always made it! Despite both the 18.25 and the later 21.45 Blackpool trains being plagued with Black 5 substitutions I did manage three further catches: 70016 *Ariel*, 70034 *Thomas Hardy* and 70051 *Firth of Forth* – the grim reaper relieving me of the ability to catch runs with 70003 *John Bunyan*, 70018 *Flying Dutchman*, 70026 *Polar Star* and 70041 *Sir John Moore*.

The following month, the remaining all-year Barrow/Blackpool worked trains were to be dieselised and I vividly recall leaning out of a window (an actively deemed unacceptable nowadays due to Health and Safety rules) in the leading coach of the Barrow train upon departure out of Crewe, savouring the Brit accelerating her train, smoke and steam swirling into the cold night air amid the overhead wires whilst passing through the small stations of Winsford, Hartford and Acton Bridge. The exhaust was music to my ears, allowing me to soak up this transient moment in time. This, my hobby, was being taken from me. There would be fewer and fewer occasions such as this to enjoy. We didn't think back then that anything like the number of main-line steam trains that proliferate today's UK railway network would be run. We thought our world was ending.

As an aside, when reading the news or watching TV these days as a result of the geographic knowledge acquired during those steam-chasing days, whenever a town is mentioned I can frequently visualise its location and, usually to my wife's annoyance, can brag about having been there. She often retorts 'but did you go out of the station?' On the occasion of catching *Firth of Forth* in February 1967, having alighted at Warrington Bank Quay at 22.49, I did venture out of the station, walking to the Central in order to travel over to Manchester for that night's 01.00 sleeper portion. Making the most of the twenty-minute waiting time, I bunked the sub shed (of Trafford Park), finding 9E-allocated 45316, 48350 and 48763 all in light steam.

With Stockport having little work for their Brits, they were placed in store at the now closed shed at Upperby until, joy of joys – because, selfishly, I still required three of them, they were transferred some months later to Kingmoor to replace some of their more poorly sisters. Meanwhile, Brit 48, missed in last year's August extravaganza, was condemned!

There was an obvious reduction in the summer Saturday steam services in 1967 but perhaps not as bad as might been have expected – the now missing Brit-worked Barrow and Blackpool trains leaving large voids during certain times of the day. An unexpected catch of 70035 *Rudyard Kipling* on a Sunday morning 01.00 Manchester to Wigan sleeper portion, normally the preserve of a Patricroft Standard 5MT, brought the number of active Brits required down to four.

With most of the summer-dated services having ceased to run the previous weekend, *Golden Arrow*-famed Brit 14 *Iron Duke*, seen passing Dock Street signalbox on Saturday, 9 September 1967, finds employment on a southbound freight – Preston's magnificent signal gantry in the background.

Whilst station hopping between Preston and Lancaster that July, 70014 *Iron Duke* called for water at Lancaster with a northbound extra. I was on the southbound platform and frantically dashed through the subway (or was it a footbridge) and, despite platform staff calling out that it was not a 'passenger' train, jumped aboard. There was no way I was letting her go! I quickly positioned myself (behind the door) in a toilet but leaving the door on vacant – a trick I had learnt to avoid ticket checks. Sure enough, both the platform staff and guard came rampaging through, kicking the toilet door open articulating 'he's not in here!' before reluctantly giving the right away. After *Iron Duke* got going I referred to the LMR STN notice and ascertained the train was a 09.30 Parspec Euston to Keswick and reasoned that to access the branch the train would stop in the platform at Penrith, thus enabling me to alight. Venturing out into the train itself, I was astounded to find that all its occupants were nuns – who were just as amazed as myself upon sighting me. Oh well, with no seats available, I 'window hung', thoroughly enjoying the Brit's labours up Shap. After being asked for my ticket by a party organiser (non-railway staff) I produced one of my BR Free Passes (was it Weymouth to Perth perhaps?) he, being satisfied I was alighting at Penrith, allowed me to continue my journey! The continuation of this train (not being Brit-orientated) can be found on page 185.

A week later, and having come over Ais Gill with Holbeck's Jubilee 45593 *Kolhapur* on the 06.40 ex Birmingham, we arrived some one and a half hours late at Carlisle, resulting from brake trouble earlier in the journey at Wath. With *Kolhapur* having disappeared towards Kingmoor the train was effectively stranded – booked DL failed perhaps? After what seemed an eternity we saw a Brit backing down. It was only one of my three remaining requirements, namely 70021 *Morning Star*. What were the chances of that happening – an absolute winner! For whatever reason (family get together on the Sunday perhaps?) I wasn't intending to stay out a second night as was the norm and had to return home to Kent that day. A quick reference to the ever-present timetable showed that I was able to go with *Morning Star* to the first stop of Dumfries, where she eventually dropped me off at 15.40, i.e. 109 minutes late. I had originally planned to head south on the steam-operated 14.00 Glasgow to Manchester/Liverpool service that Saturday but had to 'suffer' a DL journey over Shap. Steam mileage sacrificed for a new Brit – no problem.

On Friday, the 28th Brit 10 was working the 13.27 Liverpool–Scotland Class 1 train. She was, however, a little short of steam and had to be nursed into the Lancaster stop. Word was sent ahead to Carnforth for a replacement loco and after crawling into the loop south of the station, Brit 32, off of that morning's 08.35 Barrow portion, was substituted. She was in far better condition and, having stormed Grayrigg, speeds reached the 70s through the Lune Gorge. Shap was never going to be an obstacle and was topped, unassisted, at 30mph. Had she have required a banker, the 'crow' whistle repeatedly executed approaching Tebay was the agreed method and would have spurred a crew into action with one of their ever-ready steeds. On the down grade through Harrison's Sidings *Tennyson's* safety valves were already lifting, heralding an eventual thirty-four-minute late arrival into Carlisle. This scenario perfectly illustrates that every steam locomotive is an individual. In tip-top condition miracles can occur but when not feeling well she will endeavour to do her best.

With news of 70015 *Apollo's* demise this left just one more to catch – 70039 *Sir Christopher Wren*. Over the next four weeks, with all my

I am fortunate that Keith Lawrence was on hand to record my final (thirty-ninth) Brit catch. Here at Preston on 26 August 1967, 70039 *Sir Christopher Wren* is readying herself for departure to Liverpool, having had a Manchester portion detached, with 1M38 the 14.00 from Glasgow. (Keith Lawrence)

colleagues having had her, she was seen frustratingly reported/observed working services that either didn't call at the station I was at or was passed in the opposite direction – until the August Bank holiday Saturday that was. Having completed a grand circuit from Carlisle (02.22 with *William Shakespeare*), over to Leeds (45198) for the Birmingham–Glasgow (*Alberta*) I had doubled back from Preston to Lancaster, having had a required 45279 over Shap for the following 1M38 14.00 ex Glasgow. This, a train she had worked twice that July, was to prove a decisive move. Only fellow 'chasers' can fully understand the absolute joy, euphoria even, of 'scratching' the final requirement of any particular class of steam locomotive. Number 39,

Bank Holiday Monday, 25 May 1981 and the preserved *Britannia* herself works the Nene Valley Railway's 13.05 departure out of Wansford for Orton Mere.

my thirty-ninth Brit. Summoning up the chase, I reasoned that I caught as many as I could – amassing more than 8,000 Brit miles in the process. I still caught Brit-operated trains afterwards but only by default when attempting to increase my Black 5 statistics.

The final timetabled (although it ran under STN arrangements a week later) 02.22 Carlisle to Crewe on Saturday, 9 September heralded the near demise of Britannia-worked passenger trains. Powered that morning by Brit 11 *Hotspur*, this was to prove my twentieth and final southbound ascent of Shap. The three remaining services booked for Brit haulage after that date were the 08.35 (EWD) Barrow to Lancaster portion attached to a Carlisle–Euston service, the 17.47 (FO) Manchester Exchange to York, and the 01.00 (MO) Manchester Exchange to Wigan – all three regularly being reported with Black 5MT substitutions. For sure, during the remaining months of 1967 they were sometimes utilised on Blackpool Illumination traffic emanating from Scotland and short-notice replacements for DL failures. Freight and parcel traffic also kept the ever-decreasing numbers occupied. On Boxing Day a footex was powered by one into Blackpool and the last known movement (other than Brit 13), that of 70045 *Lord Rowallan*, on a Rose Grove to Wigan freight in the early hours of 1 January 1968 has been well documented throughout the railway press over the years. Then there was just one, the now preserved 70013 *Oliver Cromwell*, which was transferred to Carnforth for many specials culminating in 1T57 in August 1968.

Many years later, on the Nene Valley Railway at Peterborough, I caught, courtesy of the hundreds of hours spent by volunteers in returning her to working order, my fortieth – 70000 *Britannia* herself.

9

THE PRESTON PORTIONS: 1966–67

Preston, the administrative centre of Lancashire, was, in the boomtown days of the Industrial Revolution, a densely populated engineering town with more than fifty cotton mills. Preston, which holds a civic celebration every twenty years to commemorate its Guild status, became the first English town outside of London to be lit by gas. In the 1840s it was the scene of serious rioting – the workers protesting against poor working conditions and low wages. Situated on the north bank of the Ribble, its extensive docks seriously contributed to the economy of the area and as such during the railway mania years attracted a myriad of companies striving to reach them.

Before moving on to the subject of the chapter heading, just a few more nuggets of extraneous gen are thrown in here. Preston, awarded city status in 2002, was bypassed by Britain's first motorway (opened by the pro-road Transport Minister Ernest Marples) in 1958. Nowadays part of the M6, a link off of it, the M55, takes all Blackpool-bound traffic over the former Marton direct trackbed. Preston North End is the town's team but alas, to date, their only claim to fame is winning the FA Cup at Wembley in 1938, when they beat Huddersfield Town 1-0. And finally a selection of famous notables born there are Wallace and Gromit creator Nick Park, cricketer Freddie Flintoff, footballer Sir Tom Finney and one-time (2015–17) Lib Dem leader Tim Farron.

The first rail service in Preston was from Wigan and was opened by the North Union Railway in 1838. Two years later the Preston & Longridge

Railway, the Lancaster & Preston Junction Railway and Preston & Wyre Joint Railway arrived on the scene – all, because of various contractual difficulties, using different termini. Two further railway companies, with running rights over existing lines, joined the fray at Euxton (Bolton & Preston Railway in 1843) and Farington (Preston & Blackburn Railway in 1846) Junctions – the latter, quickly absorbed by the East Lancashire Railway, subsequently building their own access line to platforms adjacent to the main North Union's station. Upon receiving further services from Ormskirk (1849) and Southport (1882), the entire area was reconstructed into one station during the late nineteenth century and by 1913 this had expanded to thirteen platforms. Finally, completing the scenario I was to witness during my travels, the circuit via Lostock Hall and Farington West Junctions (thus enabling trains from the north to run, without reversal direct to Blackpool) was completed in 1908.

As a result of the contraction of services in the late 1960s and '70s, Preston station has subsequently shrunk to a mere eight platforms. The former East Lancs platforms have been completely demolished to make way for a new Butler Street entrance to the station. The result was short-listed for the 2017 Carbuncle Cup, an annual prize awarded to the UK's ugliest building constructed during the previous year, and was likened to a 'deadening cake tin slapped on its side'!

By the time I first set foot on Preston's platforms, the nearest steam shed, Preston (24K) itself having closed in 1961, was at Lostock Hall – some 2¾ miles to the south. I am certain that the Lancashire & Yorkshire Railway Company, upon opening it in 1882, never for one moment envisaged that it would become such a place of strategic importance some eighty-six years later, when its pivotal location put it at the heart of the final days of the British steam locomotive. The shed's fifteen minutes of fame surely came on that first weekend in August 1968 when most of the six rail tours in circulation that Sunday, the 4th, had locomotives resourced from there. Formerly coded 24C, until 1963 it came under the Carnforth umbrella and was accorded 10D until its closure. Although revenue-wise the freight and parcel traffic were the depot's bread-and-butter work, the geographic position of the nearby Preston station with its associated portion workings soon brought it to the attention of like-minded chasers such as myself.

For sure, by the time I came across the scene the normal diet was that of LMS Stanier 5MTs – but beggars can't be choosers and, with the foreman's indiscriminate propensity for dispatching whatever was to hand, this led to locomotives whose home allocation was at a depot without booked

Friday, 2 June 1967 and at Liverpool Exchange, Aintree's Black 5MT 44816 awaits departure time with the 09.00 for Scotland – a train she will take the 27½ miles to Preston. This was the first of ten occasions I was to travel on this portion – often a fertile source of locomotives from depots without passenger duties.

passenger work being much valued by enthusiasts upon seeing it back down on its train. The 5MTs' monopoly was, however, occasionally broken by the appearance, particularly for the Wigan locals and Blackpool portions, of one of 10D's handful of LMS tanks, either Stanier and Fairburn, or an Ivatt 'Flying Pig'. Visiting Patricroft Standard 5MTs were also in the mix. I would belatedly like to thank the Lostock Hall foreman for provided such an entertaining cross section of motive power for all of the aforementioned trains. The 'never know what's going to turn up' scenario made the long journeys and the seemingly endless nights all worthwhile.

So now, if the reader will permit, I will list, in time order,[11] the portions, some of which only ran on Fridays and Saturdays during the summer service, I was to travel on over those final two years. I can't profess to it being a comprehensive list as, unlike a lot of more fortunate gricers who resided within the region, my visits were dependent on London connections.

---

[11] All 1966 timings – minor variations in both 1967 and '68 timetables.

First up is the 09.00 Liverpool Exchange to Preston. This five- or six-vehicle train combined at Preston with a similar-sized 09.00 from Manchester Victoria – the entire Brush Type 4-worked service going forward to Glasgow Central with a portion detached at Carstairs for Edinburgh Waverley. This, by default, became more frequented during 1968 – being the only daylight guaranteed steam portion to which all roads led following many unproductive hours overnight. Happily, representatives from sheds such as Aintree, Springs Branch and Rose Grove often lifted my demeanour.

The Manchester/Preston portions, all of which called at the 1838-built Bolton Trinity Street station, were fortunately mostly steam worked. Regularly frequented trains departed Victoria at 13.27 and 17.45 – the southbound counterparts out of Preston being at 12.12, 15.45 and 19.00. Having regrettably missed Newton Heath's usage of her last Jubilee 45654 *Hood* just prior to her demise in June 1966, Black 5s from any shed could turn out on these, although perhaps 9D and 10D examples predominated. As can perhaps be immediately sussed by any basher, the ideal out and back (if based at Preston) would be the 12.12, due at Manchester at 13.00, and the 13.27 return – the often late-running southbound train meaning having to bale out at Bolton. A similar scenario would occur in the afternoon with the 15.45 out and 17.45 return. However, with the 12.12 out of Preston being the only all-year runner, careful study of the notations in connection with wavy-lined, short-dated entries at the bottom of the relevant timetable page had to be made.

There were two EWD Blackpool South portions, at 12.44 and 20.45, detached from Euston to Carlisle services – the locomotives sent out for these lightweight trains always being looked forward to with eager anticipation. The condition of the few remaining LMS tanks at Lostock Hall, by the summer of 1966, meant their appearances were becoming less frequent – Black 5s often being substituted. With my attention elsewhere during the winter of 1966–67, upon my return to the area, to my delight, 10D had been bestowed with a second batch of Ivatt Moguls– these in turn having been displaced at Tebay by Standard 4MTs.

Personally frequenting the evening portion more than the daytime at the end of a hard day's bashing of WCML services, what better than a 'Flying Pig' to round it off – the occasional usage of a visiting Rose Grove/Speke Junction-allocated Black 5 or Patricroft Standard 5 raising our expectancy!

Although catching a couple of her sisters on Class 2 services out of Preston, 16-year-old 42096 somehow escaped me. On Saturday, 20 August 1966, displaying a chalked 73F (Ashford) smokebox allocation – a shed she resided at in the 1950s – she was on station pilot duties; withdrawal would come at the year's end.

The south end bay at Preston on Friday, 26 May 1967 sees 18-year-old Ivatt mogul 43029 resting between duties whilst acting as that day's station pilot. Having spent 6½ of those years at Tebay, she had been, as were several sisters, displaced by an influx of more powerful Standard 4MT 75xxx the previous month.

Friday, 2 June 1967 and another 'new kid on the block', in this case from Carnforth, is 'Flying Pig' 43004 at Preston. She wasn't to stay long at her new home – being withdrawn just twelve weeks later.

The influx of Ivatt Class 4MTs at Lostock Hall, although displacing its LMS tanks, during 1967 were, from a chaser's point of view, most welcome. Not looking in the best of condition, 43041 rests at Blackpool South on Friday, 2 June 1967 having worked in on 1P58, the 12.44 portion from Preston (off of the 09.05 Euston–Carlisle).

And finally one mustn't forget the evening portion for Liverpool booked to depart at 21.17. This train was destined to enter the history books in August 1968 as the very last timetabled train operated by steam traction in mainland Britain. As Britain became more and more steamless, this train, together with its 16.53 Sunday equal, attracted a cult following – enhanced by the often random provision of the occasional Caprotti Standard.

On Friday, 4 August 1967, with there being a dearth of required locomotives in circulation, the opportunity to visit Lostock Hall shed was taken. Having arrived into Preston at 11.00 with D5712, one of the short-lived Metropolitan Vickers Type 2s, I failed to document how I journeyed to the shed: Ribble bus or taxi with others? Not equipped with the necessary permit, the foreman usually, upon production of our BR Identity card when requesting permission to wander around, often replied, 'I haven't seen you,' thus exonerating himself should any mishap befall us. It seems I didn't stay long because the next entry in my notebook indicates that I caught the 11.47 service from Lostock Hall station itself with Edge Hill's 44838 working that day's 11.00 Liverpool Exchange to Blackpool North. As an aside, I often noted withdrawn locomotives in locations such as this with sacking over their chimneys. Would you believe it was only very recently I learnt it was to prevent birds nesting in them!

The August 1966 allocation of passenger locomotives at 10D had been six LMS tanks, five LMS Ivatt Moguls and ten LMS Stanier 5MTs. A year later all the tanks had been withdrawn, the number of Flying Pigs remaining static but the number of Blackies having doubled to twenty – the main donors being Crewe South and Shrewsbury.

On Saturday, 5 November 1967, having travelled behind A4 60019 *Bittern* on a Leeds to Newcastle rail tour, I made my way via the Waverley route to Preston for that evening's 20.48 Blackpool portion. Ivatt 2-6-0 43106 was that bonfire night's power – seen here forty-nine years later at Ropley during her visit to the Mid Hants 2016 Autumn Gala.

Friday, 4 August 1967 and at Lostock Hall (10D) 20-year-old Fairburn tank 42187, having been withdrawn some four months previously, awaits the call of the cutter's torch.

04/08/67	10D Lostock Hall at 11.30
On shed	43019, 43029, 43119, 44942, 44971, 45149, 45227, 45345, 45373, 45444, 48062, 48077, 48164, 48307, 48323 (10F), 48637, 48669 (9F), 75058 (10A)
Withdrawn	42187, 42297, 42546, 42611, 45339, 45402, 48266, 48320, 48707, 78020, 78021, 78037, 78041

Although theoretically not portions, with the majority of the lesser stations along the WCML north of Weaver Junction having been closed by the early 1960s, those remaining were served by a handful of Class 2 services, which I chanced across and are worthy for a mention within this chapter.

The first of them, literally, was the 05.35 all-stations Preston to Crewe. After many uncomfortable, often cold, hours spent at Preston station overnight, the wonderful sight and sound of the locomotive and the three vehicles arriving to form it was most welcome. Being part of a Crewe South duty, the locomotive had worked north earlier that morning on a 23.40 freight from Crewe and was often used to run in those recently out-shopped from the works. Indeed, during February 1967 the final steam locomotive to be overhauled at Crewe, Brit 70013 *Oliver Cromwell*, was noted on it. During the following month the preserved A4 4498 *Sir Nigel Gresley* was utilised on three separate occasions. I usually alighted off of this train at Wigan, then spent another one and a quarter hours of mind-numbing boredom awaiting the following Brit-hauled 06.10 ex Blackpool South. If the 05.35 was a not required machine or a DL, I caught the 05.30 DMU to Kirkham & Wesham, boarding the Blackpool train earlier in its journey.

Ivatt Mogul 43029 still proudly retaining her Tebay smokebox shedplate – withdrawal coming just two months' hence.

Opposite above: Withdrawn 13-year-old Riddles-designed Standard 2MT 78021 had spent most of her short life at Midland line sheds, having only arrived here the previous November. Vulcan Foundry 1936-built 2-8-0 8F 48062 was more fortunate – surviving to the very end in August 1968 at Rose Grove.

Opposite below: Chester-allocated Stanier 5MT 45231, in ex works condition, is seen bringing the stock into Preston station on Saturday, 25 June 1966 for the 05.35 all stations service for Crewe. I was subsequently to have runs with her again, both on her home territory the following year and in preservation.

The second shot, in more favourable light, sees her awaiting time at Wigan North Western. This was the second, out of sixteen, occasions I was to travel on this train.

Another move was, if the overnight Edinburgh–Birmingham Brit-hauled train was no more than an hour late into Crewe, to double back down the WCML on the 06.25 Liverpool-bound EMU the 14½ miles to Acton Bridge to intercept it there. The last occasion I travelled on it was Friday, 1 September 1967. I understand shortly afterwards that it became steam on Mondays only – then, of course, Crewe South closed to steam that November.

The intermediate stations of Balshaw Lane & Euxton and Coppull (both closing in 1969) situated along the 15¼ miles of WCML between Preston and Wigan were served by just seven local trains, each way, per day. Although five of them were formed of two-car DMUs, the rush-hour services, to cope with the demand by workers at the extensive Leyland Truck Company factory adjacent to the station, were made up of four (usually ex LMS short wheelbase) vehicles – and were, certainly during the summer of 1966, steam operated. Northbound out of Wigan, they ran at 06.48 (unadvertised) and 07.00, returning from Preston at 16.22 and 17.45.

5B's double-chimneyed 44766 is seen at Crewe on Saturday, 5 August 1967 having arrived with the 05.35 ex Preston. It was a close call: she was withdrawn fourteen days later!

Opposite: Timetable extract showing the 05.35 Preston to Crewe that, although not indicated here, was routed via Earlestown, one of the two remaining triangular-platform stations, calling there at 06.40.

Table 50

Weekdays

NOT Saturdays 18 June to 3 September

Carlisle to London Euston

			A	B MO ✕ ⚏	C MX ✕ ⚏	MO ✕ ⚏	MX ✕ ⚏	D SX ●	E SX ⓡ	
INVERNESS .. .. .. d										
133 PERTH............ d										
133 GLASGOW CENTRAL .. d										
133 EDINBURGH........ d										
CARLISLE .. .. d										
PENRITH FOR ULLSWATER ...... d										
SHAP............ d										
TEBAY.......... d										
OXENHOLME .. .. a										
109 WINDERMERE .. d										
OXENHOLME .. .. d										
MILNTHORPE ...... d										
CARNFORTH ..... a										
107 BARROW-IN-FURNESS .... d										
CARNFORTH ...... d										
BOLTON-LE-SANDS ..... d										
HEST BANK .... d										
LANCASTER CASTLE .. a										
108 MORECAMBE PROMENADE .. d				06 15	06 15					
LANCASTER CASTLE .. d				06 26	06 26					
GARSTANG & CATTERALL .. d										
PRESTON .. .. a										
104 LIVERPOOL EXCHANGE .. a										
98 MANCHESTER VICTORIA..... a										
106 BURNLEY CENTRAL .... d										
106 BLACKBURN ..... d										
98 BLACKPOOL NORTH .... d										
98 BLACKPOOL SOUTH...... d										
PRESTON† .. d			05 35							
LEYLAND† ...... d			05 42							
BALSHAW LANE & EUXTON .. d										
COPPULL ..... d			05 55							
WIGAN NORTH WESTERN .. a			06 07							
89 MANCHESTER EXCHANGE .. a										
94 LIVERPOOL LIME STREET .. a			07 23							
93 SOUTHPORT CHAPEL STREET ...... a			07 39							
WIGAN NORTH WESTERN† .. d			06 17							
WARRINGTON BANK QUAY† .. d			06 52							
ACTON BRIDGE .. d		06 45	07 07							
HARTFORD .. .. d		06 50	07 13							
WINSFORD .. .. d		06 56	07 21							
CREWE .. .. a		07 06	07 34							
63 LIVERPOOL LIME STREET .. d				06 10	06 10					
94 MANCHESTER PICCADILLY ...... d				06 37	06 37	07 20	07 20	07 50	07 55	
CREWE .. d				07 45	07 45					
STAFORD.......... a		07 00		07 55	07 55	08 00				
			07 23				08 22	08 22			
57 WOLVERHAMPTON HIGH LEVEL .. a		08 06								
57 BIRMINGHAM NEW STREET ...... a		08 44				09 01	09 01			
						09 23	09 23			
96 STOKE-ON-TRENT .. d			07 00			07 40	07 40			
STAFFORD.......... d						08 25	08 25			
RUGELEY TRENT VALLEY .. d			07 35							
LICHFIELD TRENT VALLEY .. d			07 50							
TAMWORTH LOW LEVEL .. d			08 04							
POLESWORTH .. d			08 13							
ATHERSTONE .. d			08 19							
NUNEATON TRENT VALLEY .. d			08 32							
RUGBY MIDLAND .. a			08 50							
57 WOLVERHAMPTON HIGH LEVEL .. d	06 08	06 51		08 36	08 54					
57 BIRMINGHAM NEW STREET .. d	06 49	07 30								
57 COVENTRY .. d	07 35	08 04								
RUGBY MIDLAND† .. d	07 59	08 26		08 58	08 58					
NORTHAMPTON † .. a	08 20			09 25	09 25					
BLETCHLEY† .. a	08 43			09 48	09 48					
WATFORD JUNCTION† .. a	09 19			10 22	10 22					
LONDON EUSTON† .. a	09 43	09 30		10 02	10 02	10 10	10 10	10 25	10 30	

Heavy figures denote through carriages;
light figures denote connecting services.
For general notes see page 11

† For complete service between Preston and Leyland see Table 98. Wigan and Warrington via Earlestown see Table 89. Rugby and London see Table 52.

A Via Earlestown

B 11 July to 15 August. ✕ ⚏ and through carriages from Heysham. Ship dep. Belfast 21 40, arr. Heysham 05 00

C ✕ ⚏ and through carriages from Heysham. Ship dep. Belfast 21 40, arr. Heysham 05 00

D Not on 30 May, 29 August, 26 and 27 December ● First Class only

E Not on 30 May, 29 August, 26 and 27 December

b Via Wigan North Western and Wigan Wallgate. Passengers make their own way from one station to the other

u Stops to pick up only

175

On Thursday, 31 March 1966 the stock and loco to form the 16.22 for Wigan NW awaits platforming at Preston. Fairburn 2-6-4T 42235 is that day's power and, although missing out of a run with her when allocated to Lostock Hall, I was more successful just over a year later in the Bradford area – she having been transferred to Low Moor. (Alan Hayes)

On Saturday, 30 July 1966 10D's 42105 storms away from Leyland with the same 16.22 ex Preston train. The first nine years of this 16-year-old tank were spent on SR metals – finding her way to 10D in October 1965.

10

STEAM'S LAST HURRAH ON THE WCML: 1967

In May 1967 the BRB announced that the railways ran at a loss of £134.7 million during 1966 – the unions not necessarily helping the situation, having shrewdly negotiated two 3½ per cent pay increases together with a reduction in the working week! Although the government of the day was investing in electrification, shiny new locomotives, modern diesel depots, power signal boxes and colour lights it was a two-edged sword as, at the same time, millions were being spent on expanding the countrywide network of motorways for the bourgeoning increase of more affordable cars.

So we come to what we steam aficionados had dreaded/feared was the final summer of British steam. We didn't want to acknowledge that it was nearing the end. Surely a reprieve might occur – after all, the Southern end of steam date had been put back twice. To summarise the 1967 WCML steam scene I have to say that most of the short-dated wavy-lined timetable entries that were steam last year remained so – the notable absence of the all-year Blackpool/Barrow to Crewe Class 1 and Preston/Wigan Class 2 trains making the waits just seem longer. Obviously dominated by Stanier Black 5s, the best we could hope for, to generate increased interest, was the occasional appearance of one from depots whose workload was predominantly freight or parcels.

Within the LM timetable that year, Table 50 (Euston to Carlisle) had, as customary, the Saturday pages segregated from the remainder of the week – in this year's case the dates applicable being 17 June to 2 September. There

Nuneaton Trent Valley on Sunday, 26 February 1967 sees Oxley's 44944 about to work the 33½-mile leg of The Severn and Dee Rail Tour. This hitherto-unseen (by me) Blackie didn't see the year out, being withdrawn at Crewe South that October.

were therefore twelve weeks in which to get what you could before it all disappeared – to soak in the atmosphere of Britain's final steam-worked railway. It is not my intention to swamp the reader with a list of catches I made during that frenetic period and therefore will only home in on some of what I considered the highlights as the summer progressed.

That May saw The Beatles release their absolutely brilliant *Sgt Pepper's Lonely Hearts Club Band* LP while Procul Harum's 'A Whiter Shade of Pale' spent weeks monopolising the top spot all of June. Politically, France's Charles de Gaulle vetoed (again) the UK's application to join the EEC, stating 'Britain lacked commitment'. I am proofreading this book just weeks after Prime Minister Boris Johnson, acting on behalf of the 2016 referendum decision to leave the European Community, has stated that the UK will leave the EU on 31 October 2019 – deal or no deal. Meanwhile, also relevant to 1967 was the continuing furore over nuclear disarmament and, along with many of my colleagues, I could be seen adorned with the black and white CND badge affixed to my jacket. We, however, had hijacked the significance as 'Campaign for No Diesels'!

The first Saturday, 17 June, saw quite a few of us on a 07.17 Failsworth to Liverpool Wakes extra. As always keeping an eye on the weekly STN publications, this train traversed by that date rare steam track via Oldham Mumps, Rochdale, Bolton and Wigan Wallgate – wonderfully double-headed the 11 miles to Rochdale by 44679 (8F) and 44690(10F). Making our way to Preston, it was there that, dependent on our needs, we usually went our own ways. That was how it was back then – occasional sightings of each other during the day, jumping on and off trains, using Preston as the axis. At least, unlike the enforced night-time waits, the buffet was open and hot soup or beer in a warm, weather-proofed environment was available. Everyone knew it was the last full summer of steam and there would never be another one like it. The leading vehicle of those being worked by the run-down, filthy Iron Horses were wedged full of tape-recording enthusiasts hanging their microphones out of all available outlets. We had come to witness the death throes of BR steam in order that we could brag to the next generation 'I was there!'

Twenty-two-year-old 4-6-0 44899 arrives into Warrington Bank Quay on Saturday, 24 June 1967 with the 08.10 Barrow to Euston. This Kingmoor locomotive escaped the mass cull there at the end of that year – being dispatched to Rose Grove for her final eight months of life.

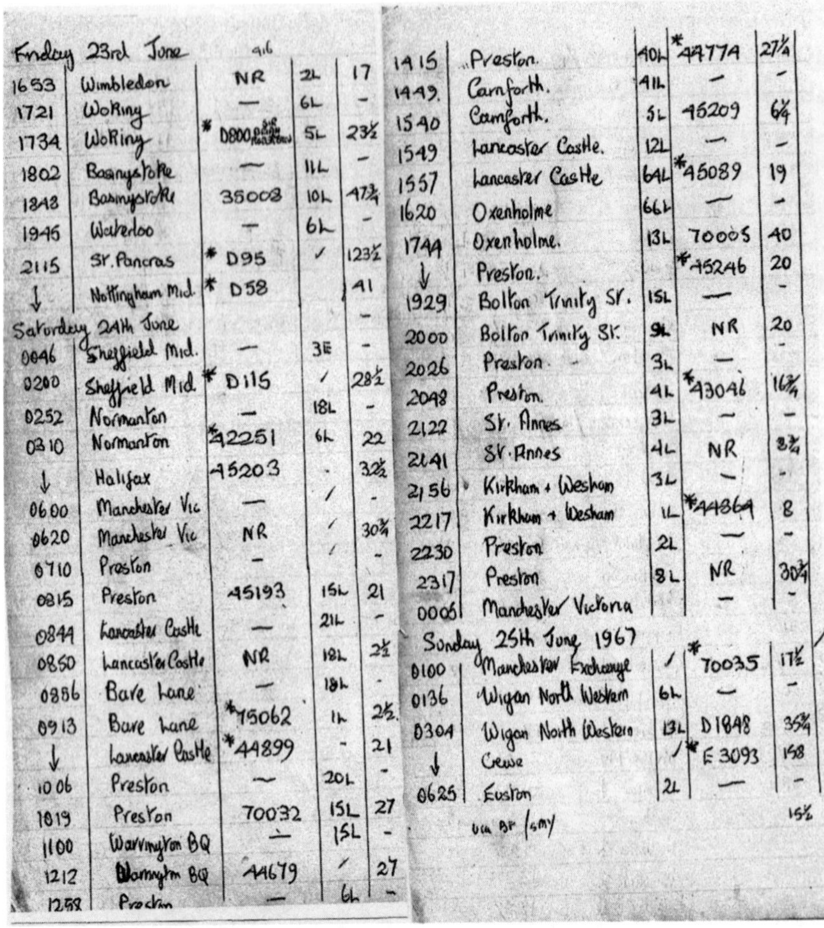

Friday 23rd June	9.6					1415	Preston.	40L	*44774	27¼
16 53	Wimbledon	NR	2L	17		1449.	Carnforth.	41L	–	–
1721	Woking	–	6L	–		1540	Carnforth.	5L	45209	6¾
1734	Woking	* D800	5L	23½		1549	Lancaster Castle.	12L	–	–
1802	Basingstoke	–	11L	–		1557	Lancaster Castle	64L	*45089	19
1843	Basingstoke	35003	10L	47½		1620	Oxenholme	66L	–	–
1946	Waterloo	–	6L	–		1744	Oxenholme.	13L	70005	40
2115	St. Pancras	* D95	✓	123½		↓	Preston.		*45246	20
↓	Nottingham Mid.	* D58		41		1929	Bolton Trinity St.	15L	–	
Saturday 24th June						2000	Bolton Trinity St.	9L	NR	20
0046	Sheffield Mid.	–	3E	–		2026	Preston.	3L	–	–
0200	Sheffield Mid.	* D115	✓	28½		2048	Preston.	4L	*43046	16¾
0252	Normanton	–	18L	–		2122	St. Annes	3L	–	–
0310	Normanton	42251	6L	22		2141	St. Annes	4L	NR	3¾
↓	Halifax	45203	·	32¾		2156	Kirkham + Wesham	3L	–	–
0600	Manchester Vic	–	✓	–		2217	Kirkham + Wesham	1L	*44864	8
0620	Manchester Vic	NR	✓	30¾		2230	Preston	2L	–	–
0710	Preston	–	✓	–		2317	Preston	8L	NR	30¾
0815	Preston	45193	15L	21		0005	Manchester Victoria		–	–
0844	Lancaster Castle	–	21L	–		Sunday 25th June 1967				
0850	Lancaster Castle	NR	18L	2½		0100	Manchester Exchange	✓	*70035	17½
0856	Bare Lane	–	18L	–		0136	Wigan North Western	6L	–	–
0913	Bare Lane	*45062	1L	2½		0304	Wigan North Western	13L	D1848	35¾
↓	Lancaster Castle	*44899	–	21		↓	Crewe		/* E 3093	158
1006	Preston	–	20L	–		0625	Euston	2L	–	
1019	Preston	70032	15L	27			via BP /5MY			15½
1100	Warrington BQ	–	15L	–						
1212	Warrington BQ	44679	✓	27						
1258	Preston	–	6L	–						

Into July and to avoid full-on depression with regards to my home region's impending cessation of steam, The Kinks' 'Waterloo Sunset' surely being more than a coincidence, I headed north out of Euston on the 13.20 for Glasgow on the first Saturday of its running that year – 1 July. Whilst last year it was rostered for steam, it wasn't until I saw the recognisable outline of a Britannia tender reversing from her hiding position around the corner on the Chester lines at Crewe that I gave out a huge sigh of relief. A glorious almost non-stop 141-mile over Shap with 70025 *Western Star* was followed, albeit after a six-hour fester, by a returning 02.58 Parspec London service with Kingmoor's 44727 taking it to Crewe. A total of 282 steam miles: who needs the SR!

With the Southern Region dispensing of their BR Standard 75xxx 4MTs that month, this left the residue, the majority of which were allocated to depots without passenger work, mostly inaccessible to a haulage basher. A slim hope, however, were those at Tebay (on banking duties) or Carnforth. As far as I can ascertain, the only train they were rostered to work was the 09.10 SO Morecambe Promenade to Lancaster portion and of the four instances I was aboard it only two, 75062 (24/06) and 75034 (15/07), were captured – the others being inevitable Black 5MTs.

70025 /8c/ —			P	610	28/5		Clifn	136 00	75
Crewe	000		Ox.	6425	43½/55/48		Ed. V L	136 43	77½
Coppenhall Jn	517	si½	B+B	6527	58½/67½		Pen.	138 21	69
M. Vernon	702	63	Brock	7113	43		Plon	143 22	75½/73
Winsford	922	67	Gar+C.	7325	63		Colk	145 13	79½
Winsford Jn	1032	68½/71	Scoul	7515	68/70½/69/75		South	147 50	82/82½
Hartford	1308	67	B.Horse	7823	74½/77½		Weecy	149 41	75/77
Acton Br.	1525	71½/74	Quebeck	8035	76½		Cor No 13	153 05	82
Weaver Jn	1705	72½	Lanc No1	8206	75		Carlisle	157 28	
Norton X	1934	77	Lonc e	8258	73/39				
A.Grange Jn	2143	69/61½	MSH Jn	8510	51				
Walton N Jn	2246	63½	Hest B.	8626	63				
War B Q	2333	63/50½	BLS	8743	68/25				
Warwick Jn	2758	59	Carn.	9003	41 /9335				
Golborne Jn	2953	38½	MP 9½	9702	32½/9346				
Colborne	3145	44½	BH	9837	56				
Bamfurlong Jn	3421	64	Miln	10212	66				
Wigan NW	3844	12 (u)	Hin L	10900	62½/61/62½				
sigs	4017 / 4223		Oxen	10733	60/57				
Boars Hd.	4643	34½	Lam.	11246	58½				
Standish Jn	4813	4)	Mose	11434	35				
Coppull Sdg	4953	53	LC	11651	55½/70½				
Coppull	5102	60/66/63	Tebay	12043	68				
Balshaw Lane	5349	54½	S Green	12343	50/31				
Euxton Jn	5509	62	Shap S	12735	37				
Leyland	5627	63	Shap.	12847	65½				
Farring. Jn	5731	71	Haw Sdy	13118	67				
Shaw Brdy	5857	33	T.Grany	13237	70½/75½				

With the majority of Brit-powered journeys over Shap being made during the hours of darkness, they went unrecorded. The only occasion I timed a Brit over Shap was on Saturday, 1 July 1967 - as shown on this extract from my notebook.

The wonderful vista of two 'Flying Pigs' as seen after their arrival into Keswick on the 09.30 Parspec from Euston on Saturday, 15 July 1967. According to the STN, the train was booked to split upon arrival into Penrith and run as two separate portions down the truncated Cockermouth branch! Seemingly inseparable, both Horwich-built Ivatt Moguls had spent the first eleven years of their lives at Cricklewood, being dispatched to Heaton Mersey in December 1963 before finding their way to Kingmoor in June 1965. However, like any long-term relationship death separated them: 43120 being withdrawn just five weeks later, while 43121 hung on until the November of that year.

Now that the SR steam scene had finished we all headed for the WCML every weekend – on this occasion top and tailed by visits to the NER and ScR.

It was the final *amateur* tennis championships at Wimbledon that year and Australian John Newcombe and the USA's Billie Jean King beating all other contestants was broadcast, for the first time on TV, in colour. The film *Bonnie and Clyde*, starring Warren Beatty and Faye Dunaway, was released and in the charts Procul Harum *still* held the top spot, keeping Engelbert Humperdink's 'There Goes My Everything' in second place.

We move on to 15 July – the highlight of that weekend being the double-headed Ivatt Moguls to Keswick. As detailed in Chapter 6, I had jumped the 09.30 Parspec Euston to Keswick at Lancaster because one of my four remaining required Brits, 70014 *Iron Duke*, was working it. The STN showed the train as being split at Penrith with two trains into Keswick but in reality the entire train, with two of Kingmoor's 'Flying Pigs', went through undivided. You could see that Keswick station was once a quite splendid

Penrith on Saturday, 29 July 1967 and former ER Brit 70038 *Robin Hood* takes a breather having just surmounted Shap with the 13.27 Manchester Victoria to Scotland. The Manchester portion was normally placed on the rear of the 13.27 ex Liverpool Exchange but on this day they were running as complete and separate trains.

Warrington Dallam's 45312 is seen in the centre road at Lancaster on a wet Saturday in July 1967. I red-lined her two months later – catching her working the evening portion for Liverpool out of Preston. Note the stanchions still *in situ* on the once electrified but now deceased Green Ayre line in the background.

canopied building as befitting a once-important gateway to the Lake District. Neglect, however, was showing through with weed-infested, unused tracks and bay platforms without rails – the end coming as late as 1972.

Absolutely euphoric at not only getting one of my final Brits but also a by then rare steam trip down the Keswick branch, I have to admit it took some time, the irregular branch-line services being hours apart, to return to Preston for that evening's portions. After relating my exploits to anyone who cared to listen, quite a few headed north for the return train the following Saturday. Alas, although 2-6-0 43139 worked the Keswick–Penrith section she was accompanied by Long Pong D213 *Andania* – which then worked the train over Shap. Oh dear, what a shame – some you win, some you lose! That's how it was back then: right time, right place.

Returning to the 15th, midnight found me at Wigan predictably waiting for the 03.04 homebound train to London. A haulage chaser's main priority is to obtain a run behind as many locomotives as possible and *whenever* a 'requirement' materialises you go where it's going. To this end a double-headed relief, 44758 (10A) and 44878 (12A), from Paignton to Glasgow for whatever reason deigned to stop there. It was at 00.52 on the Sunday morning and I jumped aboard not even knowing, or caring, where the next stop was. I fail to remember if it called at Preston, but having been on the go for more than thirty hours, the next thing I knew was arriving into Carlisle! Making the most of the situation, there being no London-bound trains until mid-morning, I then caught a Brit-worked relief into Glasgow, went across to Edinburgh and headed home on the 10.00 Deltic-powered departure for King's Cross – diverted via Carlisle due to a derailment at Acklington. A fifty-hour outing; 1,417 miles, 517 of which were steam with eighteen different locomotives – oh boy, we were living the dream.

In the news that month was the nationalisation of British Steel, while chart-wise Procul Harum had finally been ousted off of the top spot by The Beatles' 'All You Need is Love'. With NER steam services receiving my attention on the 22nd, it was the last Saturday in July (29th) that saw me board a 02.22 steam-hauled departure out of Carlisle. It was one of the starting services I, and many others frequented, for a summer Saturday bash over WCML metals. The 23.50 Glasgow–Birmingham train would, throughout the year, have a portion from Edinburgh attached at Carstairs. However, with the demand sufficient enough on Fridays from mid July to early September to warrant a complete train from Edinburgh, it ran as a separate entity – and was booked for a Kingmoor Brit south of Carlisle to boot. If one had had the Friday off to sample Scotland's steam trains, as I had on this occasion, it was easy enough to connect into. With darkness precluding any times and speeds of the trains progress being recorded, we all tried to sleep through the journey in order to conserve the stamina required for the up to fifteen hours of steam chasing that was to follow. With it being a very crowded train we were often confined to a couple of compartments and, although sleep can be obtained whilst in a seat, sometimes one or two of us would climb up into the luggage racks in order to stretch out. Upon arriving into Crewe on one occasion we (a collective decision) decided not to wake Bob (aptly nicknamed Doze), who was fast asleep in the luggage rack, thus allowing him to collect unwanted EL mileage to Birmingham – the camaraderie amongst us somewhat lacking on his part upon meeting up with him later that day!

If I had worked at my Wimbledon office on the Friday then the connection into this service would have been on northbound *Highlander* when calling at Carlisle for its unadvertised crew-change stop at 01.30. There were, however, a couple of occasions when, having taken the Friday off, I had crammed in a bash in the Preston area before heading north to Carlisle. Twice I had to rely on the right-time running of the *Northern Irishman*, which was due in at 02.18! On one of those instances it was only because someone slammed a door that I came to my senses, dashed over the footbridge, and jumped aboard the 02.22 departure not knowing until three hours and 141 miles later which Brit was on the front!

The first weekend that August saw a group of us spend the Saturday night at Heysham. Having arrived there just after 23.00 on the Belfast Boat Express, how we passed the hours, what comfort there was, waiting room or platform, I didn't note. The reasoning behind the move was a 05.35 (Relief) to Birmingham which, because of engineering work, was diverted via Carnforth, Hellifield and Blackburn – the line between the latter two points being then freight only. Indeed, the Ribble Valley line, as it is now marketed, has had a very chequered history. Not helped by the partial collapse of Whalley Viaduct, the line was eventually opened through Clitheroe to Chatburn in 1850. It would be a further thirty years before the L&YR, who had taken over the various warring parties, completed the line north to Hellifield. Stopping passenger services between Blackburn and Hellifield ceased in 1962, after which, as in our case that Sunday, although retained for freight it was, and still is, used for diversionary services. After a public campaign the line between Blackburn and Clitheroe was reopened in 1994 – north thereof seeing a Sunday Dalesrail train each week.

Anyway, back to 1967 and a wonderful 121-mile sunny Sunday morning ride through Britain's beautiful countryside, initially with the Forest of Bowland's wide expansive moors on one side and the Yorkshire Dales on the other, and finally interweaving with the River Ribble. The train locomotive, 4-6-0 44971 (10D), however, was not a well bunny and had to have assistance, in the form of Carnforth's 45072 from Whalley – both locomotives being replaced at Lostock Hall Junction by 44675 (12A).

This and the next two shots were all taken on Saturday, 5 August 1967. Observed by a solitary spotter, Kingmoor's 44675, the rescuer of the Heysham boat train, caught the following morning, races through Wigan North Western with a northbound freight.

My next two August visits to the WCML centred on the steam-saturated Saturdays we enthusiasts had travelled from all parts of the country for. On the 12th, having taken a half day's leave on the Friday and travelled into Scotland on a 13.52 (Relief) Euston to Glasgow before returning to Crewe during the early hours, the sixth steam catch of the day produced a run over Shap (the third within twenty-four hours) with the sole surviving, out of four, named Black 5MTs – 45156 *Ayrshire Yeomanry* – on yet another Anglo–Scottish relief. Returning to Preston later that day, perhaps now is the time to regale the scene usually being enacted by us chasers during the summer/ autumn of that year.

Warrington Bank Quay and Brit 70051 *Firth of Forth* is looped (with the iconic Unilever factory as a backdrop) whilst working a northbound parcels service. Warrington Bank Quay station received media coverage in 2009 resulting from signs having been erected at the drop-off point outside the entrance prohibiting kissing 'to avoid queues during busy times'. Following widespread media condemnation they were taken down three weeks later – profits from their sale going to Comic Relief.

Large numbered, doubtless resulting from her six-year sojourn on Scottish metals, Springs Branch-allocated, Armstrong Whitworth-built 45281 waits at Crewe to take the 11.20 ex Euston forward to Blackpool South.

During 1966 the evening Blackpool portion's first stop was St Annes-on-the-Sea but come the summer 1967 timetable changes, Kirkham and Wesham, at 20.58, was called at. With the majority of the regular crowd I was usually with having just turned 18 (I by then being an ancient 20!), any opportunity to imbibe the now legally obtainable alcohol was eagerly seized upon and, having spotted a pub (The Railway Hotel?) within sight of the station *and* with the knowledge that the steam-operated 21.55 Blackpool North to Liverpool Exchange called there at 22.17, a mass invasion of the pub every Saturday night was par for the course. One of my lifelong friends, Jo, called it a 'meeting of mateage'. It wasn't all about the beer. Stories of the day's exploits were exchanged, the participants each having 'done their own thing' dependent upon their own needs. Did you see that one? Haven't you had a run with her yet – she's so …

This is Oxenholme and having just arrived on the depicted train minutes earlier I ran hell for leather to the overbridge in order to take this shot of Stanier 4-6-0 45285 departing with 1M31, the 09.10 Dundee to Blackpool North. The date was Saturday, 19 August 1967 and the locomotive on the left is younger sister 44858 – which was to work the Windermere portion of the 11.55 Euston to Carlisle an hour later.

Also at Oxenholme, a bunch of aficionados I was proud to call my mates. (Alan Hayes)

common! It was all to do with one-upmanship and, although conducted in a friendly banter, some of us secretly cursed other's luck. We had our own language, which, to an outsider, must have seemed completely alien. This in itself helped to create a bonding procedure amongst us; over-inquisitive adults nearby being unable to comprehend! After necking as many pints as the barman could cope with during the seventy minutes, we had all raced out to catch the 22.17 departure with cries of 'not that old rustbucket' (or worse!) upon seeing Edge Hill's 44809, a locomotive annoyingly monopolising the train, to Preston, where a change was made for the DMU to Manchester and the predictable 01.00 Wigan sleepers.

Perhaps the highlight of the day's catches the following Saturday (19th) was an ailing 44915 (10D) worked 10.45 Blackpool North to Dundee being piloted, rather than banked, the 18½ miles from Oxenholme to Shap Summit by Tebay-allocated Standard 4MT 75040. Having been thwarted earlier in the day by the 09.10 Morecambe portion *not* being one of these elusive locomotives, this somewhat made up for it. Later that day Lostock Hall's Ivatt 43088 worked the evening Blackpool portion, but having heard before departing out of Preston an announcement to the effect that the 17.26 Glasgow to Manchester/Liverpool was running ten minutes late and given that a very much required (by us all!) Standard Caprotti 73140 was waiting to work the 21.25 Liverpool portion, we immediately doubled back from Kirkham for it. So you can see the priority there – steam over beer!

As to some further non-railway news that month, Scott McKenzie's 'San Francisco' was riding high in the charts (flower power/hippies/hallucinatory drugs being topically headlined by the papers of the day) and Monday, the 14th, saw the pirate radio ships being outlawed, subsequently prompting the BBC to set up Radio 1.

The August bank holiday, three years into the trial period having been moved from the first weekend, was now upon us. It was only fitting that I made the most of it and embarked on a four-night-long bash. On the Saturday a run of five requirements, including not only my fastest speed (88mph) with a Black 5MT through Milnthorpe and my last Brit, 70039 *Sir Christopher Wren*, certainly seemed to justify it. Lady Luck seemed to have deserted me after the Brit capture and with fewer trains on the Sunday to choose from, a three-hour afternoon sojourn at Blackpool's seafront was undertaken prior to returning to Preston for the late-afternoon portion into Liverpool.

BR 31021/1

No. 34

BRITISH RAILWAYS

LONDON MIDLAND REGION

(NORTH WESTERN LINES)

SPECIAL TRAFFIC NOTICE N1

SATURDAY, 26 AUGUST,

TO

FRIDAY, 1 SEPTEMBER, 1967

EXPLANATION OF REFERENCES

The references appearing in the Working Time Tables are applicable plus the following—

Adex—Day Excursion.

C—Station named to provide Coaches or other Stock.

Evex—Evening Excursion.

Garex—Guaranteed Excursion.

G—Station named to provide Guard.

Halfex—Half-day Excursion.

K—Refreshments.

N—Tickets to be collected.

P—Station or Depot named to provide Power.

PR—Propel.

Parspec—Unadvertised Party Special.

T—Stops for ticket examination only.

V—To be reported to Line Control in the same way as controlled expresses or divisions thereof.

Z—Lavatory purposes.

Δ—Columns so marked will contain Two Trains.

DESTINATION INDICATIONS

The indications appearing in the Working Time Tables are applicable plus the following—

I
L } Special trains running within the London Midland Region.

Z—Inter-regional special trains.

R. ARNOTT

MANCHESTER   **MOVEMENTS MANAGER**

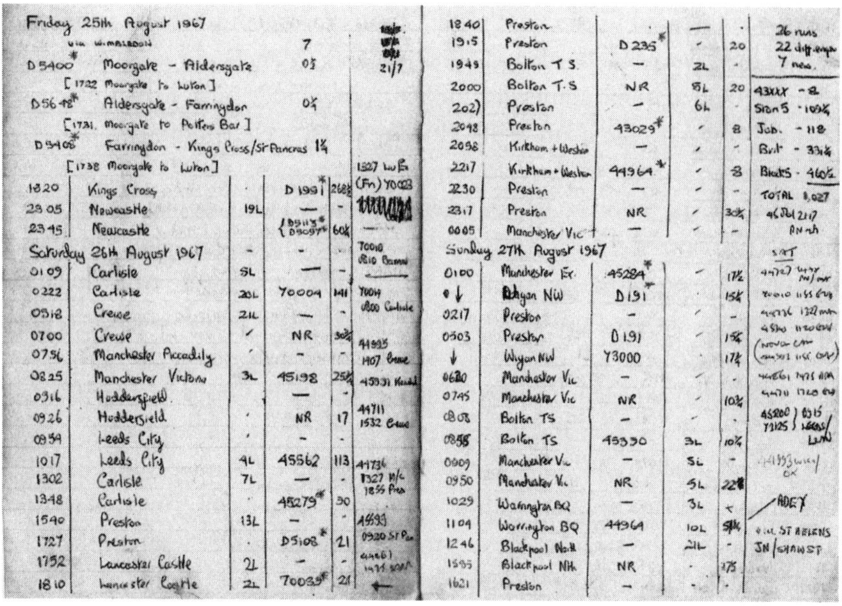

Friday 25th August 1967
via Wimbledon 7
D5400* Moorgate - Aldersgate 0½ — 21/7
[1722 Moorgate to Luton]
D5648* Aldersgate - Farringdon 0¾
[1731 Moorgate to Potters Bar]
D5408* Farringdon - Kings Cross/St Pancras 1¼
[1738 Moorgate to Luton]

1820	Kings Cross	.	D1991*	268¾	1327 [illegible] (Fn) 70023
2305	Newcastle	19L	—	-	
2345	Newcastle		{D5113* D5057*}	60¾	—
Saturday 26th August 1967		-	-	-	70010 [illegible]
0109	Carlisle	5L	—	-	
0222	Carlisle	20L	70004	141	70014 1800 Carlisle
0518	Crewe	21L	-	-	
0700	Crewe	✓	NR	30¾	44895 1907 Crewe
0756	Manchester Piccadilly		-	-	
0825	Manchester Victoria	3L	45198	25¾	45331 [illegible]
0916	Huddersfield		—	-	
0926	Huddersfield	.	NR	17	44711 1532 Crewe
0959	Leeds City	.	-	-	
1017	Leeds City	4L	45562	113	44736 1327 [illegible] 1855 Pres
1302	Carlisle	7L	—	-	
1348	Carlisle	.	45279*	30	
1540	Preston	13L	—	-	44893 0920 St P[illegible]
1727	Preston	.	D5108*	21	44461 [illegible]
1752	Lancaster Castle	2L	-	-	
1810	Lancaster Castle	2L	70035*	21	←

1840	Preston		—	.	26 runs
1915	Preston	D235*	-	20	22 diff. engs 7 new.
1945	Bolton T.S.	—	2L	-	
2000	Bolton T.S	NR	8L	20	43XXX - 8
2021	Preston	—	6L	-	Stan5 - 103¾
2048	Preston	43029*	-	8	Jub. - 118
2058	Kirkham + Wesham	—	-	-	Brit - 33¼
2217	Kirkham + Wesham	44964*	-	8	Black5 - 460½
2230	Preston	—	-	-	TOTAL 1,027
2317	Preston	NR	-	30¾	[illegible] 2117 [illegible]
0005	Manchester Vic	—	-	-	
Sunday 27th August 1967					
0100	Manchester Ex.	45284*	-	17½	44727 [illegible]
↓	Wigan NW	D191*	-	15¾	70010 1155 [illegible]
0217	Preston	-	-	-	44736 1328 [illegible]
0503	Preston	D191	-	15¾	[illegible]
↓	Wigan NW	73000	-	17¾	[illegible]
0620	Manchester Vic	—	-	-	44661 [illegible]
0745	Manchester Vic	NR	-	10¾	44711 [illegible]
0803	Bolton TS	—	.	.	45200 } 73125 } [illegible]
0858	Bolton TS	45330	3L	10¾	
0909	Manchester Vic	—	5L	-	[illegible]
0950	Manchester Vic	NR	5L	22¾	
1029	Warrington BQ	—	3L	-	ADEX
1104	Warrington BQ	44964	10L	[illegible]	via ST HELENS JN / SHAW ST
1246	Blackpool North	—	21L	-	
1535	Blackpool Nth	NR	.	175	
1621	Preston	—	.	.	

The last big steamy British Bank Holiday bash.

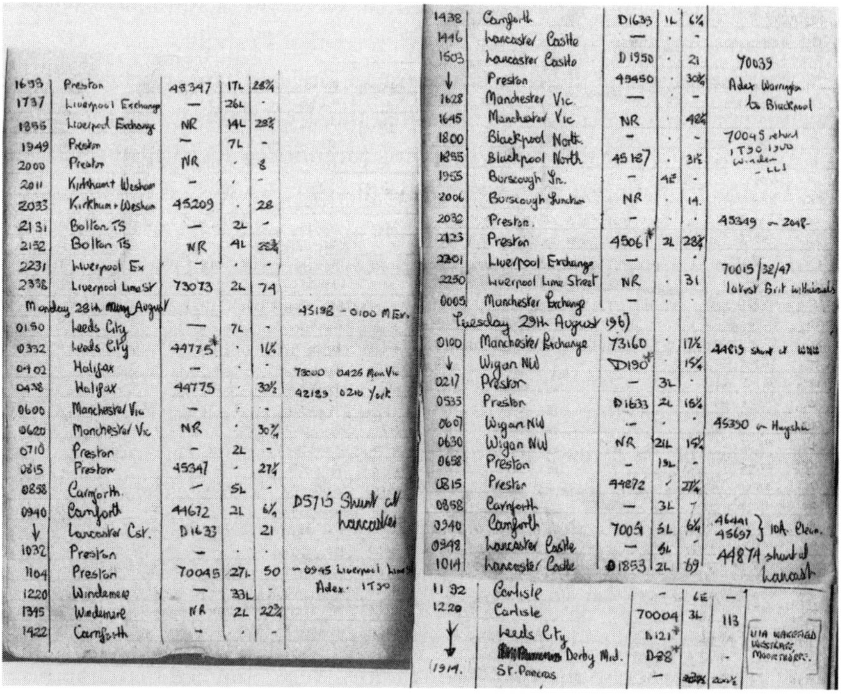

1633	Preston	45347	17L	28¾	
1737	Liverpool Exchange	—	26L	-	
1855	Liverpool Exchange	NR	14L	28¾	
1949	Preston	—	7L	-	
2000	Preston	NR	.	8	
2011	Kirkham + Wesham	-	.	-	
2033	Kirkham + Wesham	45209	.	28	
2131	Bolton TS	—	2L	-	
2152	Bolton TS	NR	4L	28¾	
2231	Liverpool Ex	-	.	-	
2338	Liverpool Lime St	73073	2L	74	
Monday 28th August					45198 - 0100 M Ex.
0150	Leeds City	—	7L	-	
0332	Leeds City	44775*	.	16¾	
0402	Halifax	—	.	.	73000 0426 Man Vic
0438	Halifax	44775	.	30½	42189 0210 York
0600	Manchester Vic	-	.	.	
0620	Manchester Vic	NR	.	30¾	
0710	Preston	-	2L	-	
0815	Preston	45347	-	27¼	
0858	Carnforth	—	5L	-	
0940	Carnforth	44672	2L	6¼	D5715 Shunt at Lancaster
↓	Lancaster Cst.	D1633		21	
1032	Preston	-	.	.	
1104	Preston	70045	27L	50	- 0945 Liverpool Lime St Adex 1T50
1220	Windermere	—	33L	-	
1315	Windermere	NR	2L	22¾	
1422	Carnforth	-	.	-	

1438	Carnforth	D1633	1L	6¼	
1446	Lancaster Castle	—	.	.	
1503	Lancaster Castle	D1950	.	21	70039
↓	Preston	45450	.	30¾	Adex Warrington to Blackpool
1628	Manchester Vic.	—	.	-	
1645	Manchester Vic	NR		48¾	
1800	Blackpool North	-	.	-	70045 [illegible] 1T50 1300 Windermere - LL1
1855	Blackpool North	45187	.	31¾	
1955	Burscough Jn.	-	4E	.	
2006	Burscough Junction	NR	.	14.	
2032	Preston.	-	.	.	45349 — 2048
2123	Preston	45061*	2L	28¾	
2201	Liverpool Exchange	-	.	.	70015/32/47 latest Brit withdrawals
2250	Liverpool Lime Street	NR	.	31	
0005	Manchester Exchange	-			
Tuesday 29th August 1967					
0100	Manchester Exchange	73160	.	17¾	44815 shunt at WNW
↓	Wigan NW	D190*	.	15¾	
0217	Preston	-	3L	.	
0535	Preston	D1633	2L	15¾	
0607	Wigan NW	-	.	.	45330 on Heysham
0630	Wigan NW	NR	21L	15¾	
0658	Preston	-	13L	-	
0815	Preston	44872	✓	27¾	
0858	Carnforth	—	3L	-	
0940	Carnforth	70051	5L	6¼	46441 45697 } 10h. Clean.
0948	Lancaster Castle	—	5L	.	
1014	Lancaster Castle	D1853	2L	69	44874 shunt at Lancaster
1132	Carlisle	-	6E	-	
1220	Carlisle	70004	3L	113	VIA WAKEFIELD WESTGATE MOORTHORPE
↓	Leeds City	D121*			
	Derby Mid.	D28*		-	
1914	St. Pancras	—	[illegible]	[illegible]	

After then, passing the next night's hours more comfortably than usual aboard the Liverpool–Leeds and Leeds–Halifax–Manchester circuit of trains, which provided, albeit somewhat broken, some three hours' sleep, I made my way to Preston to see if any Bank Holiday extras were running.

It was only Brit 45 *Lord Rowallan's* working of a 1T90 09.45 Adex Liverpool Lime Street to Windermere that staved off complete disillusionment. I had blitzed the area over the past three months – was there anything left of interest to lure me back on any further occasions? After heading into Manchester on a portion, back-tracking to Blackpool and yet another portion into Liverpool, I was to be found, on that fourth night out, on the unavoidable 01.00 Manchester to Wigan. After a three-hour fester at Preston even the usually reliable 05.35 stopper to Crewe let me down – D1633 at its head. I had noted in the STN a 09.56 (Relief to the Thames-Clyde Express) Glasgow to St Pancras, and with hope in my heart in this 'you never know what's going to be turned out scenario', the move paid off handsomely. Ex *Golden Arrow* Brit 70004 *William Shakespeare* worked it the 113 miles over Ais Gill to Leeds, with me staying aboard homebound to London.

As if to substantiate the fact that I had exhausted the supply of requirements, on a three-night bash over the final weekend of summer services a paltry three further required Black 5s were all that I caught.

So statistically how did that final summer fare as regards catches? Of the twelve weekends available to me, I visited the WCML on ten of them. The answer was a total of fifty-nine, obviously dominated by forty-three Black 5MTs. Was I satisfied? That's a hard one to answer – missed opportunities such as being at the wrong time in the wrong place, oversleeping and locomotive failures, all playing a part. Retrospectively I was grateful in participating in chasing what was becoming an endangered species – the results providing the info necessary to be able to pen books such as this. Was there life after the cessation of the summer timetable? Please read on …

That September saw Engelbert Humperdinck's fittingly titled 'The Last Waltz' dominate the airwaves, not being ousted from the top spot until the following month by The Bee Gees' 'Massachusetts'. On TV, the complexity of Patrick McGoohan's cult series *The Prisoner* had many viewers mystified as to why and what he was escaping from. Manchester United football club, with the iconic George Best, went on to win the 1967–68 championship, with Preston North End just avoiding relegation and Crewe Alexandra being promoted. Both the *QE2* and Radio 1 were launched that month.

Having brought me over Shap on 1M21, the 11.05 from Glasgow Central, on Saturday, 26 August 1967, Kingmoor's 5MT 45279, after completing the circuit via Lostock Hall/Farington Junctions, is caught about to run non-stop through Preston en route to the train's final destination of Blackpool North (Keith Lawrence).

On Bank Holiday Monday, 28 August 1967 Brit 70045 *Lord Rowallan* is seen on the buffer stops at Windermere in the days when the station was a true terminus (with turntable) rather than the single-tracked bus shelter now *in situ*. This Pacific, having arrived with the 09.45 Adex from Liverpool Lime Street, delivered new to Holyhead in 1954, was withdrawn at the end of that year upon 12A's closure.

Brit 70013 *Oliver Cromwell* was destined for a lifetime of preservation – not that I knew that when she had worked into Lancaster with the 08.35 portion from Barrow on Friday, 1 September 1967.

Two further scenes at Carnforth on 1 September. Somehow escaping the predilection most 9Fs had in wearing a coat of limescale, 12-year-old 9F 2-10-0 92056 calls at Carnforth, when it had platforms on the WCML, for a crew change. Note the nuclear flask in the consist.

Springs Branch's 44819 takes the Furness branch at Carnforth with a Barrow-bound freight. This Derby-built 23-year-old had attached the 01.00 Manchester portion onto the rear of the 00.45 Liverpool–Scotland service at Wigan North Western two days earlier – all movements count!

A gloriously sunny Saturday, 2 September 1967 saw me at Morecambe Promenade catching the 09.10 (portion to Lancaster) departure for Euston. Hoping for one of the elusive 75xxxs, I collected a run with Carnforth's 45017 instead. Oh well, it was the last day of the train's running and at least it was steam!

Later that day saw some of us haulage bashers congregate at Warrington Bank Quay. We had all just alighted off of the 08.00 Carlisle to Birmingham (70035 *Rudyard Kipling*) and were awaiting the 09.10 Euston to Blackpool South (44933) – they being just two of the twenty-five steam trains caught on my three-night bash. Wonderful unforgettable times amongst like-minded friends. (Alan Hayes)

There were just under two dozen 75xxxs shared between Carnforth and Tebay sheds during 1967 and to get one working a passenger train you had to be really lucky. Perhaps for that reason I never took a photograph of an active one. Here Tebay-allocated 75037 is caught in camera banking a lengthy freight past Scout Green on Saturday, 16 September 1967. (Keith Lawrence)

There was an increasing number of English Electric D400s (later designated Class 50) appearing on the scene, together with train formations being tarnished with a mix of blue and grey (the new order) vehicles. What was a steam chaser to do? More and more we were being banished to the dark, cold nocturnal hours' schedules.

That October was a month of extremes; the first and third weekends being low on catches and mileages, the second and fourth high. Saturday, the 14th, saw me arriving into Manchester at 6 a.m. on the Calder Valley mail train with Newton Heath's 45221. After catching a DMU across to Liverpool, there was time for breakfast before boarding the LCGB-organised Castle to Carlisle tour, which departed out of Liverpool Exchange at 09.15. It was just as well I did because; resulting from poor patronage in an attempt to recover losses, there was no buffet car provided – only pre-packed ham salad (8*s* 6*d*) or chicken salad (10*s* 6*d*) available, and that had to be ordered in advance! A polite reminder for participants not to 'hog the buffer beam' or climb signal posts when at photographic stops was also included within the typed A4 sheet allegedly masquerading as the tour's brochure. This turned out to be my twenty-third and final northbound steam assault over Shap. Probably lured onto this train by the promise of a 9F, as sure as eggs are eggs, Kingmoor turned out an unrequired Ivatt 4MT (43121) for the visit to Riddings Junction.

After the tour, to kill time prior to the *Carlisle Kingmoor* Tour on Sunday the 15th, I caught the 01.00 Manchester portion to Wigan (Springs Branch's 45048) and had breakfast (at 4 a.m.!) at Crewe before heading to Birmingham to board this Stephenson Locomotive Society tour, originally booked for the 24th of the previous month, at its starting point. A total of 322 miles of Brit haulage, now unavailable on normal service trains, was then enjoyed. After visiting 12A the tour must have been late arriving back into Crewe because, not having originally planned to stay out a third night, a reassuring phone call home was made, before I headed for Liverpool in order to obtain a run with a Patricroft Caprotti on the 23.38 Lime Street departure and then heading into work on the Monday morning. I had recently only learnt from other enthusiasts of the existence of this train and as it had become, at 74 miles, the second-longest remaining steam worked train,[12] I felt obligated to travel on it – which I was to on seven occasions.

It was an awkward train to cover, taking into consideration Monday morning's attendance time of 08.30 at my Wimbledon office was at risk. Although on this particular occasion I was able to alight at Manchester and arrived into Euston (via Wigan, of course) well in time for breakfast in an Eversholt Street café before work, perhaps I can relate another time when things didn't go to plan.

The third weekend that October saw one of those increasingly frequent low-mileage visits. I hadn't travelled north on Saturday, 22nd – a guards' dispute having resulted in a considerable number of trains being cancelled. So on the Sunday, naively not having ascertained beforehand if the 13.00 out of Euston was affected by engineering work, upon realising at Bamfurlong Junction that we were routed via the little-used Whelley Loop (Wigan avoiding line), I began to have concerns re the connection into the 16.53 Liverpool portion out of Preston. All was well because, having eventually arrived into Preston at 16.53, the simultaneously timed portion was also retimed because of a different engineering block to depart at 17.04 – with a much-wanted 45149.

---

[12] The longest being the 76-mile 17.47 (FO) Manchester Exchange to York.

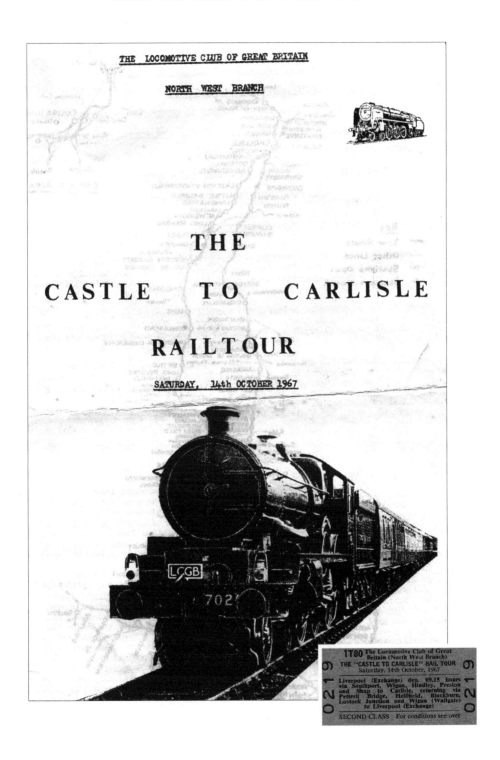

THE LOCOMOTIVE CLUB OF GREAT BRITAIN

NORTH WEST BRANCH

THE
CASTLE   TO   CARLISLE
RAILTOUR

SATURDAY, 14th OCTOBER 1967

LCGB
702

1T80 The Locomotive Club of Great
Britain (North West Branch)
THE "CASTLE TO CARLISLE" RAIL TOUR
Saturday, 14th October, 1967

Liverpool (Exchange) dep. 09.15 hours
via Southport, Wigan, Hindley, Preston
and Shap to Carlisle, returning via
Petteril Bridge, Hellifield, Blackburn,
Lostock Junction and Wigan (Wallgate)
to Liverpool (Exchange)

SECOND CLASS For conditions see over

0219
0219

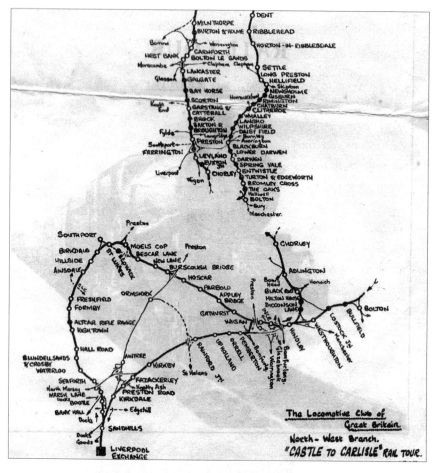

Route map of the 9F-worked section of the Castle to Carlisle rail tour.

Opposite above: A youthful 11-year-old Speke Junction-allocated 9F, 92091, at Liverpool Exchange on Saturday, 14 October 1967. This Swindon-built machine, having spent seven years of its life working GC-line 'Windcutters', was withdrawn at Carnforth in June 1968.

Opposite below: Former ER-allocated Brit 70013 *Oliver Cromwell* at Hellifield on Sunday, 15 October 1967 with the Carlisle Kingmoor Tour. This then Kingmoor-allocated Brit was dispatched to Carnforth upon 12A's closure, thus becoming the sole-surviving Brit into 1968.

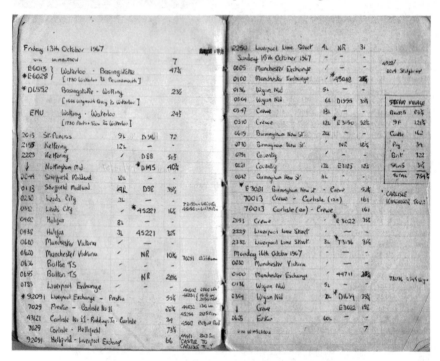

Left: The tour ticket, showing the originally planned date.

Below: Notebook extract detailing the unplanned three-nighter.

The Preston to Liverpool line, opened by the East Lancashire Railway in 1849, is sort of still *in situ*. With through Scottish expresses having been diverted via Wigan into Liverpool's Lime Street station in 1969, this route was severed at Ormskirk – the unusual sight of a large set of buffer stops in the track bed adjacent to the surviving (former southbound) single platform causing any through passengers to have to walk between the irregular DMU service from Preston onto the Merseyrail EMU forward connection. Regrettably, there are nowadays no retail outlets, unlike six years after the line opened when a group of women paid £20 per year rent to the ELR in order to sell their home-made gingerbread.

Liverpool Exchange, opened in 1850, was in fact a replacement for an earlier temporary structure just short of it at Great Howard Street. It was initially jointly owned by the L&YR and ELR: the latter's insistence of calling it Tithebarn Street (its actual location) for the first nine years, until its absorption by the L&YR, no doubt causing confusion to any prospective passengers. Damage to the overall glass roof by the Luftwaffe during the Second World War was never fully repaired and by the times of my visits the ten-platform terminus had a somewhat abandoned feel about the place. After witnessing Britain's final steam train in 1968, its demise was hastened when, the following year, all services excepting the Southport and Ormskirk EMUs, together with the Wigan and Bolton DMUs, were diverted to Lime Street. Six platforms were then sacrificed to enable tunnelling work in connection with the Merseyrail scheme diverting the EMU services direct access via Moorfields to Liverpool Central – final closure being enacted in April 1977.

Liverpool, with its distinctive scouse accent emphasising its uniqueness, was the very centre of the 1960s music revolution. Obviously spearheaded by The Beatles, one mustn't forget others such as Gerry and the Pacemakers, whose rendition of 'You'll Never Walk Alone' is sung with gusto at every Liverpool FC match. With its port once dealing with the unsavoury slave trade, together with the Toxteth riots of 1981, the city has now shed its turbulent past. In 2008 it was the European Capital of Culture.

Liverpool's grand Italianate Lime Street station was opened in 1836 as part of George Stephenson's Liverpool & Manchester Railway. Edge Hill station was his original 1830-built terminus and the twin-tracked, steeply inclined tunnel between them initially had trains hauled up by rope and controlled down by brakemen. Absorbed into the L&NWR, Lime Street was rebuilt in 1849 – further expansions between 1867 and 1880 resulting in the nine-platform terminus we see today.

Anyway, back to that night and twice, with the help of Lt Fuller's *Shed Directory* street map, that visit I walked between Liverpool's Exchange and Lime Street stations. On the first occasion I recall, just for sheer devilment, taking a short cut *through* a Yates Wine lodge, which had entrances on two streets. Rather than fester for six hours at Liverpool, for the 23.38 Leeds departure, I filled the hours with a trip over to Manchester for 10¾ miles to Bolton on the Belfast Boat Express. Whenever the capacity for a further steam trip within any visit allowed it just had to be done. You never know, it could have been a required Carnforth catch!

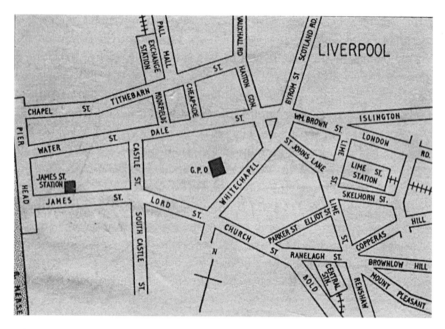

The city of Liverpool street map extract. (*Lt Fuller's Shed Directory*)

Once more returning to Lime Street I found the wait for the stock to be platformed not the most pleasant as it was cold and windy. Once in the solitary warm BSK, nestled amongst a plethora of vans, my demeanour improved. We stormed up the incline, labouring through the sleeping suburbs, travelling through Rainhill – where George Stephenson's *Rocket* was trialled 138 years previously – passing through the long-closed (1878) Parkside station – where there was a memorial[13] to the MP William Huskisson who lost his life during the aforementioned trials, before crossing the immense Chat Moss. This location comprised of an area of 12 square miles whose main consistence was vegetable matter so soft that cattle could not walk over it. The numerous viaducts and embankments constructed to navigate over it is a great credit to the Victorian engineers. On we went, espying the BR Standard 5MTs' graveyard, i.e. Patricroft shed, before, having passed the

---

[13] 1T57, the Fifteen Guinea final BR steam train, called there for ten minutes on Sunday, 11 August 1968 – ladders being provided for those occupants wishing to alight and take photographs.

Exchange station, arriving an hour later into Manchester's Victoria station. I was usually the only passenger. What possessed delusional aficionados like myself to frequent such trains during such hours? It just had to be done – the fact that it can never be replicated, that's why!

So to the final weekend of that month and, having travelled north for yet another rail tour the following day and having had the bonus, the previous evening, of connecting at Preston out of the BBE into the late-running 21.25 portion into Liverpool, I crossed over to Manchester, caught the 01.00 sleeper to Lancaster and yomped to Heysham, eventually arriving into Manchester at 08.37 having accumulated a respectable 136 steam miles even before boarding the tour.

If I recall correctly, I was a participant on this jointly organised Severn Valley Railway Society/Manchester Rail Travel Society Preservation Special Tour, which started and finished at Birmingham New Street because of its promised usage of an NER-allocated 8F on the circuit out of Normanton. No notes were made at the time due to my disappointment/joy at once again having a final run with *Alberta* – in place of a guaranteed required 8F! Although, if taking into consideration two further steam catches on the Stalybridge and Wigan portions after the tour, it amounted to a pleasing total of in excess of 420 steam miles, the achievements were tempered with a lack of new haulages.

Being the glutton for punishment that I was during that final frantic autumn, having arrived back at my Kent home at about 8 a.m., because of the clock change, after a wash and brush-up and something to eat I was able to head back north on the 13.00 out of Euston. The Liverpool portion had 10Ds 44816, the BBE had D214 *Antonia* and the 23.38 Liverpool–York 73131. It was now my third night out and fatigue was to play its part. Aboard the 01.00 Manchester–Wigan portion, no amount of shunting at Wigan, guards' whistles nor loco changing at Preston would wake me – and I opened my eyes just as we were arriving into Carlisle at 04.50. What now? I was due in work at Wimbledon in four hours' time! The steamiest way home was selected, i.e. the 08.35 ex Barrow, and to access that I boarded the all-stations 05.32 DMU departure for an 86-mile dawn ride along the Cumbrian coast. Initially considered by George Stephenson as a route from England to Scotland before deciding on the more direct one over Shap, the first 33 miles to Workington, opened in 1845, were traversed in the inky blackness of a pre-dawn autumn morning. The next 7, to Workington, caused considerable difficulties to the Victorian engineers – rock falls and high tides delaying the opening until 1847. Indeed, the *Carlisle Journal* of the day commented that the poor wretches who filled the trains must either have had their brains dashed out against the rocks at one side or be pitched head-foremost into the sea on the other – perhaps leading to the Board of Trade imposing a 15mph speed restriction. Dawn was now breaking and the true magnificence of this coast-clinging line became apparent. This section passing near to the somewhat, to me, futuristic Sellafield Nuclear Power Station, south to Foxfield was the last to be completed (1850), creating an end-on junction with the Furness Railways line from Barrow. The scenic splendour of the Lake District National Park was then witnessed before crossing the River Dudden and entering the shipbuilding town of Barrow-in-Furness.

During the eight-minute connection there I frantically located a telephone box with yet another apologetic phone call to my fortunately understanding line manager to secure a further day's annual leave, not being certain I had any left. The 08.35 Barrow to Euston train, worked the 35 miles to Lancaster by Carnforth's 45390, was my first daylight trip along this line. Completed in 1857, this line also hugged the coast, providing wonderful views with the sun shimmering on the waters of Morecambe Bay; the two river estuary crossings of the Rivers Leven and Kent being particularly spectacular. Perhaps it was made more enjoyable thinking of my work colleagues slaving away at their south London office desks!

Staying aboard the train to Preston after a one-and-a-half-hour fester, during which a Travellers Fayre breakfast was ravenously devoured, I headed into Manchester Victoria on the 12.12 portion, 45282 (8F), and walked to the Central for the 14.00 to Derby on the former Midland Railway route via Matlock. This picturesque line through the Peak District, interweaving south of Matlock with the River Derwent, was closed north of Matlock the following year, not as the result of the Beeching axe but, despite strenuous opposition, by the Transport Minister of the day, Barbara Castle. Two sections survive – the 8½-mile Monsal Trail: a cycle, horse riding and walking pathway, and the 4-mile section between Rowsley and Matlock: running under the auspicious of the Peak Railway preservation organisation.

Moving onto that November and on Sunday, the 5th, I once again made the 23.38 Liverpool departure the axis of my plan. What I hadn't planned for was, however, the hour's delay at Patricroft resulting from a locomotive failure, which dumped me at Leeds at 3 a.m. on the Monday morning. No problem, there was a 03.15 (21.55 ex Edinburgh) to St Pancras and although with its 08.10 arrival into London it would lead me to a late arrival at my office desk. At least I was able to locate an empty compartment and, taking my shoes off and stretching out, I reasoned that I could put my head down for a few hours. Presumably having had sufficient sleep replenishment, the next thing I knew was tearing through the London suburbs at about 8 a.m. Gathering my thoughts, I realised that sitting opposite me were three bowler-hatted gentlemen looking at me in disdain over the top of their pink *Financial Times* newspapers! With them watching my every move, I sheepishly put on my shoes and cosseted myself by the window pretending to admire the passing view. Blow me if several of their colleagues, who had been standing in the corridor, didn't open the door and come in to sit next to me – opening the window in an effect to dispel my obvious foot odour. It was some time later that day that I realised what had happened. The Edinburgh train had a set-down-only stop of 07.31 at Luton and these city commuters, obviously favouring a non-stop loco-hauled train over their all-station DMU, were presumably regulars on it!

On two Fridays later that month, having arrived into Manchester on the 17.30 ex Euston, the Belfast Boat Express was caught to Preston before returning for the 01.00 Manchester–Wigan – and home. Desperate measures in desperate times – I knew nothing else. Akin to an addiction, all the time there was a possibility of new haulages it seemed I was programmed to bash the scene. Those more fortunate in living in Manchester or Lancashire were spared the ever-increasing mileages behind the AC electrics and to a lesser extent DMUs I was obligated to travel on.

Even the crème de la crème of the remaining steam-powered named passenger services, the Belfast Boat Express, was not immune to dieselisation. From the last week of October 1967, English Electric D214 *Antonia*, reputedly Carnforth's only acquisition of the class, was rostered for the train – allegedly to be used until she failed. She duly obliged on 6 November and steam was returned to it from then onwards. With The Bournemouth Belle having ceased running and The Pines Express having been dieselised in that July together with The Yorkshire Pullman going DL three months later, the BBE was now the final remaining named steam train operating in Britain.

An air of despondency now settled over our hobby. One by one the final representatives of other classes were cast aside. BR 78xxx in May, Ivatt 464xxx in June and in September the last J94 and the three remaining Jintys condemned.

11

SIXTY-EIGHT IN
SIXTY-EIGHT: 1968

I could commence this, the final chapter of the Iron Horse's existence in mainland Britain, by listing all the remaining sheds at which the surviving locomotives were allocated, their transfer/withdrawal dates and a multiplicity of information about the trains they worked during the first seven months of 1968. I consider, however, that all of it has been more than adequately covered in a plethora of publications over the years and will therefore confine the contents to my personal travels.

The LMR announcement of September 1967 listing the closure dates of all surviving steam sheds only confirmed the inevitable finality my time-consuming hobby was fast approaching. Whereas when the other regions had dispensed with steam there had always been the LMR to look to in order to carry on 'chasing', with the LMR itself ending there was no getting away from the fact that all was lost.

What incentives, by the early months of 1968, remained to entice a haulage basher to venture out into the long dark cold nights of winter? Precious little. With the remaining steam-powered trains annoyingly running simultaneously, decisions had to be made at the commencement of each Friday outing as to which location to make a beeline for. If I was able to get away sharply from my workplace at Waterloo then I could make for the two evening portions out of Preston – failing that, Manchester was my destination.

As can be seen, whichever plan was adopted (steam services in bold) only three locomotives were able to be caught during the sixteen-hour itinerary – the outside chance of a locomotive changeover at Wigan in between Manchester portions sometimes enhancing the figure to a magical four! It all ended at Preston by 10 a.m. The extremely slim chance of the 12.17 Manchester and 12.44 Blackpool portions from there being steam worked was usually not worth the three-hour wait but, as will be seen as the chapter progresses, I did sometimes to kill the time prior to the Saturday evening portions, travelling widely away from the area.

Plan 1			Plan 2			Plan 3			Plan 4		
	arrive	depart		arrive	depart		arrive	depart		arrive	depart
Euston		17.30	Euston		17.30	Euston		17.05	Euston		17.05
Man Picc	20.19		Man Picc	20.19		Preston	20.33	**20.48**	Preston	20.33	**21.25**
Man Vic		20.55	Man Vic		20.55	Bpool S	**21.22**	21.30	Lpool Ex	**22.03**	
Preston	**21.55**	22.10	Preston	**21.55**	22.10	Man Vic	22.59		Lpool LS		22.50
Man Vic	22.59		Man Vic	22.59					Man Ex	00.05	
Man Ex		01.00	Man Picc		00.10	*Then either as plan 1 or 2*			*Then as plan 1*		
Wigan NW	**01.36**	**05.45**	Stockport	00.18	00.50						
Man Ex	**06.20**	06.40	Leeds City	02.25	**03.32**						
Lpool LS	07.59		Halifax	04.02	04.36						
Lpool Ex		09.00	Man Vic	06.00							
Preston	**09.36**		Man Ex		06.40						
			Lpool LS	07.59							
			Lpool Ex		**09.00**						
			Preston	**09.36**							

At the start of that year there were just over 350 steam locomotives on BR's books – the largest allocations being at Carnforth (thirty-eight), Edge Hill (thirty-seven) and Patricroft (thirty-four). Excluding one Brit and six 43xxxs, together with the 8 and 9Fs for which no Class 1 or 2 work was diagrammed, this left 151 Black and 23 Standard 5s, sixty-nine of which I required runs with, that were liable to materialise on passenger work. Keeping abreast of shed closures, locomotive withdrawals and transfers was only available retrospectively courtesy of *The Railway World* magazine. Perhaps because of this, or more likely my naivety as to where the required locomotives were allocated, I still ventured, on a weekly basis, to LMR's Manchester and Preston divisions. Research all these years later has uncovered the reasons for my limited success – the majority of required locomotives being at depots without passenger work, i.e. Heaton Mersey, Trafford Park, Bolton, Speke Junction and Stockport Edgeley!

Here then, in this chapter, is a summary, month by month, of those sixty-eight journeys made with steam trains that final year. I always set forth with high expectations but usually returned home tired, dejected and frustrated having spent hours loitering in cold draughty waiting rooms or on platform benches in the often-futile attempt to obtain anything 'new'. With hindsight I am glad I made the effort. It was a minor miracle that I obtained the haulages that I did – the elation that accompanied the successes I did achieve vindicating, to me, the reason for it all – or so I convinced myself!

It was a truly sad time for those who, like myself, had centred the steam locomotive as an integral part of their lives and who were now despondently documenting *every* steam locomotive seen in the knowledge that history (i.e. the demise of steam) was being enacted. With the majority of visits necessitating travelling through Crewe, when passing the now closed Crewe South, lines of locomotives left to rust away would be witnessed – numbers, however, too distant to note. It would have been very easy to become disillusioned with the vista I was now witnessing.

JANUARY

With The Beatles' 'Hello Goodbye' holding sway at the number-one spot and Prime Minister Harold Wilson launching the 'I'm backing Britain' campaign, encouraging workers to undertake extra hours without pay in an attempt to kick-start the economy, the first Saturday of the year saw me depart Euston in mid-afternoon for the North-West completely unaware that hours earlier a Manchester to Euston train had hit a transformer-carrying lorry at a level crossing at Hixon with eleven fatalities and forty-five injured.

The only productive result from that bitterly cold first weekend visit was that I was able to utilise the newly given flash attachment to my Kodak Colorsnap camera to photograph the three steam services caught. Having travelled on the BBE to Bolton, and rather than festering on a cold

Thirty-three-year-old Armstrong Whitworth-built 4-6-0 45134 awaits time at Manchester Victoria on Saturday, 6 January 1968 with the 20.55 Belfast Boat Express for Heysham.

Another shot of this Carnforth-allocated Black 5MT – this time making a noisy departure with 1P02 from its first call of Bolton Trinity Street.

windswept platform at Stalybridge (the waiting room having been locked up to avoid vandalism and the much-vaunted refreshment room having long since closed for the night), I caught a DMU over to Huddersfield and boarded the TPO there – thus benefitting from a far warmer environment on that cold winter night.

After collecting a run with the prototype Standard 5MT on the aforementioned portion and inevitably ending up on the 01.00 Manchester–Wigan–Euston 'circuit', I calculated that for all the hours of travel that visit my steam miles amounted to a derisory thirty-nine – behind just three locomotives. Was this the future?

Was the second weekend visit that month going to be any better? At least a required ex Chester 45353 was caught on the 17.37 (SuO) Preston to Liverpool Exchange portion. I had had several lengthy runs on the 23.38 Liverpool to York train (Patricroft 5MT to Leeds) during the latter part of 1967 and, with that train central to this visit, I killed time with 45342 to Bolton on the BBE prior to making my way to Liverpool.

It's now 00.35 hours on a freezing Sunday morning and Patricroft's prototype Standard 5MT, 73000, is at rest having arrived into Manchester Exchange with the two-coach portion (detached at Stalybridge) off the 21.50 TPO ex York.

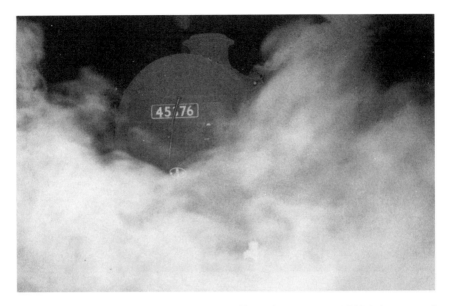

Just minutes later and long-term Edge Hill resident, Stanier 45376, is captured wreathed in steam and smoke as she heats the stock of the 01.00 departure out of Manchester Exchange for Scotland. She would work this portion, which contained sleeping cars available for occupation from 23.00, to Wigan North Western, where it would be attached to the rear of the 00.45 Liverpool Lime Street to Scotland.

To say I wasn't best pleased would be an understatement when, having wandered up to the front of the 23.38 departure, I saw Type 2 'Splutterbug' D5226 gurgling away at its head! My disappointment was probably not shared by the driver who, with his feet resting on the console, was engrossed in reading his paper – no doubt relishing the warmth and the comfort of his alternative traction to one of Patricroft's filthy Caprottis. With no option other than being stranded for several hours in the cold draughty 'tunnel' of a station (Lime Street) I reluctantly travelled across to Manchester on it. To compound my disillusionment, the 01.00 sleepers, only the previous month having been part of a Kingmoor-allocated Britannia duty on Mondays, produced a Type 4 DL, D336.

A four-hour sojourn, unsuccessfully attempting sleep on the solid wooden benches in a cold waiting room, was then endured at Wigan. For sure it would have occupied more time by continuing through to Preston and returning from there on the balancing working but, always wary of certain

The time was just before noon on a chilly Monday, 15 January at Wigan North Western and 13-year-old Standard 5MT 73053, withdrawn eight weeks later, is seen about to work the Manchester portion off the delayed 23.55 Glasgow Central to Liverpool Lime Street. The train was running 347 minutes late due to a tornado having hit Scotland together with a fatality in England.

sleeping car attendants' willingness to punch large holes in our already fragile free passes, we usually opted to fester at Wigan. At least I knew, with Standard 5MT 73053 sitting in the up bay platform, the 05.45 opposite way Manchester portion was going to be steam. It was yet another bitterly cold night and about 5 a.m. the night porter came along to tell me (I was the only fool stupid enough to be there waiting for trains at that unearthly time of the day) that resulting from a tornado hitting Glasgow, the overnight sleepers from Scotland had yet to cross the border. After consulting the well-thumbed LMR timetable, I left 73053 simmering in the up bay and walked over to Wallgate to catch the 06.53 departure into Liverpool in order to connect into the 09.00 Scottish service.

By 1968 Newton Heath's only remaining passenger working was the westbound Calder Valley mail train from Halifax on which 9D 45310, utilised on that day's 09.00 Preston portion, was turned out with monotonous regularity. I suppose I should have been grateful I was getting a steam run at all bearing in mind it had been some twelve hours since the last! After arriving at Preston I was wondering what to do – whether to wait for the 12.17/12.44 portions or go home – when what should turn up, having been further delayed by a fatality in England, but the late-running sleepers! At 10.37 (347 minutes late) Brush Type 4 D1738 took me the 15¼ miles to Wigan, where 73053 was still waiting patiently (presumably recrewed!) and an unexpected daylight journey to Manchester via Golborne Junction was enjoyed. Walking over to Piccadilly and changing at Crewe, I arrived back at Euston in the thick of rush hour at 17.00 hours. Thirty hours' travelling for 86 steam miles – an improvement of sorts on the previous outing.

Determined to better my, so far this year, abysmal steam mileage I embarked on a two-nighter the following Friday (19th) by travelling from St Pancras to Leeds for the 03.32 Halifax service on the Saturday. Arriving at a freezing Leeds City at 02.30 hours, LMS 4-6-0 44949 was the Halifax's train power that morning – the wonderfully steam-heated carriages providing a much-appreciated refuge from the bitter cold. After alighting at Halifax just after 4 a.m., I watched the Stanier berthing the stock for that day's 08.48 King's Cross departure whilst awaiting the 02.10 ex York; the train 44949 would work forward to Manchester. The crowds that used to frequent these trains as part of a wonderful six locos before breakfast scenario (as detailed in my *Riding Yorkshire's Final Steam Trains*) over the previous two years had long gone and whereas one sometimes fought for a standing room space, a one-and-a-half-hour slumber comfortably stretched out in a compartment to myself was relished.

Although having been informed by a platform-ender upon arrival into Manchester that I had missed a required Stockport-allocated 45269 on the 01.17 ex Piccadilly, the 09.00 portion out of Liverpool that morning produced a compensatory sequentially numbered 45268. I convinced myself that the 01.17 was an awkward train to return into Manchester off and that this Newton Heath-allocated sister was a far easier catch – whatever else was to occur that weekend, a happy gricer was noted celebrating with an ear-to-ear grin upon alighting at Preston. It soon, however, faded when, having waited three hours, the 12.17 and 12.44 portions were both diesel. Researching *Railway World* Motive Power Reports for this book I learnt (in the March issue mind) that both trains had become steam worked Mondays to Friday *only*! Although nine steam movements were noted during the three hours spent at Preston, the reader might remember I was *only* after haulages. I then had to make a decision whether to go home or fester at Preston for eight (yes eight) hours awaiting the next steam activity.

Notebook extract of a typically barren steam outing. Just 111¾ steam miles with four locomotives for thirty-five hours' travelling – par for the course during the final year.

I decided to embrace the embryonic new British Rail double-arrowed scenario in that I went south to Crewe and shuttled to/from Stafford several times red-lining the AC Electrics. Sad but time filling – completion of all AC Electric classes 81/5/6/7 eventually being achieved during the 1970s, considerably assisted by a three-and-a-half-year residency at Crewe. Returning to Preston on the 17.05 ex Euston, the Blackpool portion that evening had Rose Grove's 44848 on it. What a catch; one that made the day's lengthy wait bearable – she being withdrawn four weeks later! An announcement prior to our departure from Preston was to the effect that the 17.26 Glasgow to Manchester service was running late. So we (for once I was not alone!) doubled back from Kirkham *just* (by dashing through the subway between platforms) making a two-minute connection into the twenty-two-minute-late-running 45444-worked Liverpool train. A smart walk (chasing steam kept you fit) across to Lime Street and over to Manchester for the, yes you've guessed it, inevitable 01.00 sleepers was then undertaken. Caprotti 73136 was heating the stock but unbelievably was failed, being replaced by Peak D169. At least 1M12 homebound was on time and warm. Thirty-five hours' travelling for 84 steam miles was OK, but more importantly two more Black 5s were red-lined.

No steam travels were undertaken during the last weekend of January because, being 21 years old on the 27th, my parents had pre-booked a table for my brother and I in a smart London restaurant, which I was obviously obligated to attend. They had, bless them, no idea of the seriousness of the disappearing steam scene 'oop north'!

Non-railway events that month included an intensification of the Vietnam War and the democratic election of Alexander Dubček as the Czechoslovakian president. Here in the UK the Ford Escort was introduced as the Anglia's replacement and The Love Affair's 'Everlasting Love' had knocked Georgie Fame's 'Ballad of Bonnie and Clyde' off of the top spot. Film-wise, *Carry on Doctor*, the thirteenth of an eventual twenty-eight in the series, was a box office hit.

FEBRUARY

There were still a considerable number of locomotives in circulation within the North-West, on paper at least, which I had yet to travel behind and so once again I set forth on the first Saturday of the month (3rd) out of Euston in the afternoon heading for what was becoming the last-chance-saloon location of Preston. There were still a number of colleagues who, similar to myself, were making the effort to capture fresh haulages and upon meeting them at Preston I learnt that that morning's 05.45 Wigan portion had had Standard 5MT 73050 working it – an entry in my *Locoshed* book yet to be red-lined. This news, together with unrequired locomotives being turned out for the two Preston portions that evening, did nothing to lighten my mood as once again I crossed the Pennines to connect into the westbound TPO out of Huddersfield.

Edge Hill's 45284 was dispatched by Patricroft foreman for the Stalybridge portion and similarly allocated sister 45187 for the 01.00 sleepers to Wigan – in lieu of the hoped-for 73050 but at least the latter was steam! Just for something different I then headed north to Lancaster for the Belfast Boat Express, festering en route one and three-quarter hours at Preston and two and three-quarter hours at Lancaster. For my sufferings I was rewarded with a delightful 51¾-mile, one-and-a-half-hour journey aboard Britain's final steam-hauled named train. I thoroughly enjoyed this lengthy run with steam on Class 1 timings. The Lancashire countryside passed through that Sunday was wreathed with early-morning mist with the sun breaking through upon coming through the North-West Manchester suburbs. Mood lightened, I snacked at a café en route across Manchester before catching the 10.00 London departure out of Piccadilly.

World news that month was dominated by the continuing Vietnam War, whilst here at home free milk for secondary-school pupils was ended by the Education Minster Mrs Thatcher (thus giving rise to the sobriquet Thatcher the milk snatcher) and the Home Office launched a campaign with the motto 'watch out, there's a thief about'. Musically, Manfred Mann hit the top spot with 'The Mighty Quinn'.

Desperation was now setting in and with a ten-day European steam bash planned from the 16th, an additional midweek overnight, to and from work, was undertaken on the 6th. Leaving Euston on the 17.30 for Manchester, delays caused by worsening weather conditions, with the snow becoming noticeably thicker from Nuneaton onwards, and preference given to two Type 2s on the snow plough at Crewe, eventually led to a forty-minute-late arrival into Piccadilly. Having obviously missed the 20.55 BBE from Victoria, I was effectively left with the sole possibility of steam on the 01.17 Piccadilly to Cleethorpes service as being my only hope. I couldn't risk the 01.00 Exchange sleepers because the connecting 1M12 inevitably delayed arrival into London, Scotland being badly affected by the weather, and would have meant a late arrival at my desk at Wimbledon – and I was already running a yellow card for timekeeping irregularities! With Type 2 D5064 powering the Cleethorpes departure that morning, the decision was made for me. Returning south on the Irish Mail from Crewe, I pondered the possibility of applying for extended sick leave pleading insanity citing the loss of a night's sleep in a comfortable bed to travel nearly 400 miles in late-running trains during the freezing darkness of a winter's night without collecting any steam mileage!

So to my final visit to the area that month (9th). I travelled once more on the 17.30 ex Euston – this time, courtesy of a right-time arrival into Piccadilly, connecting into the BBE out of Victoria, which was unusually powered by Lostock Hall's 44683. I noted, when passing Bolton shed, a required home-allocated 73069 that was tantalisingly appearing to be saying 'you can't catch me; I don't *do* passenger work'. To rub salt further into the wound, having arrived at Preston one of the country's six remaining Flying Pigs, 43027, was on the sleeper attachment duties, seemingly enticing me to sneak aboard for the shunt – all movements count! I returned to Manchester noting the same DL as three days previously on the 01.17 Cleethorpes departure before crossing the Pennines for the Calder Valley mails with – yes you've guessed it – 45310!

Having been advised by fellow gricers, upon arrival into Manchester, that Carnforth's pet 45025 was on the morning BBE, I travelled over to Liverpool for the 09.00 portion to Preston. No. 45447 from Rose Grove, a shed with no booked passenger work, was that morning's stallion. What a winner, the abortive midweek trip was forgotten. Whatever else was going to happen that weekend, the trip was worthwhile.

The 09.00 portion from Liverpool Exchange to Preston, where it was attached to the 09.00 Manchester Victoria to Scotland, was a much-frequented train that winter. Usually having spent many hours over the previous night in either cold waiting rooms or on platforms, here at least was a daytime run on a warm non-stop steam-hauled train. OK, you might say, it was only thirty-six minutes for 27½ miles but we were grateful for any small mercies back then. Having somehow missed her when allocated to Shrewsbury and Carlisle, here Stanier 4-6-0 45447, now Rose Grove-allocated, is waiting the right of way on Saturday, 10 February 1968.

It was just as well I had that attitude because nothing else did happen. Killing time before the 12.44 Blackpool portion, a fill-in trip to Lancaster was undertaken that, because of a broken rail at Scorton involving SLW, I nearly didn't return to Preston for it in time. It was to no avail, the 12.44 being a DL, and so to fill the eight-hour wait for the evening portions I once again headed south to shuttle between Crewe and Stafford in order to red-line further AC locos. Upon returning to Preston and realising nothing required was coming out of 10D, I despondently replicated what was becoming a tiresome inescapability, i.e. crossing the Pennines to Huddersfield for the westbound TPO. For my efforts I was bestowed runs with Standard 5MT 73142 on the Stalybridge portion and 45187 (again!) on the sleepers. I suppose I should have been grateful they were steam. If it wasn't for the prospect of a great many steam haulages throughout Europe in a ten-night bash I'm sure that I could have descended into full-on depression!

MARCH

That month there was serious rioting by students in Poland demanding greater freedoms, whilst here, in London, a confrontational anti-Vietnam War rally, with many arrests and injuries, was held. Musically, 'Cinderella Rockefella' by the Israeli duo Esther and Abi Ofarim hit the number-one spot before being dislodged, for one week only, by Dave Dee, Dozy, Beaky, Mick & Tich's 'Legend of Xanadu', after which the all-conquering Beatles took over with 'Lady Madonna'. Football-wise, the League Cup Final at Wembley saw Leeds beat Arsenal 1-0.

Having been spoilt by the steam successes of a pan-European trip, I wondered if Britain had anything left to offer up that March. There had been a further reduction in steam-hauled services, i.e. 09.00 Liverpool Exchange had become MSO, 12.17 Preston MO, 12.44 Preston SX, 20.48 Preston SO and finally the 03.32 Leeds/04.38 Halifax MX.

On the first Saturday in March (2nd) a wholly non-eventful visit was undertaken. In fact, for sixteen hours' travel I only managed a 27½-mile run with 45436 on the 21.25 Preston portion. It really was the sign of the changing times because not only was the 01.00 on the Sunday morning a DL (D5199) but the connecting Euston-bound train gave me my first run with a newly delivered English Electric Type 4 D402 – which was to be classified under the TOPS system as a Class 50. The sheds at Buxton, Northwich and Trafford Park all closed their doors to steam from midnight.

The following Friday (8th) I was able to travel north on an earlier than normal train from Euston, thus allowing a greater amount of time to cross Manchester for the BBE. My job at DMO Wimbledon, having been displaced under one of the many reorganisational changes I was to endure throughout my career, was now a wagon-auditor. This involved, taking into consideration it was pre-TOPS days, visiting various far-flung locations such as Ludgershall and Hamworthy Goods and reporting back all wagons present – normal procedures being reliant on the resident shunters.

Just to break the monotony, that night I travelled on the BBE all the way through to Heysham. The next train I boarded was at 04.05 at Carnforth (the southbound Scottish sleepers to Liverpool and Manchester) and reference to my old tattered, but treasured, notebook indicated that I had caught a Lancashire and Heysham route 89 to Morecambe bus station, changing there to a Ribble-operated route 745 forward. What times they ran and where the majority of those five hours were spent I can't say. After the prototype Standard 5MT 73000 had been taken into Manchester, I crossed over to Liverpool for the 09.00 Preston portion – rumour control having gone into overdrive, indicating it was now part of a Rose Gove duty. Dare I hope for another required example from a shed nominally void of any passenger services? Wonderfully, 31-year-old 45382 of 10F was at its head. What a pleasing source of requirements this train was turning out to be – four out of the last five visits qualifying for the red pen to be put in use! The subsequently preserved 44932 became the *only* Rose Grove Blackie I missed – the matter being rectified in September 2009 by sneaking aboard a returning steam tour at Bromley South into London's Victoria.

At Preston occasionally, *very* occasionally, the 10.47 to Barrow, until mid 1967 the preserve of a Kingmoor Britannia, was steam operated. Today, fortunately, it was one of those rare occasions and a wonderful two-hour jaunt along the Cumbrian coast was enjoyed with Carnforth's 44963. Regrettably, the errant D1845 was repaired and hotfooted behind it to work the returning 13.40 service – on which, we (there were quite a few of us) returned to Preston.

There were now five hours to kill before the evening portions and rather than spend money in the buffet or endure mind-bending boredom, a return trip to Carlisle was undertaken – 180 miles of Brush Type 4 being endured.

Barrow-in-Furness sees its final steam-hauled passenger train? The date was Saturday, 9 March 1968 and 10A-allocated 44963 was substituting for the booked Brush Type 4 at short notice on the 10.47 ex Preston. The errant D1845, having been repaired and dispatched LE from Preston, however, powered the returning 13.40 to Crewe (for Euston).

At least it was warm and some lost sleep was regained! After all that, Lostock Hall didn't turn out anything wanted and so, for the fourth occasion that year, over to Huddersfield we trailed – reaping a run with the exceedingly common 45187 on the portion and, another DL on the 01.00 sleepers. Yet again the steam locomotive came off just prior to departure time and a non ETH DL supplanted. Over the following thirty-six-minute journey the heat dispensed by the Standard 5MT at Manchester disappeared and we were all shivering *before* enduring the wait at Wigan. It did make me wonder if the latter train had been turned over to DL haulage permanently. It was only reports from other enthusiasts that steam was still diagrammed that led me to continue to patronise it.

With the next two weekends being spent either chasing SNCF's Mountains (241Ps) in central France or obtaining new steam track out of St Pancras with *Flying Scotsman* it wasn't until the final Friday (29th) that March that I returned to the North-West. I first covered the BBE to Preston, with the subsequently preserved 45212, before travelling via Stockport to Leeds. As regards the 03.32 Halifax service, I have retrospectively calculated that there were only three out of nineteen of Newton Heath's 5MT allocation that I required. I wasn't to know that on this morning, when the much-travelled-with 44910 provided that night's sleeping accommodation. Readers must now have appreciated the limited itineraries that were available to a steam chaser during those days of pitifully few steam-hauled services and predictably, having come into Manchester at 6 a.m., I made my way over to Liverpool and, after having a run with an unrequired 10F 45397, I'd had enough and headed home – somewhat surprising my parents, who had got used to never usually seeing me until after breakfast on a Sunday!

A lesson learnt from those unpredictable days back then was *never* red line a locomotive as being hauled by it until it moves! Here Caprotti 73125 is at Manchester Exchange on Sunday, 10 March 1968 with the 01.00 portion for Wigan North Western. Suspicions should have been raised upon seeing her *preparing* to work the 20-mile journey tender-first and sure enough, just minutes before departure, she was taken off and replaced by English Electric Type 4 D307 – the Caprotti presumably being that night's station pilot! That she was one of my few remaining required Patricroft locos didn't help – at least I caught her four weeks later actually working the same train.

APRIL

With the clock counting down and with sheds closing like a pack of dominoes, off I went again on the first Friday in April (5th) on my self-imposed quest for new locomotives – I knew nothing else. For three out of the four Fridays in April (the other being a Good Friday) I departed from Euston in the thick of the rush hour and upon arriving at Piccadilly walked across to Victoria and caught the BBE departure – with 45025 on each occasion. Always returning to Manchester from Preston, it was only then that variations to each weekend were implemented – being dependent on what locomotives were in circulation. There were still a hardened core of enthusiasts in circulation and information gained from them enabled the initial moves to be formulated. On that first Friday my luck was in when Caprotti 73125 worked the 01.00 sleepers. The same locomotive, having turned at Springs Branch, was usually booked to return into Manchester with the 05.45 opposite way portion but on this occasion, after a four-hour fester at Wigan, sister 73142 was dispatched – I suppose I should have been grateful it was steam at all but there were still one or two 9H locos I needed and it *could* have been one of them. After noting a resplendent 45305 on a rail tour, it seemed my run of good fortune as regards the 09.00 Liverpool's power had obviously run its course – epitomised by the provision of another exceedingly common Newton Heath example. Further hours were whiled away at Preston until the inevitable disillusionment upon seeing the dieselised midday portion sent me homebound. Taking into consideration I was averaging one catch per month at the time, I assumed that was it for April.

Easter Monday, the 15th, saw me head to Preston for the evening's portions, only to learn from fellow enthusiasts that that Sunday morning's 00.14 from Stalybridge, a train so often frequented by me, had a required 45386 on it. Unbelievable. Any time I was aboard, unrequired locomotives were dispatched: but when my back was turned …! More worryingly, both the Saturday and Monday 09.00 Liverpool portions were diesel operated. After sampling 10D's 44942 on the 21.25 Preston portion, I undertook what had become a familiar walk across Liverpool en route to Manchester, where Standard 5MT 73069, having been transferred to Patricroft the previous week sat, mocking me whilst I collected a run with D5206 on the 01.00 sleepers! What hope was there for the return working? The extremes of downheartedness and euphoria were brutally tested during those months

Bank Holiday Monday, 15 April 1968 sees Lostock Hall's 44942 at Liverpool Exchange having arrived with the 1F51 portion, detached at Preston, off the 17.26 Glasgow to Manchester Victoria. It was this train, on 3 August that year, which entered the history books as being the final timetabled steam-hauled one in mainland Britain.

The following day, Tuesday, 16 April 1968, having arrived into Manchester on the Wigan portion with the subsequently preserved Standard 5MT 73050, we headed north to Bolton to catch the inwards Belfast Boat Express. Whilst waiting for the 07.50 departure, Carnforth's 44735 leaked through Trinity Street station with a northbound freight.

1J05, the 06.15 Heysham to Manchester Victoria, calls at Bolton Trinity Street with 10A–allocated 44894. Steam on this and the northbound BBE was to finish just under three weeks hence.

Black 5MT 44894, upon arrival at Manchester Victoria, was to end her days just one month short of her twenty-third birthday in August 1968.

and after suffering another four-hour fester at Wigan, fully expectant of DL haulage on the returning sleeper portion, the subsequently preserved, but then most wanted, 73050 was sent out! Heeding recent information as regards the possible dieselisation of the 09.00 Liverpool, I backtracked to Bolton for the BBE into Manchester before returning to Preston for either the 12.17 or 12.44 portions, the latter of which, 45444, I travelled on if only to justify my stay up north, before heading home.

The UK came second in that year's Eurovision Song Contest with the song, Cliff Richard's 'Congratulations', then being knocked off the top spot in the charts in mid April by Louis Armstrong's 'What a Wonderful World'. In Memphis, USA, Martin Luther King was shot dead, triggering widespread riots, and in Germany, Formula 1's Jim Clark was killed. Here the first decimal coins, 5p and 10p, entered circulation and Enoch Powell got himself sacked from the shadow Cabinet over his infamous 'rivers of blood' speech warning about uncontrolled immigration. On TV, the final episode of *The Man from U.N.C.L.E.* was broadcast, and an American entrepreneur bought London Bridge thinking it was Tower Bridge to recreate it in the Arizonian desert.

Having previously spent seven of her twenty-five years on Western Region territory, Rose Grove's 8F 48410 is seen entering Preston's East Lancs platforms with a northbound freight on Tuesday, 16 April 1968.

It's the early hours of Saturday, 20 April 1968 and, having arrived at Heysham courtesy of a 04.30 workman's bus from Lancaster, my flash equipment was once again put to good use in capturing Carnforth's 44758 preparing to depart with the 06.15 Belfast Boat Express for Manchester Victoria. She would work the 4½ miles to Morecambe Promenade where, upon reversal, 10A's pet Black 5MT, 45025, would take over.

One of the Fifteen Guinea locomotives, Stanier 4-6-0 44871, at her home shed of Stockport Edgeley. Upon 9B's closure to steam two weeks hence she was transferred to Bolton. Upon *that* shed's closure to steam she was cascaded to Carnforth. Now preserved on the East Lancashire Railway, I finally caught up with her forty-five years later on a Kent circular Christmas luncheon trip.

On the third Friday of that April (19th), upon arriving at Preston on the BBE I learnt from others that, horror of horrors, the normally steam-worked 21.25 Liverpool portion had been worked by a Type 4 DL. Trekking back to Manchester, I caught the 01.00 sleeper to Wigan, where after yet more time spent in the waiting room I, just for a change, headed north to Lancaster. Passing the imposing floodlit castle, once part of the Duke of Lancaster's (John of Gaunt) property but then a high-risk Category A prison, I yomped to the bus station at 04.30 in the morning, catching a Lancashire and Heysham bus route 90 to Heysham itself in order to board the Belfast Boat Express at its starting point. Worked the 4½ miles to Morecambe Promenade by Carnforth's 44758 upon reversal there, you've guessed it, 45025 took over.

Aware that 9B was closing to steam at the end of the month and, with nothing better to do, I travelled to Stockport to bash the shed and at least take some photographs of the miscreants that I might never catch. Following the directions as indicated in Lt Aidan Fuller's *Shed Directory*, often mischievously referred to as 'The Bunker's Bible', I was soon at the shed entrance. The adrenalin rush associated with the possibility of being challenged when bunking sheds, an activity defined as 'a hurried departure usually under suspicious circumstances', was missing by this late date. No one cared. An era was coming to an end. I was wandering amongst these leviathans when suddenly a safety valve lifted, drowning the air with a gushing roar for a full half a minute before smashing shut again to a penetrating silence. Then another's drain cocks opened, sending billowing steam across the yard. Steam locomotives were a visual and vocal part of our heritage – they lived and breathed. How can anyone say they aren't a living machine? After my heartbeat, having increased dramatically by these sudden explosion of sounds, returned to normal I carefully crept around avoiding all number of pitfalls (literally!) taking numbers and photographs quickly before any irate foreman might appear telling me to 'clear orf out of here' (or words to that effect).

20/04/68	9B – Stockport Edgeley at 10.00
In steam	44781, 44855, 44868, 44871, 44888, 45046, 45269 & 48170
Dead	45013, 45027, 45312 & 48745
Withdrawn	44940, 45038 & 48437

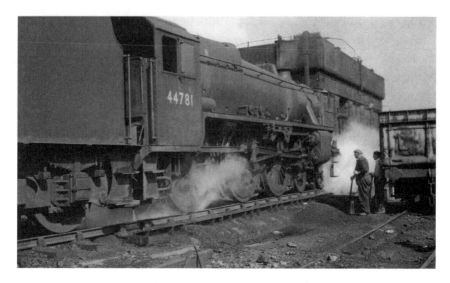

I was fortunate that 27-year-old Crewe-built 44781, another Fifteen Guinea performer, worked the following week's rail tour on which I was on board. Her end came having 'starred' in a train crash whilst participating in *The Virgin Soldiers* film the following year – being cut up soon after.

I cannot sum up the despair that like-minded steam followers felt that year better than this extract from Phil Mathison's *Shed Bashing with The Beatles* (Dead Good Publications, 2006) recalling his final visit to 9B:

> Like many before, and not a few after me, as I left I stood at the top of the steep cinder path that was a landmark of this location, and took one long last glimpse at the shed. Smoke was rising lazily from the shed vents, and the air was redolent of partly combusted coal. With this memory in mind and the acid tang of soot in my mouth, I walked thoughtfully back to the station.

Completely unaware that a rail tour from Birmingham was calling there, I was stunned to see 44949 and 45110 all dolled up for the occasion in the station. At the time I failed to document as to why I never travelled on the train. Perhaps I didn't have enough money or was spotted attempting to sneak aboard, although subsequent research has revealed it was fully booked.

After learning that a repeat tour the following Saturday was being arranged, and vowing to return for it, I continued with my plan, spending the day on Woodhead-line services catching several EM1 electric loco-motives (Class 76s) before returning to Preston for the evening's portions. Having heard what was booked and not wanting anything, I left Preston heading home for a comfortable night's sleep in my warm bed in preference to yet more hours festering at Wigan.

A week later, and having collected my sixth run with 45025 on the BBE, I travelled across the Pennines for what was to become *my* final steam journey out of the NER – the 03.32 Leeds/04.38 Halifax going DL the following month. Upon arriving into Manchester just after 6 a.m., and to fill in the time prior to heading to Stockport for the rail tour I was unable to board last week, I nipped up to Bolton for the BBE. Wonder of wonders, it was one of my last required Carnforth Blackies, 45394, prior, that was, until the Bolton displacements upon closure were reallocated there.

All dolled up in readiness to take over the jointly organised MRTS/SVRS North West Tour upon its arrival from Birmingham are two of Stanier's finest – 45110 and 44949. Having spent the majority of her thirty-two years at Holyhead, 45110 was the third celebrity Black 5MT, latterly at Lostock Hall, used on the Fifteen Guinea special. Subsequently preserved at the Severn Valley Railway, one day she will become my 290th Black 5MT for haulage! The other locomotive, Newton Heath's 44949, was a regular performer on the Calder Valley mail trains.

The sole-surviving Brit, 70013 *Oliver Cromwell*, waits at Preston on Saturday, 20 April 1968 to work the 1T85 Lancastrian No. 2 rail tour forward to Windermere. She was retained for such work and eventual preservation in preference to 70000 *Britannia* herself as having been the final steam locomotive overhauled at Crewe in February 1967.

You can't be everywhere at once and whilst I took the option of travelling on the jointly organised MRTS/SVRS North West Tour, Keith Lawrence photographed it in two locations. Firstly, with the two Black 5s in full voice, passing through Middlewood. (Keith Lawrence)

... and then later in its journey, now with two Standard 5s in charge, through Lower Darwen. (Keith Lawrence)

Heading to Stockport for the tour on a high, I found that instead of the expected locos that had been utilised on last week's tour, two completely different, but nonetheless required, sisters were provided – 44781 and 45046. I was *so* lucky because I later learnt that they had replaced the booked (not required) pairing of 44802 and 44929. The two Blackies on this jointly organised Severn Valley Railway Society and Manchester Rail Travel Society Preservation Special No. 2 tour took us to Stalybridge on a circular tour via Peak Forest, changing there for two Standard 5s. The gods were smiling on me that day because one of them was 73069 – destined to become the sole-surviving member of the class weeks later. Got her at last! The Standards took us via Huddersfield, Rose Grove (where the anticipated use of Ivatt 43027 failed to materialise because she was under repair) to Bolton. Any 8F or 9F, of which we had one of each, was a bonus in my eyes and, even after failing to win the raffle prize of a 9F smoke-box number plate, a very happy gricer eventually arrived at Lime Street at 19.00 hours aboard the last BR passenger service ever worked by a 9F. With phone calls having been made there was nothing booked out (that I wanted) on the Preston portions that night and so once again I went home early: my parents no longer surprised when I turned the key in the door at midnight.

Broadfield (Lancashire) was closed in October 1970, the line now being part of the East Lancashire Railway, and rather than take a shot of the locomotive (48652) as provided for with a fourteen-minute photographic stop, Dave (Mytholmroyd) Hill took one of the happy participants – the author 'hanging on' the station post. Great camaraderie exudes from this pleasing shot. Alan Hayes, my proofreading friend and prolific group photographer, is unusually actually *in* the shot – being in the centre of the front line. (Dave Hill)

Opposite above: I am indebted to Keith Lawrence for this and the following two photographs. He was shed bashing that April and captured Bolton's Stanier 5MT 45318 at the Trinity Street station on the 20th of that month. What was so special about this particular Black 5 you might ask for it to be included within this tome? Well, her fifteen minutes of fame was, having been transferred to Lostock Hall upon 9K's closure, that on Saturday, 3 August she worked Britain's final WTT steam passenger train from Preston to Liverpool – it goes without saying with myself aboard. (Keith Lawrence)

Opposite below: At Patricroft a wonderful close-up of a Caprotti valve gear on Standard 5MT 73134 – with the subsequently preserved 'normal' sister 73050 lurking in the shed shadows. (Keith Lawrence)

A sight that saddens any steam enthusiast's eyes. After a lifetime of service thrown aside under the guise of modernisation, a mixture of LMS 4MTs, 5MTs and 8Fs at Lostock Hall await the inevitable call to their demise. (Keith Lawrence)

MAY

The first weekend of May was based around The Slieve Cualann Rail Tour in Ireland. Departing from Euston at the height of the rush hour and connecting into the BBE, for once not 45025, a very fit 45342 attained a superb 75mph approaching Preston and 78mph at Bay Horse whilst taking a large contingent of enthusiasts through to Heysham to catch the *Duke of Lancaster* across to Belfast. The Saturday was a most enjoyable occasion with plenty of steam miles, good companionship and Guinness. I remember spending many hours in a BG-type vehicle listening to an impromptu (or perhaps it was planned?) folk-singing trio who, with their accordion and fiddles, made it a rail tour the like of which I had never been on before.

THE RAILWAY PRESERVATION SOCIETY OF IRELAND

Sliab Cualann
RAILTOUR

462 on 2.10 p.m. Market Stock Special
EX Enniscorthy at Kilcool
6.4.'57
Photo: A. Donaldson.
4th May, 1968
Souvenir 3/=
Proceeds in aid of Locomotive Fund

Below: Some of the participants grouping for a shot at Belfast – the author being fourth from right. (Alan Hayes)

Saturday, 4 May 1968 and Ulster Transport Authority's WT 'Jeep' 2-6-4T 56 is on Belfast York Road shed prior to working the 112½-mile first leg of the tour from Belfast Great Victoria Street to Dublin Connolly. In the background, but not participating in the tour, is SLNCR 0-6-4T 27 *Lough Erne*.

The scene at Dublin with the now preserved, then 79-year-old GS&WR J15 0-6-0 186 about to work the 30 miles to Wicklow.

Returning to the mainland on the same boat, we joined one of the largest gathering of haulage-bashers ever recorded, at Morecambe Promenade station. For sure there had been many occasions over the preceding years when our paths crossed, but for sheer numbers this grouping beat the lot! These were the hardened travellers from all over the UK who over the last few years had forfeited many nights in their warm comfortable beds because the authorities, in their wisdom, had restricted steam-passenger workings to the unearthly twilight hours. The reason for this mass gathering was that the Belfast Boat Express, Britain's final steam-hauled named train, was being dieselised the following day. The journey was more akin to a rail tour with photographers at every station en route together with those standing in fields or hanging over bridges to capture history being enacted.

For once I didn't mind the habitual 45025 being turned out. Looking very smart (courtesy of the MNA?), she took us into Manchester on that

The following day, Sunday, 5 May 1968, and Carnforth's pet Black 5, 33-year-old 45025, is seen at Heysham preparing to work the 06.55 Ulster Express to London Euston the 4½ miles to Morecambe Promenade. She is adorned with the Belfast Boat Express headboard because, at Morecambe, she will take over the 07.15 Heysham to Manchester Victoria. She has survived into preservation and can be found at The Strathspey Railway at Aviemore. (Dave Hill)

We now move to Morecambe Promenade. This was the largest known assemblage of haulage bashers from across the nation ever photographed. Without exception the common denominator was haulage (no copping or photographing) – we *had* to travel behind our quarry before red-lining it in our *ABCs*. (Alan Hayes)

1J05 having arrived at Manchester Victoria. (Alan Hayes)

historic Sunday morning arriving, presumably because of sheer volume of passengers, fourteen minutes late, at 09.22. What had we got to look forward to after that? Edge Hill, Speke Junction, Stockport Edgeley and Heaton Mersey sheds were all closing to steam at midnight that night – leaving just six remaining. News was also filtering through that BR had decreed that no passenger services were to be operated by steam from the commencement of the summer timetable – that being the next day. Was this true? Had my hobby, my life been snatched away from me? Read on ...

Although all the above was far more important than whatever else was going on around, I will brief the readers with a few headlines from that month.

After walking across Manchester, having arrived into Victoria, the London contingent are seen on board the 10.00 Piccadilly to Euston. (Alan Hayes)

The three Krays, notorious for their criminal activities, were arrested in London and charged with murder and fraud, Britain's first liver transplant took place at Cambridge, and the now preserved *Flying Scotsman* commemorated its fortieth anniversary by running non-stop King's Cross to Edinburgh. Abroad, 30,000 students showed their anti-American feelings by rioting in Paris. Musically, Gary Puckett and the Union Gap's 'Young Girl' ousted Louis Armstrong from the top spot and finally, in football, West Bromwich Albion beat Everton 1-0 in the FA Cup Final and Manchester City won the First Division by just two points above Manchester United.

With the BBE now dieselised and the 01.00 sleepers being erratically steam it was now not worth the effort of travelling north on the Friday evening. As I set out from Euston on the afternoon of Saturday the 11th I was wondering whether it would be worth it at all. Upon arriving at Preston in the early evening on the off-chance that the two portions still were steam operated, I learnt that all was not lost. The two sleeper portions earlier that day had both been steam (73133 on the 01.00 and 45055 on the 05.45) and it was only because 45310 failed at Leeds that the 03.32 from there was a diesel. No. 44816 worked that evening's Blackpool portion and Lostock Hall kindly turned out one of their recent acquisitions from Speke Junction, a required 44806, on the 21.25 Liverpool. My forty-eighth and mercifully final journey on the following morning's 01.00 sleepers out of Manchester Exchange awarded me with a run with 'Splutterbug' D7575. Over the past two years this train had helped my haulage scores immensely but was now so often a diesel that, together with the one-and-a-half-hour fester at Wigan for the habitually late-running 1M12 London departure, I decided enough was enough and resolved never to travel on the train again.

BR HQ had learnt that LMR's Manchester Division had flouted their diktat for the cessation of steam on passenger services and the latter were forced to issue revised duties commencing Monday, 20 May, thus causing 45310's usage on the 03.32 ex Leeds on Saturday, the 18th, and 73069 on the 05.45 ex Wigan on Monday the 20th to be the final booked steam services into Manchester.

The Preston division somehow circumnavigated this ban, it being reported that three passenger trains were to remain steam operated. They were the 20.50 SO Preston to Blackpool South, the 21.25 SO Preston to Liverpool Exchange and, surprisingly, the yet to run dated 09.18 SO Morecambe to Lancaster portion. Having been out of the country chasing West German 03 Pacifics in the Aachen area during the intermediate weekend, I was probably unaware of those machinations on the motive-power front upon heading north for Preston on Saturday the 25th. Whilst that evening's 21.25 portion was Type 2 D5251 at least the 20.50 was steam – albeit an unrequired 44816. I boarded the portion with her just to justify travelling more than 400 miles without any other purpose.

JUNE

The 09.18 from Morecambe, mentioned in the previous paragraph as being rostered for steam haulage, was the motivation for this next trip being made. With the possibility of haulage with one of Carnforth's 75xxx, having had some in the summer of 1967 on this very train, I felt it only right to catch it on its first Saturday of running this year. Departing from Euston on Friday the 14th on the 23.45 Barrow sleepers, the expected five-hour dwell time, after arriving in the area, was considerably reduced courtesy of the preceding 23.35 Euston to Glasgow failing at Hemel Hempstead. A further delay at Crewe awaiting loco and brake trouble at Acton Bridge converted a 04.28 arrival into Carnforth into a 05.30 one.

Having arrived at the then large terminal station of Morecambe Promenade just before 8 a.m., I found a café for breakfast before 'taking the air' along the promenade itself. The entire trip was centred on the 09.18 departure out of Morecambe. Needless to say, it wasn't steam – D1950 since you ask. Taking into consideration the only remaining possibility of steam was the evening portions out of Preston, some eleven hours hence; I stayed on the Morecambe service through to Euston, and home. It was the beginning of the end.

I noted every single steam locomotive seen on that outing – being so close to their imminent demise. At Warrington 45055 was on a Manchester to Chester parcels train, at Preston the station pilot was 45444 whilst 48293 passed through on a freight, and at Carnforth 44709, 44863, 45445, 45231, 70013, 75009 and 75027 were noted.

Was I bothered about non-steam events? Probably not but for those who are, General de Gaulle won a landslide victory in France despite widespread strikes and protests and at Ford's Dagenham plant woman machinists went on strike to gain equal pay, Tony Hancock committed suicide and The Rolling Stones' 'Jumpin' Jack Flash' hit the top spot. Railway-wise, as if things couldn't be more depressing, the NUR started a work-to-rule that resulted in more than 1,000 trains being cancelled and disrupted many commuter journeys to work, including mine.

JULY

On 1 July three further sheds closed to steam – Patricroft (9H), Bolton (9K) and Newton Heath (9D). Akin to the Bermuda Triangle, this left just ninety-five locomotives at Carnforth (thirty-seven), Lostock Hall (twenty-five) and Rose Grove (thirty-three), consisting of fifty-three Black 5s, thirty-one 8Fs, five Standard 4MTs, one Standard 5MT, one Brit and four 9Fs.

Whilst that was, for a steam chaser such as I, serious enough, a far greater world event was gathering pace. Russian tanks were massing at the Czechoslovakian border – eventually invading the country the following month and bringing to an end the liberalisation of Dubček's reign. From a personal point of view this thwarted my attempt to travel there (together with Poland and East Germany) in search of steam just days afterwards! Musically, the number-one spot was occupied for the first three weeks of that month by The Equals' 'Baby Come Back'. TV shows airing that month were *Dad's Army*, *Hawaii Five-0*, *Basil Brush* and *Batman*.

I had booked ahead for a couple of the final rail tours, one of which was on the last Saturday of July, having virtually given up any further attempts at catching further steam on normal services. Rumours however persisted that the 20.50 Preston portion was *still* steam-operated on Saturdays and taking into consideration Lostock Hall had received a dozen (six from each) former Speke Junction and Bolton-allocated locomotives that I required, I half-heartedly ventured forth once more out of Euston on the Saturday afternoon of the 13th. Wonderfully, completely justifying my journey, the subsequently preserved 45305 worked into Blackpool that evening. This was the locomotive that had worked an Aintree special to the Grand National earlier that year with race-goers not the slightest bit interested in what power was at the front and it had also been witnessed by myself powering a Liverpool area rail tour in April. Returning into Euston on the 1A00 Barrow sleepers at 02.40, it was of little consequence that I got soaking wet having walked across London to Victoria for my Crompton-hauled (Class 33) newspaper train home to Orpington.

With renewed optimism (subsequent research retrospectively fully justify-ing further visits, revealing that there were still fifteen 'required' Black 5s that I had yet to have a run behind) I repeated the exact scenario the following Saturday (20th) and, unbelievably, with 45212 reportedly booked for the 21.25 portion, 10D again came up trumps turning out a required 45388 on the Blackpool train. With a delayed arrival into the seaside town of 21.42, I was, however, unable to get back home so early this week, having to wait for a 02.23 London-bound departure – worked to Crewe with a by then 9-month-old English Electric Type 4 prototype D400.

Third time lucky perhaps? Perhaps Des O'Connor's 'I Pretend' put the kybosh on it! Taking into consideration I was to travel on a rail tour out from Manchester on the Sunday, I was always going to cover the portions on the 27th – 45388 was, however, turned out once more. Recently docu-mented was the fact that the driver 'failed' a DL to get 45388, so I shouldn't have moaned! With the Farewell to BR Steam tour not departing out of Stockport until 09.41 the following morning, I headed south to the all-night buffet at Crewe for both warmth and sustenance.

More time occupation during the early hours of that Sunday saw my final journey on the Manchester portion of the Scotland–Liverpool sleepers – once the preserve of Patricroft's Standards but now just another pesky 'Splutterbug'! I can't recall why I went to Stockport for the tour – perhaps just to kill time! The tour, 1L43 – 08.00 ex Birmingham New Street, was worked by a Brush Type 4 from Stockport to Manchester Victoria, where Brit 70013 *Oliver Cromwell* took us the 95 miles from to Carnforth via Wigan and Blackburn. There, two of Carnforth's Standard 4MTs, 75019 and 75027, worked the 37¾ miles across to Skipton. The usage of these 4MTs, the catalyst for my participation, was to be their swansong on passenger work. A required 45073 (ex Stockport) together with the sole remaining named Black 5, 45156 *Ayrshire Yeomanry*, then took over at Skipton for the 79 miles to Rose Grove via Blackburn, where the subsequently preserved 8F 48773 completed an excellent day's catches with a trip over Copy Pit to Manchester Victoria. Although the 8F was booked to work the tour through to Stockport, not being suitably attired for work the following morning and needing to get home that night, I alighted at Victoria and speed-walked across to Piccadilly in order to catch the 20.00 London departure.

AUGUST

And so this was it – the final weekend of the steam locomotive in mainland Britain. There was always an obvious inevitability as regards the death of steam. We all knew it was coming. Like life itself, it had to end sometime. It was always seemingly 'in the future'. Well it was here now and there was no getting away from it. You couldn't avoid it. Arriving at Preston on that first Saturday of the month, that evening the place was packed with enthusiasts – if it wasn't so sad an occasion passers-by might have thought it a carnival atmosphere. Mates, travelling colleagues, call them what you like, from around the country were all there. Whilst the crowds obviously exceeded the gathering at Morecambe two months previously, it was nonetheless the final meet with like-minded friends. No more would we come across each other on steam trains, often at unearthly times during the twilight hours, the width and breadth of Britain. No more we would exchange notes and swap stories of catches made or missed. No more would 'our' hobby, so ruthlessly destroyed by the faceless bureaucrats in London, be able to be followed. There was no Facebook or email to enable us to maintain communication with back then. But then again, the reasons for our friendships was about to disappear. Coming from all parts the UK, it was the common denominator of steam that kept us together. The thrill of the chase, even during those grim, disheartening days particularly during the early part of that year, was over.

Returning to that night, the station was a seething mass of humanity. Two bearded gentlemen appropriately clad in black top hat and tails reverently shouldered a mock coffin daubed with slogans depicting the demise of steam along the length of the platform. Was the Lostock Hall foreman going to do us proud? The good news was that local management, perhaps as a 'two-fingered rebuff' to higher authority, had ensured both the Blackpool (1P58) and Liverpool (1F51) portions were to be steam – an occurrence not always guaranteed during the last few months. Indeed, evidence came to light over the following days that the 21.25 was diagrammed for a DL. Intriguingly a Secondman had been also rostered and 'dispose; coal and place on ashpit' had been handwritten on the bottom of the 461 duty concerned!

At 20.15 former Kingmoor, now Lostock Hall allocated, 45212 (cleaned only on one side due to a police presence at 10D on crowd-control duties) slowly came into the station. The roars of approval from the masses, together with the noise of cameras clicking and the accompanying flashes, were the like of which I had never seen before. Like a celebrity on the red carpet at a Leicester Square film launch she, and the crew, lapped it up. She had been spruced up courtesy of the MNA organisation.[14]

But wait, what was the locomotive that had crept into the south bay platform 5A for the 21.25 Liverpool? Unbelievably it was, for me, a required ex Bolton 45318. During her wait for her portion she had a makeshift head-board that read 'The End of LMS Steam' fixed on her smokebox. After the 20.50 Blackpool portion had departed, every window occupied by enthusiasts wielding recording equipment and cameras, attention turned to the star of the evening, namely Stanier 4-6-0 45318.

This *was* the last regular timetabled steam passenger normal service train in Britain. I hadn't paid 15 guineas to be on this train. I doubt if I paid at all! As soon as the Glasgow train arrived and before the rear portion itself had been detached I made a beeline for a corridor space on it. There was no way I was going to miss this train. Others, having taken a shot of the Black 5 whilst coupling up then squeezed on board this seriously overloaded seven-coach train. Where had they all been during the final six months or so? There were many occasions when, during the cold winter/spring earlier that year, I was the only enthusiast on a steam service. It crossed my mind at the time that they were 'once a yearers', a term loudly spoken by pub regulars of those never seen at other times of the year coming in for their free drink on Christmas Day.

There was insufficient space to even open my notebook to record the run. Others, with presumably more elbowroom, fortunately did and a max of 78mph (claimed by some as 80mph) at Maghull was duly recorded. Thirty-three minutes and forty-eight seconds later it was all over – the squealing protestations from the tender's hot box falling silent. The arrival at Liverpool

---

[14] MNA stood for Master Neverer's Association – a group of, mainly Midland-based enthusiasts who toured the railway network in order to externally clean (the authorities at each location usually turning a blind eye) steam locomotives, for the benefit of lineside photographers en route, which were allocated to work last services. I personally witnessed their efforts at Alnmouth in June 1966 (K1 62011), Bradford in September 1967 (B1 61306) and Aberystwyth in March 1967 (BR 4MT 75033). In order to travel to these varied destinations on the occasions when trains were used it is alleged that they never paid any fares, thus giving credence to the middle legend. In a *Railway Magazine* article (2018) the organisation stated that the word never referred to giving up on a master (photographic) shot.

has been well documented enough over the years for me not to repeat it here, with the aforementioned coffin and send-off scenes, other than to say, with 'Auld Lang Syne' and 'God Save Our Gracious Steam' ringing in my ears, *I was there.*

As regards my own personal achievements, 45318 was my 283rd Black 5, which, with it being just over a third of the class, was, in my mind, a fitting closure of haulages with the most versatile class of steam locomotive ever built.

For sure, as has been well documented, 45212, upon arrival back at Preston, LE from Blackpool, replaced 44806 as the station pilot and subsequently shunted the sleepers off the overnight from Euston and placed them in a bay platform, heating them until 08.00. When is a shunt a train? Were there any passengers aboard? All the plaudits I have read since still 'award' 45318 the distinction of being *the* last steam-operated, timetabled passenger train.

The following day I was booked on one of the six specials circulating throughout the North-West — the LCGB-organised Last Day of Steam Rail Tour. This tour utilised five different steam locomotives — a feat unmatched by the others being run that day. Train 1Z74 was to start out of St Pancras at 08.30 and so I caught the 00.10 Lime Street to Crewe, enjoying my final meal at the all-night buffet, before arriving into London with ample time to walk along the Euston Road to the former Midland railway terminus. After yesterday's euphoric atmosphere at Preston, I found today's train was somewhat subdued. A great many of those aboard were not what I would consider recent travellers — the age profile perhaps indicative of a previous generation. They, of course, were the lucky ones by having travelled throughout the 1950s and early '60s when steam was the king on every main line. We all, however, had come to pay our last respects at the end of steam's reign. As regards the train itself, after gradually losing time en route, not helped by SLW at Marple, we eventually departed Manchester Victoria forty-eight minutes late, at 14.18, with Brit *Oliver Cromwell* and 44781 in charge.

Routed via what is now marketed as the Ribble Valley line, having initially traversed the spectacular Tonge Viaduct, we listened in awe to the efforts of the two locos as they climbed to the line's summit in the 2,015-yard long Sough tunnel. After which we descended past the now closed (February 1966) Lower Darwen shed to Blackburn, where the Brit was exchanged for 8F 48773.

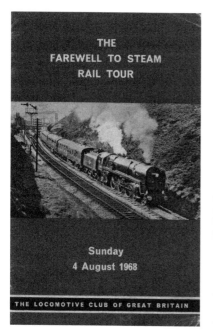

Sunday, 4 August 1968 and the LCGB-organised Last Day of Steam Rail Tour, with Brit 70013 *Oliver Cromwell* leading Stanier 5MT 44781, is seen crossing Entwhistle viaduct. (Keith Lawrence)

The tour is now at Blackburn and the headboard is being transferred on to the Brit's replacement – the subsequently preserved LMS 2-8-0 48773.

Arriving at Carnforth more than an hour late, a rapid tour of 10A was undertaken by the train's participants. Enthusiasts were clambering over the silent dead locomotives akin to maggots feeding off decaying carcasses – anything detachable being secreted away within their clothing. A great many chalked embellishments adorned these fallen comrades – perhaps the most heart-rending one I read being 'Goodbye Cruel World'.

The Carnforth reversal was completed in twenty minutes instead of the allotted thirty but for reasons not recorded (probably attributable to a combination of tiredness and the onset of full-on depression) we somehow lost even more time, with 45390 and 45025 coming off at Lostock Hall Junction nearly two hours late. Further time was dropped before arriving into Euston at 00.14 (135 minutes late), after which I caught the 01.02 from Blackfriars to my Kent home, enabling just a few hours' sleep prior to heading to my Waterloo workplace – wondering what steamless future lay ahead of me. At least it wasn't as late as a following RCTS special, which arrived four-and-a-half hours late into London at 02.15! So that was my sixty-eighth (British) steam run that year – thus justifying the chapter title.

Ron Herbert, a Preston controller at the time, has since written that the train plan provided proved to be unworkable with too many specials mixed in amongst the booked services. Other factors such as insufficient signal boxes being opened together with water-supply issues exacerbated the problems.

Even if we could have afforded it, all my travelling colleagues boycotted the following week's BR-organised Fifteen Guinea Special. Colourfully described by one of them as a plastic farrago, it was a blatant rip-off and with just 470 passengers, some of whom were LMR managers on a 'jolly', it would seem that a lot of others agreed – the load being reduced by one vehicle (fifty seats having been unsold). It was subsequently reported that BR was roundly criticised for demanding 15 guineas – 'a blatant exploitation putting the tour out of financial reach for many prospective participants'. Suddenly, although BR had banned steam north of Carnforth and Skipton since the beginning of the year, *they* were allowed to run to/from Carlisle. The train was well documented within the media and, I have to admit, it was only pride (together with three weeks' wages) that kept me off of it. All bar one, Stanier 4-6-0 44781, of the locomotives used on it have survived the years – she being cut up after partaking in a train crash whilst filming *The Virgin Soldiers* the following year.

We are now at Carnforth and, although Black 5MT 45134 (seen in action at the beginning of this chapter) is in light steam, I doubt if she ever turned a revenue-earning wheel again.

Having spent time at Gloucester and Croes Newydd, 1951 Swindon–built 4-6-0 75009's (the longest lived of the class) final shed was here at Carnforth – having arrived in June 1967.

This 10-year-old 9F 92167, having spent time at Saltley and Birkenhead, had arrived at Carnforth in November 1967. She had become a 2-8-2 the previous June, having dropped a connecting rod while en route to Carnforth with a freight service from Leeds.

So here it is – my last ever run in Britain with steam. Or so we all thought back then. Carnforth's 5MTs 45025 and 45390 prepare to work the tour's 61¼ miles via Skipton to Lostock Hall Junction.

RAILWAY WORLD

OCTOBER 1968

Three Shillings

IAN ALLAN

Photo feature — the last week of BR steam

The front cover of the October 1968 issue of *Railway World* depicting 1T57.

Was there any other news that mattered that first week? Musically Tommy James and the Shondells had taken the top spot with 'Mony Mony' but the one that really struck a chord, was Mary Hopkin's 'Those Were the Days', which said that those days would never end. Well they had. Some of the films I could watch to fill in the massive void the elimination of steam had conferred on me were *The Good, The Bad and The Ugly*, *Planet of the Apes* and *The Italian Job*.

The majority of the footplate crews at those last three depots received a brief, impersonal, curt letter from the DMO Preston advising them their services were no longer required as from 05.08.68. No thanks for their often lengthy years of railway service. Similar to their uncared-for steeds, they were tossed aside. For sure, for a 'fortunate' few training on new traction or a transfer miles away was offered. The majority, however, turned their backs on BR and left for alternative, probably non-shift, work elsewhere.

Although I did make several further European journeys, it was the week nights and weekends that were suddenly void of activity. Eventually, during 1969, the enthusiasm, on par with the continuing demise of the steam locomotive throughout Europe, began to fade. After all, at 22 years of age I was still a 'young' man and the, albeit far more expensive, discovery of the opposite sex was an easily distracting alternative.

Had it all been worth it? There were times, particularly during the final year, that I certainly didn't think so. The pathetic sight of once fine machinery, in a dilapidated condition, struggling to keep trains moving was a heart-rending, miserable affair. For sure there were many pleasurable moments of a personal nature, such as haulage by a rarely seen locomotive, or the camaraderie at the many meetings of like-minded colleagues. The downside was the long cold waits at stations for the increasingly dieselised trains. The disappointments, the euphoria – I wouldn't have missed it for the world. But whilst there was something left, however meagre, the lure of steam drew me back. Some of us could not see a future without steam. The reason and way of life was disappearing. What on earth would we talk about to other people? Most weekends over the last few years had been spent chasing steam anywhere and everywhere.

Fortunately anyone who worked for British Railways in those days were considered as 'part of a family'. I retained a good circle of friends via my workplace and with their counselling I began to reintegrate into civilian life. The Who were seen at Soho's Marquee Club, I attended the first ever free concert at Hyde Park featuring The Rolling Stones. I passed my driving test and bought a Ford Prefect, which cost £150 and had only three forward gears and vacuum-powered windscreen wipers! To fund the associated motoring costs I started working as a barman at a local pub – a location at which romance blossomed. So life after steam wasn't as bad after all. Retrospectively, I will forever be grateful to my parents for the freedom they allowed in order for me to follow my hobby. Would present-day parents allow their children to roam the railway system as we were able to do?

DIMINISHING RETURNS

Date	Running Total Standard 5MTs	Required	Running Total Stanier 5MTs	Required
01/01/68	23	8	151	61
31/01/68	20	7	140	55
29/02/68	20	7	131	48
31/03/68	17	6	114	33
30/04/68	12	2	102	33
31/05/68	7	1	84	23
30/06/68	1	0	53	17
31/07/68	1	0	46	12[15]
12/08/68	0	0	0	0

Month (1968)	Hours of travel	Miles (Total)	Miles (Steam)	(Required) Catches
January	81	2,008¾	236¾	44848 (10F), 45268 (9D), 45353 (10D)
February	74	2,053½	215¼	45447 (10F)
March	90	2,477	465	45382 (10F)
April	114	2,815	596¼	44781, 45046 (9B), 45394 (10A), 48652 (9K), 73050, 73069, 73125 (9H), 92218 (8C)
May	42	1,821¾	175¾[16]	44806 (10D)
June	19	538	0	
July	67	1,987	314	45073, 45305, 45388 (10D), 48773 (10F), 75019, 75027 (10A)
August	36	1,069¼	165¼	45318 (10D)
Total	523	14,770¼	2,168¼	21

---

[15] Of the final twelve 'missed', three have been caught in preservation; 45110 so far escaping my clutches.

[16] Excludes 285 Irish miles with two locomotives (186 and 56).

AN AFTERTHOUGHT

My hobby, of careering around Britain in search of the fast-disappearing steam-hauled passenger train, came to an abrupt halt in the August of 1968. It was as if my best friend had died. I thought, at the time, that I would never witness the like again. How wrong I was! As a semi-retired steam gricer, I still derive great pleasure in striking through a locomotive number indicating haulage behind her. There are still quite a few, and indeed some 'new' examples being built, locomotives to catch.

I was fortunate to have been amongst the most travelled teenagers of our generation in pursuit of what we thought of at the time as the dying steam locomotive. Thanks, however, to thousands of dedicated volunteers, hundreds of steam locomotives have been saved and brought back to life for both the present and future generations to enjoy. For sure, with a greater certainty of expectation courtesy of modern-day technology, the thrill of the chase, i.e. not knowing what will turn up (if at all), is missing. That, however, is a small price to pay. The wonderment on the faces of small children brought by their parents to the line side or station to witness the steam locomotive in all its glory perhaps is an adequate compensation.

Personally, over the intervening years, dependent upon family commitments, a great many preserved lines have been visited and a selection of LMS-orientated locomotives caught on them are shown here.

Nowadays the steam bug, although somewhat muted, is only stimulated upon a 'required' locomotive being in circulation at one of the many galas held on the more than fifty preserved railways or working a special out of London – the couriers on the latter well used to me asking for a single fare to the first stop! Statistically my current totals are 1,268 locomotives at 101,645 miles. How are yours?

Unless otherwise stated all images are from my collection. To view my website please visit mistermixedtraction.smugmug.com, then select one of twenty galleries, click on slideshow, sit back and enjoy. Anyone wishing to purchase copies of the images contained therein please visit ANISTR. com where, under featured photographers you will find my name and my complete photographic collection.

Whilst en route to relations at Matlock in April 1987 I called in on the Midland Railway Centre. Here the (young) author poses in front of 61-year-old former Edge Hill resident Jinty 47357.

The three loves of my life at Matlock in March 1997. One of the eighteen preserved Black 5MTs, visiting 45337, is running round her train at Matlock Riverside – she having been withdrawn at Kingmoor in January 1965.

Book signing callings at the Bluebell Railway in February 2010 neatly coincided with a visiting, from the GCR, Standard Mogul 78019. Having spent six years on the Pennine Stainmore line, she had been withdrawn at Crewe South in November 1967.

Withdrawn at Carnforth in January 1968 after just eight and a quarter years of operation, BR 9F 2-10-0 92212 arrives into the Mid Hants station of Ropley in October 2010.

Attending the 2014 MNR's Gala was 72-year-old former Northwich resident Stanier 2-8-0 8F 48151 – seen here at Dereham.

Having spent seven and a half of her ten-and-a-half-year life at Lower Darwen, Standard 4MT Mogul 76084 looks resplendent running round her train at Holt whilst participating in the NNR Gala of March 2015.

Book signing commitments led to a visit to the North Yorkshire Moors Railway during their April 2015 gala. At Grosmont, BR 4MT 75029, having been withdrawn at Stoke in June 1967, is seen arriving with a Whitby to Battersby working.

The only Duchesses I had seen were a line of condemned ones at Crewe in August 1964. Withdrawn at Edge Hill earlier that year, the Midland Railway Centre's 46233 *Duchess of Sutherland* awaits departure time at King's Cross with The Lindum Fayre train in December 2015.

The Mid Hants 2016 Autumn Gala hosted the visiting 4-6-2 46100 *Royal Scot*. Withdrawn at Nottingham in October 1962 after spending many years at Butlins (Skegness) and Bressingham Museum as a static exhibit, she was restored (for a second time) to working order in 2016.

The Spa Valley Railway hired the 120-year-old L & Y 0-6-0 52322 during the early part of 2018. Withdrawn at Lees (Oldham) in August 1960, she is seen at Eridge on Saturday, 5 May waiting to work the 14.30 for Tunbridge Wells West.

Withdrawn at Springs Branch (Wigan) in December 1966, LMS Mogul 46447 visited the Isle of Wight during 2018. Here, on Saturday, 26 May, she is at Wootton having arrived with the 14.41 from Smallbrook Junction. She had to work with Mickey Mouse 41298 as her vacuum-braking system was not compatible with the air-braked stock.

Having spent nearly five of her short eleven-year life allocated to former GC sheds it is fitting that Standard 5MT 73156 has been restored at the Great Central Railway. Here, at the autumn 2018 Gala, she is seen at Loughborough having worked in on the 15.13 from Rothley Brook.

SOURCES

Ian Allan British Railways Gradient Profiles

The *LCGB Monthly Bulletin*

The Railway World magazine

Longworth Hugh, *BR Steam Locomotives 1948–1968*

BR Database, sixbellsjunction.co.uk

Lt Aidan L.F. Fuller's *British Locomotive Shed Directory*

and countless others over the years that, if omitted, I apologise.

ACKNOWLEDGEMENTS

This book is dedicated to the many people in my life who have made it one of which I have been glad to have participated in – my ever-understanding wife Joan being at the top of the list.

Then there is John Bird (ANISTR.com), whose miracles on fifty-year-plus negatives have made them worthy of inclusion here. I am grateful to Keith Lawrence for supplementing my own photographic offerings and to The History Press team for putting it all together. Then there is *Steam Days* magazine editor Rex Kennedy, who in 2004 published my first article, thus kick-starting a late-life career as an author

Finally, to my lifelong friend and travelling buddy from those wonderful years, Alan Hayes, who not only offered up his photographs for inclusion here but also proofread the result.

GLOSSARY OF TERMS

Adex	Advertised excursion
BBE	Belfast Boat Express
BR	British Rail (ways), 1948–97
BSK	Brake standard corridor
CLC	Cheshire Lines Committee, 1862–1922
DL	Diesel locomotive
DMU	Diesel (mechanical) multiple unit
DSL	Diesel Shunting Locomotive
ECML	East Coast Main Line (King's Cross to Edinburgh via York)
ECS	Empty coaching stock
EL	Electric locomotive
ER	Eastern Region of BR, 1948–92
EMU	Electric Multiple Unit
F	Power ratio for freight traffic
FO	Fridays only
Footex	Advertised excursions run in connection with a football event
FSO	Fridays and Saturdays only
GCR	Great Central Railway, 1897–1922
GER	Great Eastern Railway, 1862–1922
GNR	Great Northern Railway, 1846–1922
GWR	Great Western Railway, 1835–1947
K&WVR	Keighley & Worth Valley Railway
LE	Light engine

LCGB	The Locomotive Club of Great Britain
LMR	London Midland Region of BR, 1948–92
LMS	London Midland & Scottish Railway, 1923–47
LNER	London & North Eastern Railway, 1923–47
L&NWR	London & North Western Railway, 1846–1922
L&YR	Lancashire & Yorkshire Railway, 1847–1922
M&GN	Midland & Great Northern Joint Railway, 1893–1922
M&SLR	Manchester, Sheffield & Lincolnshire Railway, 1847–97
MLR	Manchester & Leeds Railway, 1839–47
Mogul	Locomotive wheel arrangement (2-6-0)
MR	Midland Railway, 1844–1922
MT	Mixed traffic (passenger and freight)
MX	Mondays excepted (Tuesdays to Saturdays)
NER	North Eastern Region of BR, 1948–67
Nunex	A Keswick Convention Special
P	Power ratio for passenger traffic
Pacific	Locomotive wheel arrangement (4-6-2)
Parspec	Advertised excursions run for private parties
RCTS	The Railway Correspondence & Travel Society
S & D	Somerset & Dorset Railway, 1862–1922
ScR	Scottish Region of BR, 1948–92
SLS	The Stephenson Locomotive Society
SO	Saturdays only
SR	Southern Region of BR, 1948–92
STN	Special Traffic Notice
SuO	Sundays only
SX	Saturdays excepted (Mondays to Fridays)
T	Tank
TPO	Travelling Post Office
WCML	West Coast Main Line (Euston to Glasgow via Crewe)
WR	Western Region of BR, 1948–92

APPENDIX

LONDON MIDLAND REGION MOTIVE POWER DEPOTS

Date	Shed closed to steam	Running Total
01/66	Annesley (16B)	53
02/66	Fleetwood (10C), Lower Darwen (10H)	51
03/66	Bescot (2F)	50
04/66	Mold Junction (6B), Lancaster Green Ayre (10J)	48
05/66		48
06/66	Nuneaton (5E), Leicester Midland (15A), Wellingborough (15B), Southport (8M)	44
07/66	Stourbridge Junction (2C)	43
08/66		
09/66	Burton (16F)	42
10/66	Banbury (2D), Llandudno Junction (6G), Bank Hall (8K), Kirby-in-Ashfield (16E), Westhouses (16G)	37
11/66	Tyseley (2A), Agecroft (9J)	35
12/66	Machynlleth (6F), Holyhead (6J), Carlisle Upperby (12B), Barrow (12C), Colwick (16B)	30
01/67		
02/67		
03/67	Oxley (2B), Saltley (2E), Shrewsbury (6D), Derby (16C)	26
04/67	Skipton (10G)	25
05/67		
06/67	Chester (6A), Croes Newydd (6C), Sutton Oak (8G), Aintree (8L)	21
07/67		
08/67	Stoke (5D)	20
09/67		
10/67	Warrington Dallam (8B)	19
11/67	Crewe South (5B), Birkenhead (8H)	17
12/67	Springs Branch (8F), Tebay (12E)	15
01/68	Carlisle Kingmoor (12A), Workington (12D)	13
02/68		
03/68	Northwich (8E), Trafford Park (9E), Buxton (9L)	10
04/68		
05/68	Edge Hill (8A), Speke Junction (8C), Stockport Edgeley (9B), Heaton Mersey (9F)	6
06/68		
07/68	Newton Heath (9D), Patricroft (9H), Bolton (9K)	3
08/68	Carnforth (10A), Lostock Hall (10D), Rose Grove (10F)	0

THE TOP TEN TRAINS TRAVELLED ON

Train	Total	DL	Dates	Booked
01.00 DLY Manchester Ex–Wigan NW	48	6	07/66–05/68	9H–S5
02.10 EWD York–Manchester Vic ($)	25	1	07/66–04/68	9D–B5
20.55 DLY Manchester Vic–Heysham	23	1	06/66–05/68	10A–B5
20.45 ★ EWD Preston–Blackpool South	18		08/66–08/68	10D
05.35 EWD Preston–Crewe	16	1	05/66–09/67	5B–B5
04.20 ★ EWD Manchester Vic–York ($)	13	2	07/66–11/67	9D–B5
21.17 ★ EWD Preston–Liverpool Ex	13		08/67–08/68	10D–B5
00.12 ★ SuO Stalybridge–Manchester Ex	11	2	07/66–03/68	9H–S5
09.00 EWD Liverpool Ex–Preston	10	1	05/67–03/68	10F/9D–B5
05.25 ★ DLY Wigan NW–Manchester Ex	10	1	05/67–04/68	9H–S5

B5 – Stanier 4-6-0: S5 – Standard 4-6-0 ($) – LMR section only

(★) Note minor variations to timings occurred in both the 1967 and '68 timetables

NUMBER OF OVERNIGHTS SPENT CHASING STEAM THROUGHOUT BRITAIN

	Jan	Feb	Mar	Apr	May	Jun	Jul	Aug	Sep	Oct	Nov	Dec	Total
1964			1	1			2	1			1		6
1965				2		3	4	1	2				12
1966		1	3	2	5	5	10	11	8	4	4	4	57
1967	1	3	7	8	6	8	9	12	6	9	9	1	79
1968	4	4	4	4	4	1	3	1					25

Grand total of 179, 84 of which were Fridays and 63 Saturdays

NB – A further 47 (1968 = 33, 1969 = 14) were spent in Europe.

BY THE SAME AUTHOR ...

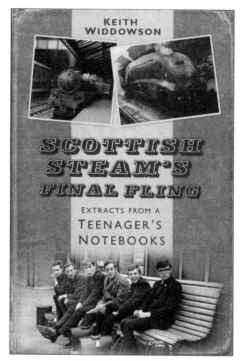

978 0 7509 7022 8

In May 1967, Scotland became the third of the six British Railways regions to dispense with the steam locomotive, bringing an iconic era of Britain's transport heritage closer to its demise. Living 300 miles away, a teenaged Keith Widdowson set out on a series of marathon journeys to catch Scottish steam's final fling.

REVIEWS OF *SCOTTISH STEAM'S FINAL FLING*

'Keith's narrative is lively and engaging from the start ... what [he] does best in this very personal account is to recapture the sense of travelling into the unknown as far as steam haulage was concerned ... a hunt which relied on knowledge, intuition and often pure luck ...Very highly recommended indeed.'

Steam World Magazine

'The author displays a lovely turn of phrase without, relaying a story with warmth that brings the story to life, elevating this publication way above what you would expected from the book's subtitle. Recommended.'

Steam Days Magazine